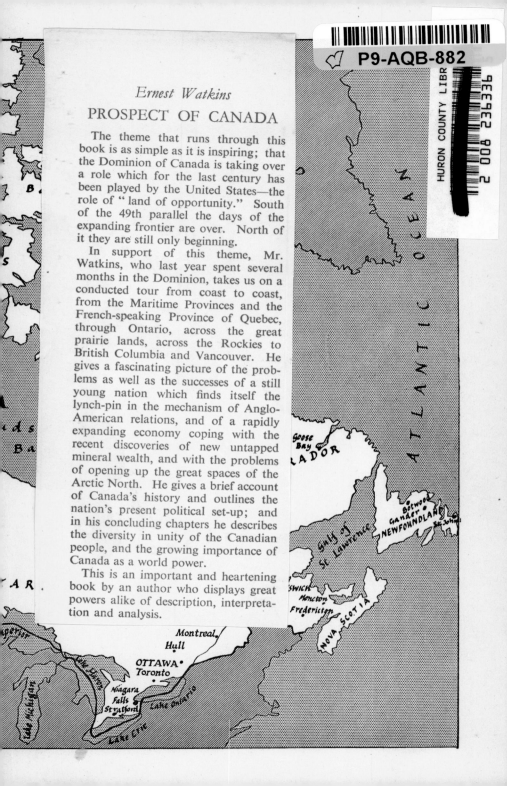

Ernest Watkins

PROSPECT OF CANADA

The theme that runs through this book is as simple as it is inspiring; that the Dominion of Canada is taking over a role which for the last century has been played by the United States—the role of " land of opportunity." South of the 49th parallel the days of the expanding frontier are over. North of it they are still only beginning.

In support of this theme, Mr. Watkins, who last year spent several months in the Dominion, takes us on a conducted tour from coast to coast, from the Maritime Provinces and the French-speaking Province of Quebec, through Ontario, across the great prairie lands, across the Rockies to British Columbia and Vancouver. He gives a fascinating picture of the problems as well as the successes of a still young nation which finds itself the lynch-pin in the mechanism of Anglo-American relations, and of a rapidly expanding economy coping with the recent discoveries of new untapped mineral wealth, and with the problems of opening up the great spaces of the Arctic North. He gives a brief account of Canada's history and outlines the nation's present political set-up; and in his concluding chapters he describes the diversity in unity of the Canadian people, and the growing importance of Canada as a world power.

This is an important and heartening book by an author who displays great powers alike of description, interpretation and analysis.

Prospect of Canada

Prospect of
CANADA

Ernest Watkins

London
SECKER & WARBURG
1954

MARTIN SECKER & WARBURG LTD.
7 John Street, London, W.C. 1

First published 1954
Reprinted 1954

PRINTED IN GREAT BRITAIN
BY WESTERN PRINTING SERVICES LTD. BRISTOL

To
My Wife
JENNY
with my deepest love

Contents

page

List of Illustrations

Thanks are due to the following for permission to reproduce photographs: the Royal Canadian Air Force, for Nos. 7 and 13; the National Film Board, for Nos. 4, 6, and 16; Canadian Pacific Railway, for No. 1; Canadian National Railways, for Nos. 3 and 11; Arrow Surveys Ltd., for No. 12; Arnott & Rodgers, for Nos. 2, 5, and 15; Aluminum Co. of Canada, for No. 10; George Hunter, for No. 14; and Consolidated Mining and Smelting Co., for No. 9.

ix

Foreword

WHEN I told Hamish McGeachy, of the Toronto *Globe and Mail* equally known to Canadians on radio and television, of my intention to write a book, he said—and they were his last words before I left Toronto: "Don't make generalisations; Canada is a more complicated place than you think. And for Heaven's sake, get your facts right."

Of course I agreed and of course I have not been able to follow his advice. I like facts and I like generalisations. I sincerely hope that the facts I have collected are correct, But I am sure that all my generalisations from them cannot be. I am sure I have seen in Canada the things I wanted to see and that, some Canadians may say, my misconceptions reach at times the proportions of remarkable blunders. I do not care—and that insouciance is not only an attempt to ward off criticism in advance. At bottom, this is a book of impressions, and if I had been in Canada a longer, or a shorter, time I doubt if my impressions would have been so very different. Indeed, I might as well nail my colours to the mast here and now; I should be a happy man if I were able to die a Canadian citizen. So, if this book persuades any reader to interest himself in Canada a little more in consequence, it will have served the purpose I had in mind.

No foreword is complete without a tribute to those who have aided the author in his work, and, having now some experience of book-writing, I know that nothing in any book can be more sincere than such a tribute. Authors can only expect to be put to some trouble if they set out on that kind of undertaking; the extraordinary thing is how much willing help they are so frequently given—as I was—by so many people who cannot really be very much concerned in the project itself.

Sunday Morning in Banff

1. Getting There

ALL the way from the Azores to the mainland of America we had flown in sunshine. We seemed still to be climbing an hour after take-off when we passed over Corvo, the most westerly of the islands of the Azores, an island that is no more than a dead volcano cone, its western wall already half eaten away by the sea, its eastern slope a patchwork of terraced fields. The clouds beneath us then were cottonwool balls, with grey-blue sea below, but gradually the spaces between the puffs filled with a grey transparent sheet which thickened as the clouds themselves spread. By the time we had reached the further coast we were flying above the familiar white, flossy quilt of cloud, above the snow-fields of the sky. Nova Scotia, if it existed at all, was an abstraction, an outline printed in black on a navigator's chart.

The captain sent a message back. It read: "We should be in at Dorval, Montreal, at five-forty-five, local time. Please put your watches back four hours."

The aircraft was an R.C.A.F. transport "North Star". The captain was tall and lean, his co-pilot shorter and bulging a little at the belt of his tunic. The radio officer was coal-black, from the Carribean. They were the three commissioned men among the crew; the oldest member, the flight engineer, a sergeant, middle-aged, was the only one among them with ribbons from the last war. The passengers, other than myself, were eleven R.C.A.F. service personnel, two wives and three children, returning home. To them, this journey was—but what could I know of their hopes or fears or acceptances? All I knew was that I was possessed by the excitement of curiosity, for me as powerful an excitement now as it was when I was a child.

By two, Montreal time, the lower half of the sky ahead was a wall of yellow haze, and beyond, grey ridges of high cloud were climbing above it. These spread across the sun and down the sky on either hand, so that at last we were alone in an empty space between two levels of cloud. Beneath, the whiteness had gone. I thought suddenly of the Lake District at Easter, halfway up Helvellyn, with the mist above and grey rain beneath. It was, after all, April.

We flew on. Twelve hours, the flight engineer had said, from the Azores to Montreal, and I had thought that a long time. And then I had thought of all the others who had set out from the Azores to cross the Atlantic. On the wall of the waiting-room in the airport building there they have painted a vast mural, to show the routes of all the Portuguese explorers—none of the others— up and down and across the Atlantic, and I had never realised until then how many Portuguese explorers there had been. What would they have thought of twelve hours to Canada? Or the others—Cabot, Jaques Cartier?

Twelve hours; and eight of them gone. One of the children was crying but I could not hear his voice over the roar of the engines. Well, if anything happened now, we would not fall into the sea and be drowned. We would run into a mountain and be burnt.

At last I felt the aircraft begin to lose altitude, to run down-hill, as I had always thought of it, and as always the sound of the engines seemed to become more powerful. The clouds beneath were closer and we raced over them and into them and thin channels of water traced themselves across the glass of the windows, each with a single black edge of shadow. At times the clouds fell away from the aircraft, becoming mounds of grey smoke below and around us, and then I saw the dark shadow beneath one mound become even darker and change from shadow to substance, and in its centre, far below, was an irregular grey outline, with faint traces of yellow in it, set against a deep bluey-brown background. Land: hills, tree-covered, still in their mid-winter colours, and set among them a lake, its ice sullied by thaw but still unbroken. Was this my first sight of Canada or were we still over the State of Maine?

The clouds swept over the brief landscape and it was gone.

Monotony returned. And then, suddenly, we were right through and below the cloud and the ground was clear beneath, save for some sheets of falling rain. I was caught by that moment. It is there now in my mind, with other moments when I first saw new land, bright and vivid, uncorroded by time; an evening in June 1940, sailing into Reykjavik Bay, a morning in July 1944, when the mists lifted and there was the coast of Normandy. This was Canada.

April in the Province of Quebec. No sign of green. The land was a dead brown, with patches of ochre and orange earth dotted with trees and outcrops of rock, and straight yellow lines running north and south, the gravel roads marking out the boundaries of each section, and as we came lower I could see that these roads were flanked with occasional buildings, the largest barns painted a dark red. Another road appeared, running diagonally across the landscape, almost parallel to our course, and alongside it a railway. Another railway came in from the north and curved westwards to join the first. And then, at the top of the picture framed in my window, there was a river, dirty yellow, running northeastwards. It was wide and seemed to grow wider as we flew towards it. The St. Lawrence.

Each of the servicemen in the aircraft now found a window on the starboard side and I craned my neck to see as far forward as I could. The river had moved into the foreground and I could see the beginnings of a long girder bridge come from under the wing and cars driving up the incline towards it. Someone said—perhaps they all said: "Montreal."

In a moment the city was in sight. Another bridge, tall buildings, ships tied up at the quays, lines of white smoke from railway tracks, a wooded hill, rows and rows of streets, brightly painted houses and darker patches around them, a church with a vast dome, and beyond the city a grey-green countryside. How far outside Montreal was Dorval, the airport?

The note from the engines changed and our speed checked as the flaps went out and down. The ground came nearer; fields, a road, poles and wires, a glimpse of a tarmac runway. The wings swayed a little, as though the pilot was giving them their last free movements before holding them rigidly level for the landing. The engines spluttered. A single bump, another, and then the vibration of wheels running over concrete. We taxied over to a one-storied building, with a door to the right and a luggage ramp to the left. The clock-face on a tower at the corner of the building said ten minutes to six. Someone wheeled out the landing-steps and the door opened. This was Canada; Dorval on a damp winter's afternoon.

The aircraftsman in front of me ran down the steps, knelt down and kissed the wet tarmac. Then he turned and grinned at me.

"Like to buy any pound notes?" he said. "Two dollars each."

2. By the Bow River

Some six weeks later, I was in the town of Banff, in the Rockies themselves. Banff is the tourist centre, neat and clean and looking as though it breakfasted on porridge. Around it are the mountains and the forests and, since it is now a National Park, the moose and the mountain sheep and, so they said, even bears. Banff is crowded in summer but I was there before the season had begun and the town was almost empty. It was Sunday morning and the sun was hot so I went for a walk.

In Canada, distance is the first impression. After that comes another; in the end, perhaps no stronger in the Rockies than elsewhere, but it was at Banff that I experienced it the most vividly. It is more than an impression. It is the real challenge of Canada.

All over the British Isles, with the possible exception of those parts of Scotland that are very difficult to reach, one is always sensible that here is a country that has been lived in for a very long time. The fells of the Lake District can show their Roman roads. On the bare hills of Devon and Wales there are mounds and fortifications raised by a former race. Even the Pennines have their dry-stone walls, so old that they seem a natural part of the landscape until one asks oneself who can have laid them. The countryside of England is full of what the economist would call capital improvements and the writer our national heritage; the parklands, the mill-ponds, the neat plantations, the network of lanes, ditches and bridges. All that has its charm and there are many Canadians who envy the English for the shape of the land in which they live.

Do they really envy the English for positive reasons, or is their feeling no more than a reaction from their own so different country? Banff had its sign-posted footpaths and its romantic walks, carefully fenced at the more dangerous points, so that the visitor might have the illusion that he was free to roam at will while the locality remained safeguarded against the bad publicity a broken holiday leg would cause. But let the visitor walk out of the town on something other than a beaten track and at once he is in the true Canada, the unlived-in country. He pushes aside a branch, mounts the rotting trunk of a tree that fell fifty years back, and immediately he thinks: "Am I the first man to have trodden on this square of earth?"

That is how the challenge of Canada first expressed itself to me and time and again the challenge was repeated. A mile out of Grand Falls, in Newfoundland, or beyond the Jordan River on Vancouver Island, at the end of a drive north from Montreal or Ottawa, even among the metal caps that mark each producing well in the oilfields around Edmonton, always no more than a hundred yards or so from the existing track there is a section, a wood, a tangle of undergrowth, a vista of uninhabited prairie, that contains the challenge of the totally unknown. To most Canadians that is the real adventure of their country. They may seek in England the relief of contrast, the relief that comes from a slackening of this awareness, but few of them can turn their backs for long on their own adventurous home.

I sat down by the Bow River on that Sunday morning and I tried for the first time to separate the ingredients in the excitement I felt simply because I was there. This quality of "newness", of the untouched and unexplored, was certainly a part. But not all. I am, I suppose, romantically minded. At that moment I knew that I was capable of sharing the emotions that are reputed to have moved Cortez in Panama even while the more prosaic side of my mind, in its rather tired voice, was telling me that the rock on which I sat watching the torrent and the falls had surely been used for the same purpose year after year by hundreds of other tourists. But I was looking beyond Banff. I was looking northwards and my mind took me beyond the confines of that valley to the lands I had not seen but of which I was already deeply aware. So I began —not that the process ended there in Banff—to try to identify to myself all that lay behind the pull I already felt towards Canada, its prospects and its orders of society.

I can think of no better way of describing the ultimate sum than by saying that in Canada I found a still expanding society.

Let me put on one side for the moment the question of whether an expanding society is a good one in which to live, or not. I write as a European, one whose life began about the beginning of the century, who sees the world through European eyes, and as one who grew up in the unquestioning belief that Europe is the centre of the world and that the world's other peoples have derived more benefit than misfortune from the activities of its inhabitants (a circumstance for which these others are ceasing, unfortunately, it seems to my European mind, to be sufficiently grateful). Europe's age of expansion began about five centuries ago and ended with the beginning of this century, with, one might say, the South African War or, at the latest, with the creation of the separate spheres of influence in Persia a few years later. Since then, Europe's efforts to expand have slackened and those she has made have been generally unsuccessful. The whole climate of her life has changed; the ending of this period of expansion has not been simply a matter of geography. Today, among the Western European peoples—by which I mean peoples whose society has its origins in Western Europe—it is now the exception to find one which has any solid belief in the possibility of further expansion beyond its frontiers, physically or politically.

I belong to my age in that I dislike even the idea of any race claiming the right to rule the lives of other peoples. I believe that Europeans have given a better government to some peoples than those peoples could have given to themselves. I believe that, in some circumstances and maybe for no more than a limited time, Europeans could still give better government to others than those others could give to themselves. But even such a belief is now irrelevant. The majority of people in Europe have lost confidence in either their right or their duty to govern others, and, after all, successful government depends far more upon the self-confidence of the governors than it does on the assent of the governed.

I doubt if one can exaggerate the importance of this change in Europe's faith in itself; its loss may well have been a most important turning-point, for Europe's expansion may have been more than an expression of its vitality. It may have been a condition of its vitality. Perhaps when Europe ceased to expand it began to die, and now the whole structure of its society may be no more than a coral reef, beautifully intricate, rigid and brittle, and, worst of all, sterile. But that is a digression.

In contrast, Canada has this great advantage. She is the only country peopled entirely by Western European man which can still expand geographically within her existing legal frontiers. Her struggle is not against other peoples or societies but against physical conditions, land and water, cold and wind and stubborn rock. This battle is a clean battle. Victory will not be corroded from below, by the existence of a defeated or subject race. What is more, the struggle is in, and with, the physical conditions that bring out most strongly the best qualities of the white race. It is a curious fact that both the characters and the abilities of Europeans tend to disintegrate as they settle nearer and nearer to the Equator (which is why, by way of digression, I would rate the prospects before Canada so much more highly than those before the white peoples in Australia).

In Canada, the frozen north is both a phrase and a fact. The movement northwards in Canada is a part of the Canadians' determination to win for the rest of the world as well as for themselves all that these lands contain. But the adventure is not confined to the north. It is everywhere in Canada. It is the effort to apply the methods and skills of this century to the struggle the men of Europe took up centuries ago and prosecuted more vigorously than any people yet seen on earth. It is the struggle to make still more of the earth itself progressively more productive.

Let me be practical. The average immigrant to Canada from Europe is not going to wonder whether he will be the first to tread on a fallen tree-trunk at Banff, or anywhere else. He is going to think of what job he will get, and where, under what conditions he will be able to use his existing skills and what he will be paid for them. He will want to know about housing and education. He may very well settle down in a town in Southern Ontario, buy a car and a deep-freeze and a television set, and never see a hill higher than the South Downs. Yet, granted all that, he will move in to a country in which there are the Rockies and the Mackenzie River and Ungava and his whole life will be changed because the people around him are conscious of that, too. He will settle in a country in which this battle for physical expansion and mastery continues, fought by men and women who are his fellow-countrymen. He will not escape its impact. In countless ways his life there will be different from his life in Europe on that account.

The drive that incites Canadians to do all this springs from motives besides those of personal gain; indeed, I think it is a European disease to dismiss as pure materialism the kind of enterprise that has built up North America. To say that there is nothing of the spirit in the imagination, the experience and the enterprise that has gone into, say, the Kitimat aluminium and power project is, to my mind, to be wilfully blind. Like Mr. Attlee, I must be a Victorian at heart. I believe in the parable of the talents. If Western European man has, as I believe he has, greater powers of mechanical invention, of organising ability, of improvisation and of co-operation, than any other of the world's peoples, then he must use those talents to the full and trust to his instincts, and the instincts of his descendants, in the use that will be made of his work. If he loses confidence in this obligation, then his day is surely done.

All this, some would say, is no more than the old argument that Canada is a part of the New World, a land fit for pioneers to live in. And who would be a pioneer from choice? Civilisation itself, they imply, is not to be found in that state of development. For those of European origin, civilisation lies in Europe and can only be lived and understood in Europe. I am not so sure that the New World can be dismissed in this way, but let me answer at least a part of that question first: Why choose Canada as the section of the New World in which to live? Why not the United States?

The simplest answer of all is this: Canada is still a part of the Queen's Dominions. Either that means nothing at all or it means a great deal. If it has any meaning there at least is one adequate reason for a preference for Canada. The other parts of the question, and of the answer, are more complicated—the rest of this book is primarily intended to give anyone who reads it the kind of information he should need to enable him to answer it for himself. It is obvious that what I consider to be important considerations may seem to others to matter little one way or the other. But, for me—and here I am summarising what took far longer than an hour or so beside the Bow River to sort out—for me—

For one thing, each of us as time goes by builds up a conception in his mind of the virtues he most admires and of the vices that seem to him to be the most detestable. The admirable virtues run off the tongue at once; one knows them so much the better for not possessing them. The vices are harder to name. They are so often to be found in ourselves and, in our own keeping, we prefer to think of them as no more than amiable weaknesses. But, over time, the vice I have come most to dislike and mistrust is arrogance. Canada is not an arrogant country. Canadians are not arrogant as both Americans and Europeans, in their so different ways, can be. In Europe, an intellectual asks you a question in order that he may tell you the answer. In Canada, the man who asks will really want to have your answer to it. The Canadian has what I would call an intelligent simplicity, and the arrogance of those in Europe who assume that because they have a culture they must also have wisdom is the hardest of all things to bear.

For another, I am a political being. For the last seven years I have made a living by commenting on what can be best described as current affairs, and my curiosity over them, fed by what it likes, has grown. It is with difficulty that I resist the temptation to introduce into the beginning of a book on Canada the synopsis of an entirely different book on European, particularly British, politics. Instead, I will put my reactions to this aspect of the Canadian scene without comment. Faced with a choice between the political system in Canada and that in the United States, I cannot imagine anyone choosing that of the United States. In so far as the Canadian approach to political parties and economic relationships differs from that of the British, for the most part I prefer the Canadian. But these comments are only oblique approaches to what I became convinced is the core of the whole problem, for in Canada two beliefs came into sharper focus in my mind than ever before.

The first was that this political and economic structure built up by Western European man, this thing we call our civilisation, is in Europe very sick indeed (I did not need to go to Canada to know that, only to realise it.) The second was that, in Canada, this civilisation has its best—perhaps its only—chance of regenerating itself.

I am not overmuch concerned to attempt to estimate how good that chance is. I will not see the answer and I suffer from an inability to be deeply concerned with results that only my children will see. But I cannot conceive that anyone should be indifferent to the fact that this chance exists. Here is a civilisation, our civilisation, that has spent its day in a battle that is still only just joined, that of prescribing the power of the few over the many. Here is a civilisation that has been avidly greedy in acquisition and yet which has spread its accumulations around the globe and made them a currency for a world exchange in material progress. Here is a civilisation that has grown more from argument than from violence, more from dissent than from conformity. It contains, however imperfectly, the essence of humanity's fight here on earth. If in Europe it is in the evening of its day, the conceptions of its morning are still bright. One may hate them, or despise them, or value them; it seems impossible to turn one's back on them.

It stands its best chance of being born again in Canada for these reasons. Canada is free, democratic and Christian. Canadians are more free than the British because they have felt no need for the aids and crutches and restrictions that so many in Britain cling to with fear and devotion. Their lives are still their own. They are as democratic as the British. They vote their government into office and they remain convinced that they can vote it out again, if they are so minded. They regard themselves as Christian, and that I believe to be both true and vitally important.

I would not say that the majority of Canadians either accept without question the whole dogma of some Christian church or that they invariably follow during their waking hours all the Christian guides to conduct and relationships. But there is a majority that has faith in the values of the Christian civilisation of this last five hundred years, of which the core is the conviction that the individual is accountable in the sight of God for his actions, that there are absolute standards of value against which every individual, be he commissar, general, priest or salesman, is to be judged. That they do have this faith, I came to believe, is due more than anything else to the stubborn tenacity of the French-speaking Canadians. By keeping this faith, they hold something that Europe no longer has.

It is not that Canadians were able to start with a clean sheet. That was impossible; they have as part of themselves four-fifths of modern Europe's history. It is that they have escaped the remaining fifth, all that Western Europe has done to itself this cen-

tury. They are free from the cancer of fears and hates and smoulder-
ing resentments that holds Europe back from unity, free from the
barriers that, inside Europe, seem as solid and as immutable as
those met in a nightmare. Can one imagine what Europe would
be like if one could wipe from the mind of every man and woman
all recollection of the events recorded in its history over the last
fifty years? To Canadians, those events were a spectacle, not an
experience. Hate is not etched in the Canadian mind.

When I first went to Canada I found the wailing cry of the railway locomotives discordant and sad and I was surprised when
they said that for them it was one of the sounds that most closely
belonged to their country. Gradually I began to understand something of what it meant to them. It belonged beyond the cities,
to the homesteads and the small townships. It belonged to
loneliness and isolation. It was a reassurance that the world outside the four wooden walls was not dead nor inaccessible. It was
the sound one lay awake for in the nursery, the sound of father's
key in the lock, of mother's footstep on the staircase. Of course to
go to Canada is to go back to one's youth, to a land and a time
when there are still unopened doors. But is that a retreat or a new
beginning?

To sit on Birdlip Hill and look out over the Severn and beyond
to the mountains of Wales and to think of the generations of men
who have used those fields and roads and fought and worked and
died—oh yes, as a pilgrimage of respect to one's ancestry. But for
zest and energy to go forward—for me, Banff on a Sunday morning in May.

Western European man—perhaps all mankind—can be divided
into those who seek security, those who seek privilege and those—
a very small minority—who seek power, but there is another element in the make-up of most men. It is a desire to make some
contribution to the common stock, to posterity. It may be a tree
planted in a garden, a better education for a child, the Nuffield
Foundation. I began to wonder, from Banff onwards, whether
this was the country to which I could offer, with both humility and
self-respect, whatever contribution I could make, in the belief
that it might be of more value there than in the country from
which I had come.

2
Some Facts

1. The People

THERE were some 14,009,429 people living in the ten provinces that make up the Confederation of Canada, according to the 1951 census (it is estimated that there are three-quarters of a million more, now), and almost all of them are of European stock. In fact, only 145,559 of them were aboriginals, of pure Red Indian or Eskimo blood. Of these fourteen million people, 85 per cent, or just short of twelve million, were born in Canada.

Canada is larger than the whole of Europe, larger than the United States with Alaska. It contains 3,845,744 square miles. Of its population, over five million live in the fifteen major cities of the country, which means that some nine million people are scattered about some three and a half million square miles; three in each square mile. So, if the population of the major towns were to be excluded, every Canadian family of five, spread evenly over the rest of the country, would be almost two miles distant from its nearest neighbour. In England and Wales each family of five would find another within some fifty yards, in whatever direction it went; an unreal calculation, of course, but one which may serve to emphasise the sense of isolation that must underlie the mind of every European who sees Canada.

About 31 per cent of this population are of French origin. They are *les Canadiens*, almost entirely descendants of those who left France for Canada between the years 1608 and 1763 and who settled in what was then called Acadia, along the Atlantic coast, and up the shores of the St. Lawrence River. When France surrendered her rights over Canada to Britain, the stream of emigration from France across the Atlantic came to an end, but the French had already created Quebec.

Forty-eight per cent of the population are of British origin, and they have come to Canada at various times, in various ways and from various parts of the British Isles. The first to come chose, too, the debatable lands of Acadia or moved northwards from New England towards the St. Lawrence and Lake Ontario. Some settled in Newfoundland, but they were fewer, for permanent settlement there was forbidden by the authorities at home. Then came the rebellion of the thirteen English-speaking colonies in North America followed by a fresh wave of immigrants from the south, the Loyalists. Some settled in the Maritimes, some travelled westwards and broke new ground on the northern shores of Lake Ontario and created Upper Canada.

The proportion of people of British origin is falling. Fifty years ago it was 57 per cent; the 10 per cent difference represents people from other parts of Europe. An early settlement in Manitoba, for instance, at Gimli, was made up of people from Iceland. But most of the other Europeans have come to Canada in this century. Before 1900, Canada lost as many people by emigration as she gained from immigration. The empty lands of the United States filled up first and it was the preference for remaining within the Empire that, acting as a magnet, kept in Canada more of the British immigrants to North America. But the population of Canada of other than British or French origin is now almost one-fifth of the total, and one-fifth of fourteen million is quite a lot of people. Many have settled in groups; the country around Edmonton, in Alberta, is dotted with Greek Orthodox churches and Winnipeg would be a good place in which to learn Russian; in Trail, British Columbia, the language would be Italian. During the eight and a half years that ended on 30 June 1953, 885,999 people from outside settled in Canada; some 85,000 of them came from the Netherlands and nearly 100,000 from Germany, many of them refugees from the lost German lands beyond the River Oder. Of the immigrants into Canada now, only two out of every five are in origin from the United Kingdom.

There is one other possible classification of importance in Canada, that of religions. Forty-three per cent of the people are Roman Catholics; they are the French-speaking Canadians, plus the Scottish and the Irish immigrants who were Roman Catholics.

The United Church, which is a combination of most of the Presbyterian and some of the dissenting churches, claims 20 per cent, the Church of England, nearly 15 per cent, the Continuing Presbyterian Church, 5½ per cent, and membership of the other churches —which are very varied indeed—18 per cent.

The census figures show another problem facing Canada, that which comes from a high birth-rate and a low death-rate now matched against a small natural increase in the population during the 'thirties. The labour force of a country is generally reckoned to be those between the ages of fourteen and sixty-four. In Canada, now, for every ten people in that labour force there are six others, dependants, outside it, a proportion which is higher even than that in the United Kingdom. But in Canada the position should right itself. There are over 3,100,000 children under ten years old, and the birth-rate remains high. In ten years' time those children will begin to go to work and Canada's need to attract labour from outside will be that much less. It is the next ten years that offer the best prospects for the immigrant to Canada; indeed, preferably, the sooner the better.

That is the Canadian people, classified by reference to their countries of origin, their habits of speech and their religions; of course, such dissections of a people form as incomplete a picture as one built up solely from the card index of finger-prints in New Scotland Yard.

2. The Ten Provinces

The ten provinces of Canada lie almost in a necklace spread out along the northern boundary of the United States from the Atlantic to the Pacific Oceans, for the 3,000 miles that lie between St. John's, Newfoundland, and Victoria, British Columbia. Canada can be likened to a seed-bed, its base resting on the United States border. Its soil is the line of settlements from the Gulf of St. Lawrence along the railways westwards to the Fraser River in British Columbia, and its most recent growth, the new enterprises, climb upwards, like tendrils from the awakening seeds, along the lines of the rivers and the lakes towards the polar seas. Newfoundland, Prince Edward Island, Nova Scotia, New Brunswick,

Quebec, Ontario, Manitoba, Saskatchewan, Alberta, British Columbia; six British and four Indian names.

Prince Edward Island and New Brunswick sound solidly Hanoverian, as they were; mid-eighteenth-century creations. Nova Scotia sounds older and must come from the sometimes romantic and always literate Scots, just as Alberta can only have been a dutiful compliment to the Widowed Queen. The name British Columbia made it clear that the Yankees were not going to have the whole of the valley of the Columbia River, and Newfoundland, the oldest colony and the youngest province—its name has all the faith and directness of the Tudor age that discovered it. There could only be one New Found Land on the way to Cathay. Ten provinces, each with a provincial legislature and sending senators and members to the Federal Parliament in Ottawa.

To the north of the provinces are the territories, Yukon and the North-West Territory, which is divided into the districts of Mackenzie, Keewatin and Franklin. They contain 41 per cent of Canada's land area and are still Federal responsibilities, governed by a Commissioner assisted by councils partly elected and partly nominated, very much on the British colonial pattern. They contain some 25,000 people and a great proportion of Canada's future wealth.

In the year 1648, the Treaty of Munster brought an end to the war between Spain and the Dutch Republic, and confirmed the territorial division of the Low Countries, originally established by force of arms, as it had existed since the truce agreement of 1609. Brabant and Flanders were thus divided along, roughly, the line that now separates Holland from Belgium. In many respects the line was quite arbitrary. It paid no regard to racial unity; the Flemings of Belgium were not essentially different from the Dutch immediately to their north. The line did not divide the peoples on the basis of their religions; although the Dutch Republic had fought Spain as a Protestant country, to this day over 90 per cent of the population of the Netherlands south of the Maas are Roman Catholics. It was blind to the economic interests of the people it separated, for it left the port of Antwerp cut off from the sea. Yet that frontier has remained, fortuitous as its origin may have been. It divided a people and they went their several ways. It was strong enough to defeat the attempts to unite Holland and

Belgium under the one crown after the Napoleonic Wars. It has remained a fact, despite the attempts to erase it made in the Benelux era. The peoples are now different, and, although in the Low Countries of Europe the ties should seem to run north and south, politically they run east and west.

So with Canada. The boundary between Canada and the United States has been drawn, on the various occasions on which it was given its present position on the map, with nothing but immediate political considerations in mind, and one of the parties concerned in the final settlements, the United Kingdom, was on occasion more concerned to placate the United States than to further the interests of the inhabitants of Canada. In the hundred and fifty years or so in which it has been approximately in its present position it has become real, as with the frontier that separates Holland and Belgium, and yet its existence has not altered the fact that, in North America, the lines of interests and connection, of geography and weather, run north and south.

Nova Scotia, New Brunswick, Prince Edward Island and Newfoundland are, physically, a continuation of the Appalachian chain that stretches up the eastern coast of North America, and their peoples have moved north and south more freely than east and west. The St. Lawrence Valley below Lake Ontario is one, although the boundary between Ontario and New York State not only ignores the fact but has itself become something of a hindrance to good relations between the two countries.

Southern Ontario is a part of the community of the Great Lakes and, to many of its people, New York and Chicago have as strong a pull as have Toronto and Montreal. The social pattern of the life of the majority of people in Toronto is Eastern American. Western Ontario, from Port Arthur and Port William on Lake Superior westwards, is a land of woods and lakes, duplicated almost exactly in north-east Minnesota. Beyond Winnipeg the prairies begin, a part of the vast central wheat-growing area of North America that extends northwards and westwards along the valley of the Missouri through the Dakotas and which is matched in Manitoba and Saskatchewan. The Willison basin oilfield, likewise, is no respector of the 49th parallel. More people in Winnipeg know Minneapolis than know Montreal, and the farmers of Saskatchewan and Alberta share climate, economics, even religions, with the men of the Dakotas and Montana. In Saskatchewan

1. Alberta: Banff and The Hotel

2. Ontario: Toronto

and Alberta the 49th parallel happens to coincide with a watershed, but it is one that you can drive over without noticing it.

In British Columbia the north–south line is at its most unmistakable. The Rockies are the common property of the United States and Canada, as are the rain-rich coastal ranges of the Pacific coast. In the small towns in southern British Columbia, for instance, it is to Spokane, in Washington, that you may go to find your dentist. In Vancouver, women buy the more important elements in the spring outfits in Seattle. In Eastern Canada, you vacation in Florida, if you can afford that kind of vacation. In the West, you drive either to Los Angeles or to Santa Barbara, depending on what kind of person you are. And you can travel from Toronto to Mexico City by bus for $78 return. The one unique physical possession that Canada has is the Canadian Shield.

3. The Canadian Shield

The Canadian, or pre-Cambrian, Shield is the name given to the mass of pre-Cambrian rocks that constitute the central portion of the country. The southern limit of the Shield, the dividing line between it and the newer rocks to the south, runs westwards from the coast of Labrador, along the Laurentian Mountains north of the St. Lawrence River to Lake Superior. The northern shore of Lake Superior to the head of the Great Lakes is itself the southern fringe of that portion of the Shield, and from there the line runs northwestwards through Lake Winnipeg, Lake Athabaska, Great Slave Lake and Great Bear Lake to the Arctic. There are some 2,500,000 square miles of land within the Shield, more than two-thirds the land area of the whole of Canada.

The characteristics of the Shield are broken, hilly country covered with forest and muskeg, or semi-swamp, and dotted with great numbers of lakes and streams. The surface has been ground down by glaciers in the past, leaving the hills bare and rounded and the valleys overlain with gravel and moraine. The whole Shield tilts towards the north so that, within the Shield, the rivers flow either into Hudson's Bay or the Arctic Ocean. Little of the land there is cultivable, save round the southern shores of Hudson's Bay and James Bay. There the rocks of the Shield are overlain by sedimentary rock, itself covered with a layer of marine

C

clay surmounted by peat. This land, today, is poorly drained and is frozen for most of the year, but if drained it could produce summer crops.

But the immediate importance of the Shield lies in the mass of minerals it contains, and in the fact that it is lined with rivers that are sources of power. These minerals comprise most of the metals that mankind uses and they exist in quantity and to an extent which no man yet knows. Already the country within the Shield produces all Canada's nickel, radium, platinum and cobalt, 95 per cent of her copper, 92 per cent of her gold and over half of her silver. The iron-ore deposits in what is called the Labrador Trough may well extend in a belt thirty miles wide and 400 miles long. At Lawson, in Ontario, a vein of silver ore with 12,000 ounces of silver to the ton was found on the surface. The Eldorado pitchblende mines, taken over by the Canadian Government during the war because of the importance of their uranium content, are almost on the Arctic Circle, in the Great Slave Lake area. The concentrates are shipped 1,300 miles by river and another 2,000 miles by rail to Port Hope, on Lake Ontario, for refining. So the list continues. Man has begun to spread out over the Shield and the nature of his discoveries already is almost a guarantee in itself that he has not yet found more than a fraction of what the Shield must contain.

The Canadian Shield could not have been developed before the present century. It was inaccessible before the petrol engine; its products were unworkable before it became possible to transmit electric power over a distance. It has taken some fifty years to bring the equipments making use of power in these forms to the stage at which they can conquer the North, and that development has come at a time when there is a sharp rise in the demand for the ultimate products themselves. The pattern of technical development in the nineteenth century cannot be repeated in this northern country. Something different, both technically and socially, must come out of it, and that alone makes it one of the most exciting places in the Western world.

3

The East

1. Quebec

THE cities of Quebec and Montreal are in sharp contrast. Quebec
is a city behind a wall; Montreal sprawls around the hill that gave
it its name as though its life bubbled up at a score of different
points. Quebec is crystalline. The whole city seems to be there for
you to see in the mind from the first moment; the port, the Upper
and Lower towns, the ramparts, the history, the churches, the
grain elevators, the university, the river, the provincial government buildings. But attempt to reach out to it and you find that
the city is encased in a hard, transparent shell; of language? So
it seems at first, until you begin to realise that the barrier between
you and Quebec is more complex than that.

Montreal, by contrast, is soft, absorbent, almost like a sea
anemone. It is gay and mondaine, too busy to pay any attention to
the visitor on its streets. But this indifference is equally deceptive
for it begins to suck you in from the moment you arrive, as
though it were intent on making you an inhabitant of itself, without affection, perhaps almost as a condition of its own life. Montreal is an atmosphere to breathe.

Montreal is built around the hill of Mount Royal, and Mount
Royal is in fact a ridge, about three miles long and not very high.
When I first saw the city from the air as I flew in it reminded me
of my native city, Liverpool, and there are some resemblances. In
both the land slopes upward from the river, but in Liverpool the
edge of the escarpment itself, where the cathedral now stands,
was never quite steep enough to deter the builders. The face that
Mount Royal presents to its river is much more of a cliff and that

19

has led the inhabitants—through good sense or luck?—to keep
at least half of its crest as an open space on which one may ride
in summer, ski in winter and walk all the year round. The ridge
lies parallel to the river and at one end, standing out and facing
downstream, is a giant iron cross, a hundred feet high, a rather
grim skeleton by day and a blaze of light at night. At the other
end of the ridge is the great church of St. Joseph, a memorial to
a hospital porter who found that he could work miracles. Mount
Royal also provides the surrounding countryside with excellent
television reception from the transmitter on its summit, it contains
Montreal's largest cemetery and it is a vast handicap to Montreal's
traffic because there is only one public highway across its length.

The population of Montreal is about 1,400,000, of whom about
two-thirds are French in origin—there is also a big Jewish population. The collection of semi-independent townships that make up
this metropolitan area lies on a large island between the left bank
of the St. Lawrence (which there runs almost north and south)
and the right bank of a tributary, La Rivière des Prairies. It
stretches for some fifteen miles, making an oval with the ridge of
Mount Royal as the yoke, rather off-centre, of this vast egg. The
industrial areas, and the areas in which the French-speaking
workers live, are to the north-east and they lap up to the end of
the ridge and run a little way along its north-western slopes. On
the south-western half of the ridge is Westmount, English-speaking, elegant and expensive but losing something of its former
domination because its largest private houses are now too huge
for any one family to maintain, and beyond are the English-
speaking townships of Hampstead and Mount Royal. To complete the picture, the eastern slopes, facing the river, are dotted
with the buildings of McGill University, the tall flats along
Sherbrooke Street and the upper section of the shopping area.
The country immediately around Montreal is flat and from whatever direction one approaches the city the line of the ridge stands
out against the horizon.

The original French settlement at Montreal was a village named
Ville Marie, and it lay on the river about a mile upstream from
the Indian village of Hochelaga. They chose this spot because
there a creek made a peninsula against the river-bank, very much
as Liverpool was once a settlement on a peninsula on the banks
of the Mersey, cut off from the main shore by the Pool, and, in

Montreal as at Liverpool, this channel has now been filled in. The whaleback ridge of the former settlement has become the heart of downtown Montreal, the financial centre, dominated by the tower of the Royal Bank of Canada, at one end, at the other the French-speaking factories and offices and the market of Bonsecours, named for the sailors' church, with the Place d'Armes, the City Hall and the Cathedral of St. James in the centre between the two. But a second business centre is challenging the old rule of St. James's Street, as Kingsway rivals the City of London. When Montreal's Central Station was built, at the mouth of the tunnel under Mount Royal, the excavations for the tracks left a large open space. Slowly that is becoming an area of high buildings and open gardens, and Montreal, like so many European cities, will have a double heart.

Montreal is one of the two centres of the heroic hundred years of the French in Canada. Cartier reached the island first, in 1535, on his voyage of exploration. Maisonneuve established the first permanent settlement, in 1642, with thirty-three men and a priest who, at the first mass on landing, likened those with him to a grain of mustard seed whose branches would overshadow the earth, and his faith can be said to be justified. No more than some 60,000 settlers from France crossed the Atlantic and their descendants now number over four million.

Maisonneuve chose Montreal as the site for the second town in Canada because the Indian village of Hochelaga marked the end of the waters his ships could navigate; just upstream were rapids which the French called Lachine because they lay further along the road to China. The settlement commanded the junction of the St. Lawrence and the Ottawa rivers and each was a waterway leading towards the Great Lakes. Barring the way westwards were the Iroquois, fighting men, ruthless and delighting in torture, and for another fifty years the French fought a double battle with cross and sword. By the end of that century they could feel that they had established themselves in the face of the original inhabitants of the St. Lawrence Valley. In the fall of 1760 their rule came to an end. British sea-power extended itself up the river with sufficient force, and luck, to capture Quebec, and when the Marquis de Vaudreuil hauled down the fleur-de-lis flag there he surrendered for ever Montreal and all the lands in Canada that the French had ruled.

The men and women from France brought with them their religion and their language; whatever nostalgia they may have felt for France as a country died, for there was no way back. In North America they found land, and the care of their land and the cultivation of their family relationships were all their temporal needs. They have shown not only a power to survive. They have also shown a power to absorb and yet remain themselves unchanged. When Wolfe's Scottish regiments were disbanded after 1760 and were given grants of land in Quebec, they married among the French. In the province of Quebec today the mother tongue of a man named MacDonald will almost certainly be French. The one people they did not absorb were the English-speaking men and women who came to Montreal.

These came mostly from the south, from New England—hard, Puritan men who knew that every religion but their own was evil. They were men and women who had left the shores of England because its king was too tolerant of religious diversity for their own spiritual comfort, and they moved northwards from Massachusetts, Connecticut and New York on the newly won province of Quebec. They were the men who began the tradition in Canada that to speak English was a necessary condition precedent to the attainment of money and power, that to speak French was a sign of the hewer of wood and the drawer of water. The Roman Catholics of Quebec knew a good deal about the people from New England, and they liked them not at all. It was useless for Benjamin Franklin to spend his time in captured Montreal in 1775, writing pamphlets urging the French-speaking inhabitants to throw their lots in with the American Colonists. The loyalists in Canada might have reason for rejecting the claims of the revolutionary theorists. The French-speaking in Canada had an even more powerful emotion; they knew that the practices of these theorists represented the antithesis of the way of life they valued.

In 1774, Guy Carlton, Governor of Canada, persuaded the United Kingdom Parliament to pass the Quebec Act of that year. It was legislation hastened without doubt by the mounting trouble with the Thirteen Colonies further south, but it is remarkable in that it came into existence no more than sixteen years after the Conquest (and some sixty-five years before the Catholic Emancipation Act in the United Kingdom). In many ways it was a Tory Act. It gave government into the hands of the Governor and an appointed Council (although it limited their powers of taxation) and it restored to the seigneurs and the clergy the rights they had held under the King of France. But it gave freedom of worship to Roman Catholics, it relieved them of the need to take a Protestant oath before they could hold office and it declared that in civil matters the "Laws of Canada" should prevail (in criminal matters it established the English common law). It must, says Professor A. R. M. Lower in *Colony to Nation*, "be regarded as a great constitutional landmark in Canadian history. . . . In the province of Quebec, it gave the French an assurance of the British Government's good will and apparently its sense of justice." It ensured that Quebec would retain her ancient religion, that the way of life of the ordinary people would not be broken up by force. Would it have been better for Canada if it had?

The division is still there. The main axis of the city of Montreal is a street known as St. Catherine's. At a point somewhere near where Bleury Street crosses it, there is a zone division, almost a dividing-line. On one side, which contains the main shopping-centre, the names and labels in the windows are English, on the other the shops are cheaper and they are French. There is even a change of atmosphere, notably in the evening, for Montreal enjoys its evening life. On the English-speaking side people seem to walk with some purpose in mind; on the French-speaking side they promenade. The French-speaking find enjoyment in the simple fact that they are alive, and are living in a milieu consisting of people feeling as they do. They are supremely natural. In the suburbs they live in apartments, blocks of two-storied flats, ugly buildings disfigured still further by added outside staircases of revolting design, but full of life and gossip and neighbourly interest. The English-speaking care for the separate house and they tend their gardens and keep up appearances. Montreal is a cosmopolitan city, but not all its people are cosmopolitans.

"When I was a boy," a friend told me, "we fought any boy who spoke French", and I dare say if he had gone to a different school he would have been the sufferer. English-speaking are still intruders. For many of the English-speaking, there is at least an opaque curtain across St. Catherine's at Bleury. We don't go beyond there, they will say; it is so very French. Even in McGill University, so I was told by a French-speaking Canadian, it was the practice until recently to select lecturers in French from

France. To some of the French-speaking, the English-speaking are a species of occupation force, as the Germans were in Paris; it is permissible to make money out of them, but they are to be excluded, if possible, from the civil government of Quebec. The French-speaking are very successful at this.

There is, however, no such division in the city of Quebec; it is wholly French-speaking.

The best vantage-point in Quebec is the Château Frontenac. It is very hard to accept that this fabulous structure is no more than an hotel belonging to a railway company; it has the air of a building dreamed by Sir Hugh Casson and subsequently modified by a joint commission of the Principality of Monaco and the Committee of the Edinburgh Festival. It stands on a cliff some four hundred feet above the river. It is flanked by a statue of Champlain and a memorial to Wolfe and Montcalm. Its central tower is sixteen floors high and at its top the wind whistles into the elevator shaft like a gale in the rigging of a ship at sea. Its public rooms are the finest flower of the Canadian-Scottish baronial style, and one half-listens for the wails of tortured Sassenachs to come faintly up from the dungeons below. Immediately adjoining it is a wooden promenade, and from there one can see Quebec.

I stood there in the early morning, with the sun still low in the east and the river a dark green in the shadow from the wooded banks opposite. Downstream, hazy in the morning mist, the Isle of Orleans divided the river, and the bridge across one arm of the water was delicately pencilled in against a background of grey flecked with silver. The Lower Town was out of sight below me, but blue smoke from it drifted across the foreground. A ferry-boat moved slowly across to the further bank, to the town of Levis, and there only the churches and the colleges stood out from among the trees. Beyond the end of the promenade, away from the sun, the land rose to the crest of the old fort, a mound of freshly green grass buttressed by dark-brown stone, and beyond that were the grey roofs and the closely packed buildings of the Upper Town of Quebec. Quebec stretches solidly back into time. No other city in Canada gives such an impression of endurance.

Running down beside Laval University, in the Upper Town, there is a street that ends on the ramparts. It is narrow, and the buildings are flush with the footwalks. On the one side is the

university, a long façade of undistinguished buildings, on the
other two terraces of houses, grey houses with rough plaster
fronts, broken by one side street. The street is so narrow that one
forgets the sky save where it is a background at the further end
beyond the ramparts. When I turned into it there was a woman
in the roadway, some distance down. I had seen her before, the
dark hair tightly drawn back, the blue print skirt, almost ankle-
length, tight at the waist under a black belt, full in the skirt itself,
and below the black stockings and shoes. I had seen her in Lille,
in Le Havre, in Bordeaux.

There are two shops in this street, both with glass fronts made
up of some dozen panes of glass held in place by wood once varnished. One belongs to a butcher. Behind the glass a wooden
block contains slabs of meat, dark red in front and fading to a
darker purple in the shadows behind. The butcher is fat and
wears a blue overall and darker blue beret. The other is a cycle-
shop, its door half-blocked by a tradesman's cycle on a stand, the
window a jumbled heap of accessories, with only the bright
yellow of the cardboard covers of puncture-repair outfits giving it
any colour. The street, the shops, the inhabitants, save the one
black cat in the middle of the road, were clearly, unmistakably
and for ever French.

So is the Quebec post office, in the Upper Town. It looks as
though it had been designed by a minor engineer in the French
Postes et Telegraphes in 1890 for a provincial centre such as Dijon
and shipped, stone by stone, to Quebec as a gesture of goodwill
after the Paris Exposition of 1900.

So is the Lower Town, below the ramparts. There is the same
rutted tarmac road, the same cracked concrete footwalks, the
same jumble of houses and factory buildings, with disused and
broken windows stuffed with straw, identical with those of any
provincial French town. Not one is used for the purpose for
which it was built; each is as active and as incongruous as
a wasps' nest in an old boot. Just under the ramparts there
is what was once a smithy, ill-adapted by a man who be-
grudged the expenditure of a single franc to the handling of such
motor repairs as may be carried out by hard work and ingenuity
without recourse to either light or power. In the grass-grown
yard are two rusted horse-drawn hay-rakes and an enormous iron
flywheel from a long since dismantled local factory engine. The

hardest mental adjustment to make in Quebec is to accept that the cars in the streets will not be Citroëns and Renaults and Peugeots. And yet: nowhere else in Canada did I see a shop filled with fabrics of local weave and of such beautiful colouring and design.

The slums of Quebec are shocking. The sections of the city that began to grow fifty years ago with industrialisation show that other French characteristic, an indifference to order and neatness in appearance, to any of the practical amenities of life, coupled with an unwillingness to spend money solely to those ends. To that has been added, perhaps, a trace of North American individualism, the underlying conviction that the answer to poor housing is to encourage the people in it to work their own way out, and not to bother too much about the failures left behind. Maybe the day will come when they are tackled, and, when they are, it will be with bulldozers and the full parade of mechanisation. For Quebec cannot be wholly French, and it is certainly not in France. Where in France does the river, the one route to Paris, freeze solid for five months in a year, leaving exiles to stand until the last sail has cleared the point against the Isle of Orleans and then to climb slowly from the quays into the town and bar their gates and await their winter of cold and ice, and isolation?

Of the 4,056,000 people in the province of Quebec at the time of the 1951 census, 1,670,000 of them lived in the cities of Montreal and Quebec. The adult working population numbered about 1,500,000 in 1952, and one out of every three at work was a woman, which is a higher proportion than anywhere else in Canada. About half of them were in manufacturing industry, and the value of what they produced was some eight times that of those working in agriculture. Among these industries the two largest are wood-pulp and paper products and textiles and clothing. There are proportionately fewer strikes in Quebec than in Ontario but when they do happen they last longer. There are over a thousand separate trade unions in the province, and in 1950 they reported a membership of about half a million. If you worked in the building industry at Drummondville, which is the area with the lowest rate of pay, in 1952 your minimum hourly rate of pay would range from 80 cents as a labourer or a truck-driver to $1.30 as a bricklayer.

The old picture of life in Quebec is that described by Louis Hemon in the classic novel of the province, *Maria Chapdelaine*; the habitant, or small landowner, labouring in a harsh climate to tame the land and feed his large family from the produce of his holding, shepherded from the evils of the world, and of dangerous thoughts, by the care of the village priests. The fields along the St. Lawrence may still be in a pattern of long strips stretching back in countless parallel lines from the river-bank, for that was the original form that land division took, three centuries ago, and the shape of a country's fields changes very slowly. Nor has the life of the habitant gone, but it is no longer typical.

What has changed? Simply that, as Quebec became industrialised, the sons and daughters of the land left to supply labour for industry. It is they who, in the last ten years, have been filling up Montreal and Quebec and the smaller towns in the eastern townships of the province. The process began earlier and perhaps went more smoothly in Ontario for, as a rule, the English-speaking settler was more aware of what might be called the cash value of his activitiy and so the more ready to change it for one paying a higher return in money. The French-speaking settler felt otherwise. He cared for the land and the way of life built up around his land. He sold its produce in order to be able to stay where he was and to live as he had lived. He has not changed, but his children have and so it is from the cities of Montreal and Quebec that the ferment among the French-speaking people of Canada bubbles out.

The French people, of course, have no difficulty in living in a world of glory and a world of reality at the same time (most nations make the attempt, but the French seem to be better at it than most) and in that the people of Quebec are very French. The French in France have usually preferred talking of political democracy as an ideal to taking the trouble to make such a machine of government work; in that sense the French-speaking people of Quebec are more anglicised, but they are still happy to accept one form of democracy in federal affairs and a somewhat different variety in affairs within the province. Provincially, democracy is not just a matter of counting heads and of attaching the same weight to each vote. Since the provincial governments of Canada are mainly concerned with property rights, is it not more logical to give those with property more influence than those without?

The people of Quebec have always been disciplined and submissive. They were accustomed to see their affairs ordered by an
oligarchy of talent, and provided talent could enter the oligarchy
(Mr. St. Laurent is an excellent example of the talent that did
enter the oligarchy) should not everyone be satisfied with that?
The pattern of society was patriarchal, with good employers like
fathers and bad employers like stepfathers. The French-speaking,
long ago, established that they could run their own businesses,
such as banks and insurance companies, but a great deal of the
money needed to develop the capital resources of the province
could only be found in the rest of North America. It was deliberately attracted to Quebec by the offer of such desirable circumstances as a low level of wages and a docile population. And, if
the docile population did occasionally step out of character and
protest, they were at once told that the culprit must be some
English-speaking concern; was not the capital exploiting them
largely owned by these strangers?

This world of Quebec—still real but, I feel, likely soon to be
counting the years left in the calendar of its life—is exemplified
by Mr. Maurice Duplessis, the provincial Premier. Mr. Duplessis
is a lawyer, and a bachelor, intelligent, immensely hard-working
and scrupulously honest in his personal transactions. He likes
power, he believes that the practice of politics enables a man to
gain power and he does not believe that people go in for politics
unless they want power (and, despite their avowals that they are
solely interested in human betterment, it is hard to escape the
conviction that Mr. Duplessis is as right about many on the left
as he is of the remainder). Mr. Duplessis' convictions on the relations between the classes have the simplicity of the last century.
There are bosses and hired hands. A hired hand is free to become
a boss, if he can, but he must not seek to possess too many rights
until he has done so. Mr. Duplessis does not recognise many
limitations on the rights of those that have power to use it as their
interests dictate. If private enterprise is prepared to be enter-
prising, it is no part of Mr. Duplessis' conception of duty to curb
it unduly. But there are such things as provincial elections and
over these Mr. Duplessis relies upon his appeal as champion of
provincial rights. Many federal activities and proposals can be
described—particularly at election time—as interference in the
provincial affairs of Quebec. Mr. Duplessis has denied the right of

the Federal Government to make a grant to McGill University, on the grounds that education is purely a matter for the province. He has refused to make a tax rental agreement with the Federal Government, because these agreements are based fairly and squarely on a surrender by the province of its freedom to impose certain taxes. At the same time, he has stretched provincial rights far enough to justify a refusal to co-operate in the contruction of the Trans-Canada highway. It is said of Mr. Duplessis that he has two enemies, Ottawa and Moscow, of which either may seem the more dangerous at any one given time (yet, federally, Quebec votes solidly for the Liberals and Mr. St. Laurent).

All this would seem to describe a society which is in some way insulated from the changes affecting the rest of Canada; of course, Quebec is not so insulated and the impact of the changes of the last ten years is the most intellectually exciting thing about Quebec today. The traditional conception of Quebec as the land of the one peasant people in North America had ceased to have real truth behind it before the war. Industry had been spreading, the towns had grown and the countryside of the peasant proprietor was losing both its importance and its attraction to the next generation. But the myth remained until the war; it was the one Canadian myth that seemed to have immortality. Mr. Duplessis may not like to face this change, but it is there clearly to be seen. All the standards of the past, good and bad, are under challenge, from within.

The present generation in Quebec cannot—no one can—escape time, history, or traditions. They are Catholic North Americans, not atheistic Europeans. The working-class leaders cannot turn their backs on Catholicism and go over to Communism; they would divorce themselves from those they should lead if they did. They cannot take over ready-made the answers the left-wing parties in the United Kingdom would give them, for a policy of nationalisation depends upon control at the centre, at Ottawa. They have not that now, they are not likely to obtain it for a considerable time, and if they did attain it they would find in the end that keys made in Britain did not fit their lock. They cannot wholly accept the materialist view of the American unions, that the proper concern of trade-union leaders is that they shall be successful in their chess games with the bosses for higher wages. They feel that to be too empty a policy. They cannot wholly accept the present order of society in Quebec, for it belongs to an economic pattern that has gone.

They believe that, in some way, a trade-union movement should have political expression, but what is the right course to follow in winning it? The creation of a new party, the capture of a single existing party, infiltration into more than one of the existing parties, or operations on the basis of a series of shifting alliances with existing parties? And, while they search for their answers, there is the running battle with the Duplessis government, with big business—which does not think in terms of offering high wages from the start—and with those sections of their Church that are suspicious of any movement which they do not control. Quebec may in the end find most guidance—from Europe, that is—in the experience of the Catholic unions in Germany and the Netherlands. In the meantime, the Department of Political Science at Laval University in Quebec is to the trade-union movement in that province what the London School of Economics was to the British Labour movement thirty years ago—always bearing in mind that both the University and the trade unions are Catholic.

Quebec is a looking-glass city. What one can see suggests at first that here is a pattern of life that any European can understand. It corresponds to—seems almost identical with—one in which he has lived elsewhere. But gradually he finds it otherwise and then he comes to believe that the back of the clock may have the face of a grinning old man and that there are chessmen walking among the cinders.

I went to the City of Quebec from Park Avenue Station, in the suburbs of Montreal. The station building is massive and wildly extravagant, with a waiting-room as dignified as a private art gallery in New York City, and so overwhelming that even the news-stand avoided the coarser comics and sold only glossy magazines. By contrast, the station platform is open to the four winds and at least two of them seemed to be blowing across it. I was early for the train and there were on the platform, waiting with me, some dozen people or so who, for me, exemplify a great deal of what I saw in the province of Quebec.

Four were student priests of the Roman Catholic Church, three of them with innocent, protected faces and the fourth a cheerful numskull who must have cherished the instinct—for he looked incapable of holding a belief—that the good life consists of a long series of guffaws. He would have made, judging from his appearance and behaviour, a better travelling salesman. In a little group by themselves were three priests, middle-aged and silent, one ascetic, one round-faced and solemn, the third a great pillar of a man with short, wiry, grey hair, a lined face and eyes that would be content with nothing but the truth. There were four business men in another group, one old and dogmatic, one younger but giving the impression that he had as much law to lay down, the other two listening as men do who wait for their cue to second the resolution.

There was a student, in a blazer and carrying three books under his arm, a man in European clothes who looked Italian and a stout lady with large ankles, dressed with the elaborate unattractiveness of the middle-aged Frenchwoman. And with her was a little girl of about eleven, neat and demure. Her frock was ballet-length and frilled, her coat was of smooth blue cloth buttoned up her neck and she wore a blue straw hat, trimmed with ribbon, at exactly the right angle for an adult. At one moment she began to explore a knothole in a plank, part of the wooden platform, with the toe of her elegant, black patent-leather shoe until her mother took her hand and moved away and she walked alongside her, silently and with no change of expression.

The four business men got out at Trois Rivières. The priest with the grim, spare face sat next to me all the way to Quebec, reading his Bible. He occasionally looked up out of the window but I do not think he saw the fields in their long strips running back from the river, nor the untidy woods, nor in the distance the grey water of the St. Lawrence River itself.

There are two cities in Canada in which I should like to live, Vancouver and Quebec. Vancouver I should enjoy. Quebec would be good for both my mind and my soul.

2. Ontario

It is hard at first not to believe that the province of Ontario consists of the city of Toronto with some surrounding land. I think that is the impression that Toronto itself likes to suggest.

Toronto is supremely important, even more to Canada as a whole than to the rest of the province. From it a great many of the enterprises that have built up Canada were organised and financed. It has intelligence, knowledge and a willingness to take a calculated risk. It contains about a quarter of the population of the province, and a third of its total purchasing power. York County, which is, in effect, Greater Toronto, raises from local taxation, and spends, over $80 million in the year, and one out of every nine of the motor vehicles in Canada is registered there. In Toronto itself there are published, besides the English press, six newspapers in Ukrainian, three in Estonian and one in the Croat-Serb tongue. It is a place that drives one to express it in statistics. It is the most American city in Canada.

But that is not by any means all Ontario, not even all industrial Ontario. Northern and Southern Ontario are very different. Northern Ontario lies within the Canadian Shield, a land of woods and lakes, of forestry and mining, of the giant nickel-mines at Sudbury and of the scores of others that are a part of Canada's history. Southern Ontario is becoming the industrial heart of Canada—industry spreads through its smaller towns—but it has not ceased to be agricultural. The Lake Erie region, for instance, has large areas of light sandy soil which, by the 1920's, could no longer sustain its earlier cereal crops and was beginning to suffer from soil erosion. In 1923 they tried tobacco-growing. Now, there are some 110,000 acres under tobacco, the annual value of the crop exceeds that of all the grains grown in the province, and the tobacco-farmer, with a net income of $4,500 from each occupied farm, has the highest farming income per head in the province. Likewise the area to the immediate west of the Niagara River is not only the most rapidly expanding industrial area in the province. It produces grapes, peaches and plums and is Canada's vineyard. Toronto does not dominate Ontario as London does Southern England, for Ontario itself is a part of a closely knit community, that which circles the four Great Lakes.

Southern Ontario holds a great deal of the history of English-speaking Canada. Twelve hundred of the families who had fled across the Niagara River from the American Revolution settled in this part of Ontario and the first Parliament of Upper Canada met at Niagara-on-the-Lake, then Newark. A mile or so west of the river canyon stands the monument to General Isaac Brock, who

3. Quebec: Montreal from Mount Royal

4. Quebec: The Ursuline Convent, Quebec City

was killed in the Battle of Queenston Heights on 14 October, 1812, leading a charge against the United States troops who had crossed the river to invade Canada. That was one of the decisive battles of the War of 1812, if only because it showed both sides that Canada did intend to fight for her separate existence.

And its smaller towns all have their personalities. London is a university town of 100,000 people where all the learned societies of Canada hold their annual meetings in almost continual succession for two weeks in June each year. Hamilton has the largest blast-furnace in Canada, producing 400,000 tons of pig iron a year, and great deal of black smoke in consequence. Brantford, where Dr. Graham Bell invented the telephone, is the town in which the circuses of Canada spend their winter. The town of Stratford, with 18,000 people, has decided, after some hesitation and goaded by Mr. Tom Patterson, to back a Summer Shakespearian festival for Canada, in the uneasy belief that its name perhaps does carry some obligation. The Governor-General, Mr. Vincent Massey, opened the 1953 season. And Sarnia, on the St. Clair River, which divides Ontario from the State of Michigan, sees more tonnage pass its quays in six months than the Suez, Kiel and Panama Canals together carry in a year. Yet, in Ontario, one must begin not with any of these places, not even with Toronto, but with Ottawa.

On 31 December, 1857, Her Majesty Queen Victoria was graciously pleased to inform the Government of Upper and Lower Canada that she had determined that Ottawa should be the site of the permanent capital of the Colony. She had been asked to make the decision some nine months before, when the Government of Upper and Lower Canada, after alternating between Montreal and Toronto, had signally failed to agree on a permanent home for the provincial capital. She had seen a sketch of the place from the pencil of the Governor's wife, and had read a confidential dispatch from the Governor himself.

Ottawa [he had written] is the only place which will be accepted by the majority of Upper and Lower Canada as a fair compromise. With the exception of Ottawa, every one of the cities proposed is an object of jealousy to each of the others. Ottawa is, in fact, neither in Upper nor in Lower Canada. Literally, it is in the former; but a bridge alone divides it from

D

the latter. Consequently, its selection would fulfil the letter of any pledge given, or supposed to be given, to Upper Canada at the time of the Union. . . .

Nor was it only jealousy.

In a military point of view [the Governor continued] Ottawa is advantageously situated. Its distance from the frontier is such as to protect it from any marauding party, or even from a regular attack, unless Montreal and Kingston, which flank the approach to it, were previously occupied by the enemy. Stores and troops could be sent to Ottawa either from Quebec or Kingston, without exposure on the St. Lawrence to the American frontier. . . .

"The main objection to Ottawa is its wild position. . . ."

That seems to have been the only qualification. Child of disputes and fears, Ottawa was accepted by the Legislative Assembly in 1858 as the capital of the double province by a vote of 64 to 59. On 1 September 1860, the Prince of Wales, later King Edward VII, laid the corner-stone of the Senate building. On 1 July 1867, the city became the capital of the newly created Canadian Confederation.

Ottawa has not quite lost its wild position. It stands where three rivers meet, the Ottawa River, once called the River of the Ottawas, the Indian tribe from whom the name comes, and its two tributaries, the Rideau and the Gatineau. The Ottawa, the second longest wholly Canadian river, divides the province of Ontario from the province of Quebec and, where Ottawa now stands, skirts the limestone cliffs on its southern bank in a wide curve. In the centre of this bay is the entrance to the Rideau Canal. To the west of the canal is the Hill, on which the Parliament buildings stand, to the east the Château Laurier, part of the C.N.R.'s mystic vision of what hotels should be. The slopes of the cliffs are still wooded, with beeches, as was once the plateau at the summit, and the waters of the Ottawa still pour over the seven falls of the Chaudière.

Ottawa, like all cities that live upon the water, is best seen by night. To look across to Ottawa from the town of Hull on the northern bank at the time of the Coronation, to see its buildings floodlit in orange, its trees in green, and the Victory Tower, Ottawa's counterpart to Big Ben, dark against the sky, to watch the reflections in the brown and sepia water of the river, was to feel that what had once been wild was still untamed. The Parliament Buildings, Centre Block, East and West Blocks, and the Library, are a heavy Gothic. Individually the buildings are not outstanding. They gain something from their grouping, much more from their position high on the cliff over the river. As they stand together they have their own strength. They are more than an urban intrusion into a countryside still of great wildness and loveliness. They are a symbol of another kind of strength, of determination, of order, of union. They are less than a century old but the ideas they carry stretch back very far in time.

The Ottawa that is the Federal capital of Canada has roughly the form of a letter "L". The long leg of the letter is Wellington Street, running parallel to the river, and the main buildings of government, the Parliament buildings, Confederation Building, and the temporary buildings that at least are freshly painted, lie to the north, set in grass between the street and the edge of the cliff. On the south side of Wellington Street are the buildings that no capital can be without, the banks, the Metropolitan Life Assurance, from New York, and the Rideau Club, where everyone lunches and in which a cabinet minister can start a rumour by hanging up his hat more brusquely than usual. At the eastern end of Wellington Street is an open space, once a gully up which the locks of the Rideau Canal climbed, later half-covered by Sapper and Dufferin Bridges, and now completely filled in and carrying the Canadian National War Memorial in its centre.

The shorter leg of the "L" is Elgin Street which runs southwards from the War Memorial. Elgin Street does not go very far before it leaves the Federal atmosphere. Its dual carriage-way and general parklike intentions are shortlived, and a cinema and a garage make it clear where business Ottawa takes over. Elgin Street is still an act of faith, but one that will be justified.

Ottawa, and Hull, which is twenty-five years older, came into existence because the falls of the Chaudière compelled voyagers up the Ottawa River to make portage around the barrier. The Iroquois, hunting their enemies the Hurons to destruction, made the portage a traditional ambush. Early last century the Governor-General of Canada, the Earl of Dalhousie, persuaded the United Kingdom Government to build a canal along the line of the Rideau River to link the Ottawa River with Lake Ontario at Kingston.

The war of 1812 was still a vivid event. To the south was still a potential enemy and for Lower and Upper Canada to be dependent upon a line of communication that ran along the St. Lawrence River, in part the actual frontier, was a tactical risk the Governor-General desired to eliminate. The authorities at home agreed and Lieut.-Col. John By, an officer of the Royal Engineers, was selected to superintend the construction of the canal. He made a final survey in the summer of 1826, and in March 1827 two companies of the Royal Sappers and Miners were raised in England specially for work on its construction.

John By was not a man attended by good fortune. He was a Londoner. His father and his grandfather, officials in the Custom House, had lived in Archbishops Walk, in the Parish of St. Mary, Lambeth. He had served in Canada between 1805 and 1811, returned, and had been present at the seige of Badajos in 1812. He was, by contemporary accounts, a jovial man, of great energy and determination. At the time when he was appointed to command the Rideau Canal operation he was already forty-seven and on half-pay, and he must have thought the command his last and his most promising chance of military fame. And did not the inhabitants of the settlement where the new locks led the canal down to the Ottawa River give the place the name "Bytown" almost from the start?

Like many soldiers before and since, the career of John By was finally wrecked on the reefs of parliamentary procedure and the incompetence of War Office employees. After five years of work some £788,000 had been spent on the canal, yet only £474,000 of that money had been authorised in the normal War Office vote. Why, asked a Parliamentary Committee, has this been permitted, and the Treasury, seeking a scapegoat, called home Lieut.-Col. John By. It was useless for him to point out that the Committee had commended his economy on the ground, that the cost of the canal had been below that of any similar undertaking in America. It was no use his reading to the Treasury the glowing tributes paid to him by newspapers in Canada. He had, whether he knew it or not, whether he was responsible or not, broken the most strict of Treasury rules; all government expenditure must be authorised by Parliament before it is incurred. Lieut.-Col. John By was replaced, never re-employed, and died four years later, a bitter man.

Even his name did not survive in the place he had helped to create. In 1855, the name of Bytown was voted out of existence and replaced by Ottawa. The citizens of Bytown were already thinking in terms of capitals. Had John By been, say, John Montmorency, had he been able to claim a descent from the Normans as long as that of any of the old families of Quebec, perhaps his name might have survived, another link between Upper and Lower Canada. But Bytown—still less Byville—!

The eight locks of the Rideau Canal, that once raised barges eighty-one feet in the first three hundred yards after leaving the Ottawa River, are no longer employed. The canal was a military precaution, like the Grand Military Canal in Kent, from Hythe to Rye. It never paid and the United Kingdom Government never succeeded in persuading the province of Ontario to take it over. The locks remain the oldest part of Ottawa; the proportions of each basin are right and the work of the masons on their stones is true and exact. They have the charm of a nineteenth-century steel engraving. And the St. Lawrence itself has ceased to be a tactical risk; it has become a bone of contention instead.

After confederation? Ottawa married. The rather unruly tomboy of a girl, whose early history had been marked by a long series of fights between the established settlers and the newer Irish immigrant labourers, took a politician for husband and settled down. Domestic Ottawa now stays at home, keeps the house clean, attends to the cooking and mending, and provides a shelter for political Ottawa, the man of the house. He spends his mornings in committee, lunches at the Rideau Club, is in his place in the House promptly at three when it assembles in the afternoon, and from there goes on to a round of cocktail parties in the Château Laurier and onwards through the foreign legations. In between, he has fitted in interviews with civil servants, business men, constituents and reporters. And, when Parliament rises, he goes off on vacation. It is a reasonably happy marriage, for domestic Ottawa won the husband she bid for and political Canada found in Ottawa a pleasant spot in which to live. The remarkable thing is how little the two have changed each other over the years. But there are developments even over that; political Ottawa is buying domestic Ottawa a mink coat, by instalments.

Ottawa is a small town, interested in lumber and its products, on which has been grafted the Federal capital of a nation becoming great. It has never really disturbed Canadians that Ottawa should have all its fine buildings stretched along the cliff above the river, and that the streets that run parallel with them are dingy and crude. The factories and sawmills across the river at Hull, the yards and dumps of Ottawa itself, are the kind of thing every Canadian knows in his own town. For those who insist on a pastoral, more elegant, background in which to live, there is always Rockcliffe, eastwards beyond the Rideau River, set off by the grounds of the Governor-General's house.

Ottawa's small town is attractive in itself. It has no pretensions. It is homely and friendly. It gives shelter, board and lodging to the great who visit it and to the workers who must live there. It is neither humiliated nor dismayed by the contrasts between its own shabbiness and the grandeur of, say, the Château Laurier. It escapes snobbishness, either direct or reversed, because, when you come to live next to them, government servants, even politicians, are recognisably human, and are certainly not excessively paid. Ottawa is interested in and diverted by the activities of the politicians, and the diplomats, and it has a small-town delight in rumour and gossip; these are its own equivalent of a three-ring verbal circus. Outside the area of existing Federal buildings it has little it is not prepared to see knocked down, provided something more convenient is put in its place.

Ottawa has a town plan with a time-table of fulfilment stretching out for the next fifty years; that is the mink coat political Ottawa is buying. When the work is finished Ottawa will have been transformed. It will have used the Rideau River and Canal to give it an unrivalled urban landscape. It was once no more than Bytown. With Sir Christopher Wren it could say: "The history of my City is but beginning."

It is time to return to Toronto.

"I do not pretend to understand Toronto. All students of Canada have tried to plumb these depths, but all, so far as I know, have failed." So wrote Mr. Bruce Hutchinson in *The Unknown Country*. I read that after my first stay in Toronto and I felt grateful to him for that statement. It explained many of my earlier feelings of bewilderment and doubt and convinced me that I was in good company.

Toronto calls itself the Queen City of Canada; if that is so, it was the Queen, rather than the King, who was in the counting-house, counting out the money. Toronto is wealthy, and casually displays its wealth. It is busy and it fills its streets with so many vehicles that everything moves at a crawl. It is respectable, par-ticularly on Sundays. It has two night-clubs and one good restaurant for its 1,117,000 people. It has a history, but one which does not seem to belong to its present inhabitants. Coming to the city from Montreal and Ottawa, I had the ridiculous impression that all the people in Toronto had settled there some five years back, no longer, and that, while they had overcome their initial surprise at finding such a city ready to walk into, they had not entirely succeeded in coming to know each other as people very well.

On a rise overlooking the centre of the city there is a vast mansion that might have been built in Bournemouth by a Scottish architect to the orders of a Lancashire mill-owner who had made a fortune late in life. It has now been taken over by the city be-cause it was worth no one's while to pay the taxes on it, and the Kiwanis run Saturday-night dances there. A friend told me that he remembered having played among the ladders and piles of bricks when it was being built. I did not believe him. I don't think anybody was there when it was being built.

As a physical entity, Toronto is now a vast city on the northern shore of Lake Ontario (not until 1952 were its various townships and municipalities federated together under a central commission). It was laid out in plan by military engineers on a rectangular basis and there are very few deviations from the resulting straight lines and right angles. Its main north–south axis is Yonge Street and people claim that Yonge Street is the longest main street in the world, since it stretches over fifty miles north to Lake Simcoe. The main east-west axis is Queen Street and at one time the waters of the lake must have lapped its southern boundary. Toronto was then York Town, at the mouth of a little creek where an island off the shore gave some protection and created a harbour. There are some delightful prints of those times.

All that casual charm has now been remedied. The lake here is, fortunately, shallow. It can be filled in and made into firm ground at reasonable cost. The first filling-in process began when it was decided to carry the railway through the centre of Toronto. It

was cheaper and more convenient to follow the level line of the
lake shore and compel the lake to accommodate the tracks and
the freight yards. The railway engineers, too, must have wept
like anything to see such quantities of sand. Once the lake shore
had gone, the remaining developments were matters of pure
common sense. The next step, obvious and economical, was to
push the lake back still further and allow factories to group themselves near the railway yards, and, having created an industrial
area there, it was folly not to extend it. The small island off-
shore still exists, put to no better use than as a public pleasure
garden and park, but that, too, the present Mayor will remedy,
if he can. The obvious line for the next traffic highway is parallel
to the railway but further out into the lake. That will put the
island land to good use, that of more factory sites, and this in its
turn will build up the volume of traffic on the new road. Bay
Street, now, is what a geologist would call a raised beach.

The majority of people live in Toronto to make money. When
they have any money they buy a car and, after that, a house.
Most of the new houses around Toronto are identical, which can
only mean that many people in the city have not only identical
tastes but also identical incomes. But some of them must in time
draw ahead in this race. They will then buy another car—not
bigger, for no American car is really bigger than another—but
one with a bonnet of a different shape. If fortune continues to
favour them, they will buy a different house. There is a point,
about one-third of the way out from the centre, at which the most
pleasant and the most expensive houses are to be found, and
ultimately the winners in the contest arrive there. I do not know
whither you must move when you have so much money that it is no
longer proper for you to remain there. Probably you have to leave
Canada altogether, for Florida, if you have not already done so.

Toronto is a fair example of the fate of many North American
cities, in which inadequate public service transport encourages
the use of the private automobile, and the private automobile, by
weight of numbers and extravagance in space for each passenger
normally carried, goes far towards inhibiting all traffic movement
altogether. The logical end of that comes on the day when all
automobiles are parked so tightly in the streets that not one of
them can be extracted from its place.

Toronto ought to be a city in which the pen slipped naturally

into moving accounts of magnificent buildings and vistas. This pen
will not. There are magnificent buildings and some, far fewer,
magnificent vistas but what haunts the eye afterwards is Toronto's
splurge over the face of Ontario. The city begins to shape itself
more and more into the form of a problem in a town-planner's
notebook.

Suppose, for instance, one approaches the city from the west,
from the town of Burlington, which is some twenty-five miles away
along the shore of Lake Ontario. Burlington itself is a charming
small town. It must have been laid out by people who wanted their
pleasant house to be a part of a pleasant community, who neither
wished to pretend that they lived in isolation nor that there was
anything humiliating in the presence of a smaller house within
sight. They did not huddle together for protection nor drift apart
in imaginary social divisions. They must have been friendly,
casual and relaxed. The people who live there now may still be
that, for all I know, but I feel that the days of their peace are numbered. Toronto is bounding towards them as fast as it can along
King's Highway No. 2.

The dual carriage-way of Queen Elizabeth Way has now replaced King's Highway No. 2 as the main road west from Toronto,
so the original character of No. 2 has not been obliterated. It still
winds its way through all the stages that separate rural Ontario
from the developments of the city, and the specimens of past and
present are grouped on either side of the road like so many show-
cases.

There is the lakeside house of the early century, pretentious
perhaps, but elegant still if there is money to keep it up. There is
its modern replacement, the ranch-type house with windows
that stretch interminably under wide eaves. Round the next bend
is the cheaper version of the last, seemingly delivered to the site
in packaged prefabrication and in bundles of a dozen at a time.
There is the township shopping centre, containing the five standard shops of suburban life, the filling station, the groceteria, the
drug store, the ladies' hairdresser and the radio and television
shop. There is the Motel, or Autocourt, with its flock of bungalows-
for-the-night looking like slightly enlarged bathing-machines, and
of course the vacant lots for the sale of used autos. And the trailer
park, recognisable from afar by its forest of television masts. The
one unique sight on the road in from Burlington is an oil-refinery,

surrounded by its fleet of storage tanks, all brightly painted in aluminium. If I were building a house near Toronto I would pick a site that overlooked that.

The real centre of Greater Toronto's social life is the groceteria. The groceteria sells food, packaged, ready for the refrigerator, and very nice the carrots and potatoes look in their neat cellophane wrappings. In a groceteria, the bacon is already stripped of its rind, the steaks are boned and cut to the size of the family, and even six-pennyworth of marrow bones is wrapped up securely enough to be posted home. The groceteria is a wonderful institution. I wish they existed on the same scale in London.

The food is clean. The profit of the establishments I saw runs at a rate below 2 per cent of the total turnover, and the stores remain open until ten each Friday evening, thus allowing husband and wife to spend a happy time together filling the week-end basket. No Torontonian husband can complain that he does not know the cost of living, and, according to a *Financial Post* survey, in Toronto in 1952 he spent nearly $8 per head each week on food alone (one-fifth of it on meat). The groceteria will have achieved the summit of its social influence when it relieves the Canadian housewife of all necessity for thought in cooking food; it may well do so, for it is not hard to imagine each package sold equipped with a device which cut off the supply of current to the cooker at the right moment. And, as a social centre, the groceteria is cheaper than the public house.

All this, I feel a good Torontonian will say, is taking too low a viewpoint from which to describe the Queen City of Canada. I can't help it. It is a part of the real enigma of Toronto, its social organisation.

As a social organisation, Toronto seems to consist of innumerable circles, each having certain points of contact with others but all without a common centre. The people of Toronto seem to have no cohesion; it is impossible to imagine (although I am sure they exist) a Torontonian with the deep civic loyalty possessed, say, by every Mancunian. It is not a question of where they were born. It is that they seem to have come there by chance. Their interest in the city is still, in some indefinable way, incomplete. They are residents in a vast transit camp.

·   ·   ·   ·   ·

Toronto is a proud city and always has been, from the days of Governor Simcoe and the Family Compact. The more one experiences of Toronto the more one comes to realise that the spirit of the city has considerably more of Ulster in it than of England. It is, of course, a Tory city and it has always been a characteristic of Tories that they should link loyalty to England and the Throne with acceptance of the particular political arrangement of their designing that leaves them in absolute power. To be subversive to one is, in their eyes, to be subversive to the other. In England, there have always been Whigs and Radicals to counter them, dangerous fellows, no doubt, who occasionally win an election, just as there have always been Dukes of Wellington and Benjamin Disraelis to turn the Tories themselves away, often at the last minute, from the crest of that mad slope into the sea. In Ulster, no; and, seemingly in Toronto, no. To an Ulster Tory—indeed, to an Ulsterman, whether he lives in Belfast or Toronto—the natural form of government is the oligarchy, based on Crown, Church and Possession. Crown and Church between them can supply the sanctions with which to confound the infidels and the nine points of the law that possession gives can usually be stretched to cover the tenth for quite a time.

To the visitor, Toronto is exhilarating, for the Tory, is hospitable and generous. It is full of interesting people, circles and activities. Its board-rooms are not filled with chartered accountants and retired civil servants; it is a city of engineers and of men interested in this calculated risk. It has its musicians and its writers, its lawyers, its salesmen and its sharks. Yet Toronto remains a city of which one feels compelled to say that, disappointingly, the entirety is less than the sum of its parts.

But any attempt to explain Toronto is bound to have a despairing, frantic note in it. As for understanding it—The only suggestion I can make to Mr. Bruce Hutchinson is that he might study Belfast, in Northern Ireland, the original home of the Ulsterman. It is just possible that he might pick up some clues there.

3. The Maritimes

The Saint John River in New Brunswick is very beautiful. It is named for Saint John the Baptist, for Samuel Champlain first entered its estuary on 24 June 1604. It is 450 miles long and, at Fredericton, about a third of a mile wide, smooth and untroubled, flowing down a shallow valley to the Bay of Fundy at Saint John eighty miles away. This river was once the artery of the country. It carried the felled timber downstream to the mills, and it bore the produce coming in from the outer world to those who had settled on its banks. All the way along the river are quays and landing-places that once must have seen the excitements of comings and goings, of partings and reunions, of news from the outside world. How did the first news of Waterloo travel up the Saint John? Was it still summer and were the journals tossed ashore at each halt before the harvest was over, or had the fall already come and did the people of Fredericton read them under the scarlet leaves of the trees?

The country of the river valley is still soft and gentle. Once the land was cleared of timber, it can have changed very little. Constable might have lived and worked at Fredericton; he would not have painted the pictures we know but he would have responded to all he saw. If it were not for Moncton (and, of course, a certain caution against making generalisations). I would claim that the Saint John at Fredericton is typical of the province of New Brunswick.

I had arrived at Fredericton Junction, twenty miles away, from Montreal. An old, old man carried two of my bags along the platform; he had a high voice, a thin scrawny neck, a puffed-out striped linen cap such as all railwaymen in North America wear. It was a hot morning—a lovely day in early June I would have called it in England. A locomotive brought in the two coaches that made up the train to Fredericton. It was middle-aged and high and its stiff, slender smoke-stack gave it something of the air of an immense and proud carriage horse bringing up the family brougham to the door. We waited until the connecting train from Boston had dropped off its five passengers for Fredericton and then we were off.

Mainly through woods. The country was a little like southern Sweden, but softer and less drilled. The Swedes, although they may never have tamed their landscape, have at least battered it into submission. The train from Montreal to the Maritimes whisks its passengers—I doubt if Senator McCarran realises this—in and out of the State of Maine by night without any security check at all and when I awoke we were still in Maine, travelling through woods and marshes and lakes. Each village, and there were not very many, seemed to be no more than a clearing among the trees. The hills are low and the glaciers have left them with what the geologists call a seriously modified drainage system, which may be beautiful to the passer-by but must be a nuisance to those who have to plan communications and make a living on the ground.

This final stage from the junction seemed a more casual journey, except the last two miles into Fredericton, which are downhill, beside the river, through sidings and lines of stationary freight cars, into the southern side of the town. Those we did with a flourish, like some long-distance train completing its day with some three minutes in hand.

"You'll be staying at the Lord Beaverbrook," said the taxi-driver, without very much of a question in his voice, and I could not resist it. Who but Lord Beaverbrook and Cecil Rhodes can have had places named for them in their lifetimes on that scale?

Everyone has written of the elms of Fredericton. They are everywhere. Vancouver and Toronto may have more beautiful trees in some of their suburbs but nowhere in Canada has any provincial capital enticed so much of the countryside into its streets. Were it not for the trees the town itself would be far from handsome. It is the fashion in Canada for commercial buildings, and for some houses, to have flat roofs, sloping gently from the front of the building to the back, and it is hard to achieve any effect of elegance with what is no more than a slab of house. There are individually beautiful buildings; the cathedral, Christ Church, which was built in 1845 and of which the nave is an exact copy of St. Mary's at Snettisham, in Norfolk, and the old Government House, which stands by the river and is in the classic tradition of the eighteenth century, a kind of common ancestor of what today is both English and Canadian. It has long since ceased to be a practicable residence for any one family, or official, and it is now the district headquarters of the Royal Canadian Mounted Police, which is a happy fate, for it would be hideous as a commercial building with a neon sign along its portico.

Most of Fredericton's buildings are the old frame houses and by then they had begun to grow on me. They are all of a pattern, weather-boarded, with a covered veranda in front and, if possible, a small turret at one corner, the whole embellished with fretted corners and gutterings wherever the tormented wood can be nailed on. Heaven knows what they are like to live in. They may be warm and snug in winter. They may be ridden with creaks and draughts and I can imagine the timid mother sleepless night after night, brooding over the fire risk. They are dying out and it would be wrong to shed tears over them. So much of the country looks as though it had been bought from the one mail-order catalogue. Yet they are neighbourly. No one house puts on any airs, not even in the colour of its paint. It is difficult for any frame house to be pretentious; it merely becomes ridiculous if it tries.

Fredericton is not a city that one associates with production. There must be some activity in the town somewhere; someone must make some money. But the how and the where of it are by no means obvious. In Toronto, in Moncton, there is no question about people making money. Their eyes are filled with the dollar round the corner, and those who are not as good at it as others show their failure almost openly. They dress poorly and they look aimless. But in Fredericton no one looks poor and most of them avoid too much appearance of purposefulness. They look like traders, men who sell things to the farmers in the valley and the lumbermen in the woods, who may well be the same people for the farmer of the summer is so often a lumberman in the winter. Fredericton must draw its commission on a great many of the activities that are going on around it.

On the evening that I arrived there was a dinner of the Kiwanis Club in the Lord Beaverbrook Hotel. It was ladies' night and there was a good deal of singing and one member led them in dumb show in the songs that have cumulative refrains. There were many speeches, too, and they went on until comparatively late at night, long after the elms were silent and the river outside was the colour of a pearl. One man in particular seemed to me to exemplify so much of what I felt about the city; he left the dining-room to relieve himself, so I had a double vision of him. He was tall and heavily built. His jacket was tight and his belted trousers were low down on his stomach so that his white shirt seemed twice as long as shirts commonly do. His face was cheerful and strong and very red, and he smiled all the time. His hair was black and had a thick curl, kept in place by some sort of grease. In the Army he would have been a very successful sergeant, or a major who liked high living and was a source of anxiety to his colonel until the trouble started. I do not think any man had ever bothered him. He might have been the man who sold tractors, or a butcher. I am sure he was very pleased with himself and with Fredericton.

I should think that a great many people in Fredericton are. And why not? The President of the University there, who was then Dr. A. W. Trueman, told me that for a long time he had been wanting the authorities to do something towards paving and channelling the roads that run through the University grounds. The University is on a hill and when it rains, as it does, the water is always damaging the roadways. He asked the City Engineer— Fredericton is a city: it was created one by Queen Victoria on 25 April 1845—to serve on the appropriate committee of the University. The Engineer consented.

"Not that I agree with your ideas about improvements, though," he said. "I wouldn't change a thing about this place."

But they have made some changes. There is the Lord Beaverbrook Hotel, for one thing; that is very new. It stands by the river, alongside a small park with a statue of Robert Burns in it. I am still puzzling over why Robert Burns should have that post of honour in Fredericton. Why is not the statue one of Lord Beaverbrook himself?

There ought, some day, to be a good and a prominent statue of the first Lord Beaverbrook in Fredericton. It is not easy to attempt to assess a man's value to any community in terms of money—who could adjudicate between the contribution made to the United Kingdom by the Minister of Aircraft Production and the Proprietor of the *Daily Express*? But in Fredericton such a calculation seems, superficially, easier. There are the buildings he has given the University, the Bonar Law-Bennett section of the Library, the Law School, the students' residences, the house for the President. There are the scholarships for students and teachers at the University of New Brunswick, at Mount Allison University, at London University and at London's Institute of Teaching, by now about seventy in all. What with one thing and another, they say, his benefactions must have already gone beyond $2 million; he began as long ago as 1919. But one cannot reduce the value this will give to the people of New Brunswick into terms of cash. A man is remembered by what he does with his money, not by how much he accumulates. New Brunswick has good cause to remember Lord Beaverbrook.

I have a feeling that about one person in four in Fredericton would say that the place needs the kind of shock that a Beaverbrook scholarship holder should be able to give it—that is, if he, or she, has caught any of the infection that should go with the dollars. And any person holding that view would hold it very strongly indeed. The other three in Fredericton—well, I should think the butcher, or the dealer in tractors, at the Kiwanis' party would be among them.

Across the river, beyond the suburb of Fredericton that was once the separate village of Devon and on up the valley of the Nashwaak River, there is a mill. It might have been brought there intact from Bury or Nelson. It is not only that it is ugly. It has that true Lancashire pride in its indifference to any aesthetic criticism at all. What is worse is that its red-brick squareness is repeated in every single one of the company dwelling-houses built around it; they are scaled-down versions of the factory itself. It looks as though it has been there a long time and has every intention of staying there an even longer time yet. The best that can be said for the village around it is that it has a village green and a village hall.

If there is a town in Great Britain with an atmosphere that could suggest Fredericton, it is, perhaps, Haverfordwest, in Pembrokeshire. The farmers of Pembroke are active men, swarthy, short and lean, and they walk quickly and slyly, as though bargains were things to be taken unawares. In Fredericton there is calmness and a certainty that all business is for the best and that no man need feel doubt over his transactions. But in each town there is an air of remoteness, an air of being self-contained. The rest of the world is a long way away and, if it exists at all, it cannot be important.

It is hard to believe that all this valley, all New Brunswick, has been fought over, most bitterly. The Indians delighted in cruelty and the French and English delighted in employing Indians and their cruelties against each other. Fredericton was once St. Anne's and French. In the winter of 1759 an English party took St. Anne's, burnt it and drove the inhabitants into the woods to make their way to the nearest settlement as best they could in the snow, or to die. It was not a period when it was advisable to be on the losing side.

In the seventeenth century New Brunswick and Nova Scotia, then all part of Acadia, were French. On the eastern shores of the Bay of Fundy, in Port Royal, in what is now Nova Scotia, lived d'Aulnay Charnisay, a relative of Cardinal Richelieu and holder of the lands on that side of the bay. On the western shores, at the mouth of the Saint John River, lived his rival Charles de la Tour, who claimed trading rights over the river valley and up into what is now Maine. Charnisay had the advantage of the influence at the French Court, de la Tour of the merchants of La Rochelle, in France, and of the New England leaders in Boston. De la Tour, in fact, was a man who believed in having a foot in either camp. In 1628, his father, captured by an English ship and taken to London, had negotiated for a grant of land in Nova Scotia from Charles I and had presumably paid enough for it to receive in addition the grant of a baronetcy of Nova Scotia. His son Charles saw no difficulty in accepting both that grant and one from the French King as lieutenant-general in Acadia.

The first round in the contest went to de la Tour. Charnisay obtained a decree from the French King suspending de la Tour's title to the lands across the bay and, so fortified, called upon de la Tour to surrender his fort at the mouth of the Saint John. De la Tour refused, Charnisay's first attack, in 1643, was repulsed and there was at least a truce for the following two years.

De la Tour decided to spend the winter of 1644 in France, repairing his communications with the sources of power there, and he left his wife in charge of the fort and his domain, whilst he was away. His wife, it is said, was a woman of great beauty and courage, and possessed a considerable business ability. She was in command of the fort when Charnisay attacked again, in the spring of 1645.

The direct attack failed, and this time Charnisay resorted to guile. He suborned one of the garrison and induced him to open the defences of the fort whilst Lady de la Tour and the rest of the garrison were at prayer on Easter Sunday morning. Even so, when the alarm was raised, Charnisay found that he could not carry the whole fort. He offered terms for a surrender, promising the survivors their lives. Having procured a surrender, he at once broke his word. In the Easter week itself he hanged the

E

garrison, all save the one man who volunteered to serve as hang-
man. He compelled Lady de la Tour to watch the ceremony
with a halter round her own neck, and then he spared her life.
She died three weeks later of what might be termed a broken
heart.

It is a romantically tragic story. Nicolas Denys, the contemporary historian of Acadia, told it in this way, although it may or
may not be significant that, when he did so, Charnisay was dead
and Charles de la Tour was very much a power in the land
(Charnisay's own account, written before he died, is rather different). The sequel is another story in itself.

Charnisay too had a beautiful and capable wife. Five years
after his successful assault on the fort on the Saint John River he
himself died, from exposure after a canoeing accident. The following year de la Tour reappeared, armed with a fresh grant from
France. He took possession of his old lands along the Saint John
River, and, to procure the peace and tranquillity of the country
and concord and union between the two families, as the marriage
contract expressed it, he took possession of the widow of d'Aulnay
Charnisay. He might almost to be said to have united two nations
as well as two families, for, when Acadia passed to the British in
1654, his connections were so good—and perhaps his baronetcy
of Nova Scotia so impressive—that he was left undisturbed in
his possessions. He died peacefully in 1666, leaving five children
by his second marriage.

All this happened a long time ago, and, sitting on the bank of
Saint John, it is difficult to believe that it ever did happen. Just
as it is difficult, sitting on the banks of the Severn at Worcester,
to believe that, somewhere about the same time, the Parliamentar-
ians and the Royalists were killing each other just south of the
city with the same gusto and overwhelming faith.

The first time I flew the Atlantic, in a B.O.A.C. Stratocruiser,
there was some engine trouble after we left Gander for New York;
the outer of the starboard engines stopped with its propeller
feathered. It was early in a November morning and the sky was
full of cloud, ahead of us black and climbing far above our altitude. We went into a long right-hand turn and below I could see
a seashore with a white line of surf breaking on the rocks and
sand. The first rumour that drifted through the cabin was that we

were going to put down at Moncton, in Canada, and Moncton sounded far better than anything I could see beneath us.

Then we altered course again, swinging away to the left until we were heading far enough to the south to clear the black clouds ahead. The next piece of information was more than a rumour; it came straight from the steward's mouth.

"It's New York," he said, "or Boston if there's more trouble. Any place but Moncton," he added. "It's the most God-awful town in Canada."

I never forgot the name "Moncton". It remained a place I wanted to see.

The flight from Fredericton to Moncton, a hundred minutes or so by Maritime Central Airways, can tell you more about New Brunswick than anything else could in the same time. The statistics say that 85 per cent of the surface of the province is wooded. Looking down that is exactly what you see. There are the woods, the lakes and the marshes, the greens of the spruce, the curious grey patches where some fate has befallen a small area of trees and they have died where they stand. There are the isolated clearings and the isolated farms, and there is the one railway, the one road, the one line of power cables, and the road is straighter than the railway. New Brunswick may grow a great deal of fruit and export many tons of potatoes. What those who inhabit the place live on is timber.

That was the country we flew over, until, from under the starboard wing again, I saw the outskirts of a town unwind, and, beyond, another wide yellow river. We lost height. As we turned to come in I could see that we were heading for a runway, at the end of which was a solid block of buildings. We dropped down, landed and taxied over to the apron. This was Moncton. It said so in very large letters on the front of the building. The airport itself is on a rise outside the town and the one long runway seems to take off into the sky itself. Moncton lies a little below and beside the river.

Moncton is a rough rectangle of a town, with its streets at right angles to one another and divided diagonally by the main line of a railway. At one end of the town, the end in which the hotels are located, there is a station and a freight yard. Every train that moves into or out of any part of Nova Scotia must pass through Moncton. Any freight train that reaches Moncton spends some hours there, discarding some cars and picking up others. The rigid couplings of Canadian freight trains, and the fact that they are largely made up from natural sounding-boxes like metal box-cars, produce when the train stops a sound that is equivalent to a sharp clap of thunder immediately overhead. Indeed, it might well be in the same room. In addition, since there is a level-crossing every fifty yards or so along the track through the town, every locomotive in motion must keep its warning bell in con-tinuous operation, and the warning bell of a Canadian train re-sembles the dismal sounds Sir Ralph the Rover heard when approaching the Inchcape Rock. It is impossible not to be aware that Moncton is a railway centre of importance. Whether it was named for General Monck or not, its patron saint should be George Stephenson.

An industrial town is immediately identifiable. For instance, there are many more banks visible in Moncton than in Frederic-ton. There are more branches of the fixed-price stores and each devotes one window to the display of men's overalls and working clothes. In industrial towns the inner garments worn by ladies, as shown in the windows, have more lace attached to them. Judging from the evidence in these windows, in Fredericton they wear plain, shiny rayon. In Moncton, it is crêpe (of course, one must bear in mind that 40 per cent of the inhabitants of Moncton are French-speaking). There are more cafés and drug-stores; the young are more sophisticated. In Fredericton the young men stand at the corner of the street in groups and make sheepish comments to the girls as they pass by. The boys are roughly dressed and the girls are smart. In Moncton the boys have the family car for the evening; and the teen-age girls go about in blue jeans and tartan coats, with their hair tied with a bow at the nape of the neck. There is always more movement in the streets of an industrial town in the evening. The young have spent the day standing at a machine or sitting before a desk. In the even-ing it is time for activity. They come alive. In Fredericton, in the evening they relax. And yet has Moncton really found out what to do with its time?

I spent an hour and a half in the lounge of one curling club in Moncton, and the fruit machines, three of them, were not silent for a moment. If two out of the three were running at the rate of one throw every five seconds, at ten cents a throw, then some two

and a half dollars were going into those machines every minutes:
$150 an hour.

Jackpots from fruit machines are not a crime; indeed, they are
hardly to be distinguished from the almost universal British practice of spending the leisure hours of the week in deciding on what
sequence of marks to make on football-pool coupons. They are
no more than a sign of frustration; but frustration is not typical
of Canada.

Moncton claims possession of two natural phenomena, the tidal
bore on the River Petitcodiac, and the Magnetic Hill. The tidal
bore is real. The notice in the little handkerchief of a park overlooking the river, Moncton's one public amenity (the park also
contains a public lavatory, which is a rarity in Canada), disclaims
any dogmatism on what gives rise to a tidal bore, but says that the
tide in the Bay of Fundy, thirty miles away, is a forty-foot tide
and that it comes up the Petitcodiac twice a day in the form of a
wall of water, anything from eighteen inches to four feet in height.
It does and it is an impressive sight, even though, on the evening
I saw it, the wall was no more than two feet high, for behind it
surges the solid flood tide, moving upstream at some eight knots
and rising at the rate of a foot in five minutes.

But the Magnetic Hill is pathetic. Some five miles to the west of
the town, we left the main road as it curved away to the left over
a spur of the hill, and drove up a gravel road towards the crest.
On the left was a restaurant and souvenir store; there the road
levels off and fifty yards beyond it is a white post in the hedge. If
one stops a car at that post, it is possible, from the contours of
the surrounding ground, to imagine that the car is at the bottom
of a slight down-grade and will remain at rest. In fact, it rolls
backwards, to deposit its happily deceived passengers once more
outside the shop that sells the postcards. That is the Magnetic
Hill.

The oddest thing of all is that from this spot, still more from the
crest of the hill above, there is one of the most charming land-
scapes one can see in that part of the province. The land sinks to
the east in gentle folds, and far away on the horizon there is the
faint silver line of the sea. To the right the spur of ground closes
the valley. To the left, the valley opens out and curves gradually
away into a darker haze that is Moncton. In front, it is open
pasture-land until in the middle distance, on the further side of

the shallow valley, a low wooded crest draws its own band, a mosaic of greens, across the line of the fields. New Brunswick is an old and undisturbed country; the glaciers fined it down. From this hill it would seem that man, too, had reached a state of tranquillity. The lark should spring from underfoot and hold the world still with his song. Instead, the Magnetic Hill is a place to which one drives to see a car run backwards for thirty yards.

It seemed to me that there must be some explanation for the importance which Moncton attaches to the Magnetic Hill.

The three traditional Maritime provinces are Nova Scotia, New Brunswick and Prince Edward Island. Prince Edward Island is by far the smallest of the Canadian provinces, no more than 2,184 square miles. It is an island in the Northumberland Strait, about 110 miles long and never more than fifteen miles wide. It was first settled in 1719, became British in 1758 and a separate province in 1769. Its population is about 28,000, and that is less than it was fifty years ago. It depends for its livelihood on agriculture, fishing and an increasing tourist trade. It raises pedigree stock, farms for fox-pelts, and its seed potatoes are known all over North America. Prince Edward Island has an economy which corresponds to that of the Channel Islands, and its inhabitants must have very much the same approach to life. Jaques Cartier, its discoverer, (a native of St. Malo) said of the island: "It needs only the nightingale."

New Brunswick has an area of 18,000,000 acres and a population of 515,000. The Treaty of Utrecht in 1716 confirmed Great Britain's possession of Nova Scotia but failed to define "Nova Scotia". Britain retained her western settlements, the French Cape Breton Island. The French settlers in what is now New Brunswick, the Acadians, were claimed by both. The Acadians obtained forty years of respite by temporising; they would accept English allegiance provided they were not compelled to fight against their own flesh and blood. But, in October 1753, Charles Lawrence became Lieutenant-Governor of Nova Scotia. "It would be much better", he wrote to the Privy Council in London, on 1 August 1754, "if they refuse the oaths, that they were away". and without waiting for a formal instruction from home, away he made with them. Six thousand of the inhabitants of Acadia were rounded up and shipped southwards to the other thirteen colonies, and their homes burnt. "They went off praying, singing and crying, being met by the women and children all the way with great lamentation". So wrote Colonel Winslow in his journal of the deportation from Grand Pré which he, reluctantly, carried out.

They were scattered over the face of America, of the West Indies, even in the ports of England and France. Many made their way to Louisiana, then still French. Many waited for a chance to return to a land they could not put from their minds. Some did return. In 1766 those exiled to Massachusetts gathered in Boston, to make the pilgrimage back, and nine hundred men, women and children set out to march through the forest country along the New England shore on their way home. It took them four months to cover the four hundred and fifty miles and not all of them completed it. The survivors finally made their homes again in the country around Yarmouth, in the South of Nova Scotia. Réne le Blanc, the notary at Grand Pré, was put on shore at New York with his wife and only his two youngest children. The remaining children—and his was a large family—were scattered over the other colonies and Charles, one of them, made a vast fortune in Philadelphia. There are now, it is said, some thousands of the descendants of the Le Blancs of Acadia and they are still sufficiently Acadian to have held recently a grand reunion in Moncton itself.

With the American Revolution came a second wave of immigration, this time from the south. The people of the Saint John Valley are mostly of loyalist stock, those who sailed north after they were expelled from the thirteen colonies, who survived, which was rather more desperate, the lamentable administrative arrangements made by the English Colonial authorities for their reception at Saint John, and who later resisted the pull to accept the *fait accompli* of the Revolution and return to the communities they had left. Whatever their circumstances might have been in New England, in New Brunswick they were compelled to start again, even to clearing their own sites and building the house that was to shelter them. They found a good land, but the first generation after 1776 must have been men and women of indomitable will.

Perhaps the struggle for survival exhausted them. Perhaps circumstances were kinder thereafter; certainly, in the war of 1812 between Great Britain and the United States, the townsfolk of St. Stephen, in New Brunswick, were able to agree with the townsfolk of Calais, in Maine, immediately across the

River Saint Croix, that, whatever their respective Governments might do, they resolved not to fight each other. Certainly it is true that the English-speaking and the French-speaking in the province get on with each other better than they do in other parts of Eastern Canada. The French-speaking have not the Quebecois' insistence on the importance of race, the English-speaking avoid the touch of superiority that has coloured the behaviour of so many from Ontario. Is New Brunswick tolerant and placid or just a little asleep?

Nova Scotia is almost an island (the neck of land joining it to New Brunswick is no more than seventeen miles wide), 300 miles long and with 4,625 miles of coastline. Sir William Buchanan attempted a settlement in 1605. It failed as a settlement (Sir William died a bankrupt) but it did at least leave behind a name, a flag, the cross of St. Andrew, and an order of nobility in Britain, the Nova Scotia baronets, established by Charles I with baronial rights and jurisdiction over the plantation and costing their original grantees a payment of £1,200 each into the Stuarts' coffers (ten of these baronetcies still survive).

Nova Scotia became firmly British in 1749 with the founding and settlement of Halifax. Halifax itself was half Catholic Irish from Europe and half Protestant from men and women already in America. Lunenburg was settled in 1753 from Germany, and its people quickly became English-speaking and fishermen. Annapolis was peopled by people from Connecticut and Massachusetts, Baptists and apple-growers. The north, around Cape Breton, was settled by the Scots, Lowland Presbyterians and Catholic Highlanders, in between the surviving settlements of the earlier French. Scotland really came to Nova Scotia in the middle of the eighteenth century, in the ship *Hector*, and the crofters from Scotland, dispossessed at home, marched ashore in their new land led by a piper (who, tradition says, had stowed away on board and earned his passage by his music). Gaelic as a common language survived as long in Nova Scotia as it did in Scotland itself. In Nova Scotia the Legislative Assembly dates from 1758 and is the oldest representative body in Canada. Professor A. R. M. Lower, in his *From Colony to Nation*, says: "The Assembly, meeting in Halifax year after year, gave a centre to the province. . . . Nothing could have drawn the scattered communities so effectively to-

gether into a genuine body politic." And a genuine body politic
it has remained.

Not so prosperous as it was. In his day, the wooden-boat builder
of Nova Scotia and New Brunswick, and the men who sailed them
all over the world, were famous and prosperous. They built the
famous ship *Bluenose* and left that name as a description for Nova
Scotians ever since. They could build wooden ships in the harbours and the coves. They could not build the ships of iron and
steel, and the country became not a land so much of poverty as a
land where every man was conscious that there was a limit to the
reward he could earn from the work he could do. And, unfortunately, the transition came at the time of Confederation.

The late Professor H. A. Innis, in his *Changing Concepts of
Time*, quotes this memorial:

> We use the word Canada in its original and proper sense,
> comprising the provinces of Quebec and Ontario. It is a com-
> mon error to regard these two provinces as Upper Canada, and
> the Maritimes as Lower Canada. That is incorrect. Ontario was
> Upper Canada, Quebec, Lower Canada. Nova Scotia was never
> Canada. . . .
>
> In 1867 Canada was a crown colony. Nova Scotia was a
> crown colony. Surrounded by the sea, nurtured in the traditions
> of the sea, Nova Scotia became a great maritime power. Her
> ships were to be found in every port of the world, and they
> brought back to our people the necessities of life, industry and
> commerce, which has made them the richest per head of any
> population of any British colony on this side of the Atlantic.
> In the colony of Canada civic strife and hatreds had been
> assiduously sown. The people were divided in race, language,
> tradition and religion. In their Parliament of the two provinces
> representation was about equal. Every proposal advanced by
> one province was looked upon by the other as concealing some
> sinister motive. Suspicion was the watchword of both. . . .
>
> Down by the sea, three maritime provinces, Nova Scotia,
> New Brunswick and Prince Edward Island, had devoted them-
> selves to the industries of a maritime people, and had grown
> wealthy. Nova Scotia had outstripped them all. There were no
> divisions. They lived in harmony and good-will. It was upon
> these provinces, and Nova Scotia in particular, that Canada

now cast envious eyes. Their plight was desperate. Far out-
numbering us in population, if we could be enticed into a
confederacy, their combination would be complete, and our
revenues and sources of wealth would be at their command.

It is difficult to conceive of your Commission being unin-
formed of what followed. It is a history of legislative violence
inflicted on a loyal province, a black and evil page in British
Administration on this continent, in which Nova Scotia was
handed over—not to an imperial power to be ruled, not by
statesmen and a wise and just sovereign, but to another crown
colony, bankrupt alike in morals as in money. . . . The 'breeds'
of the Yukon, the plainsmen of the West, the bushmen of
Ontario, the Habitant of Quebec, the bucket shops of Toronto
and the gilded gamblers of St. James's Street may issue their
edicts to a British people in an island province of the Atlantic,
and proclaim to them that they are forbidden to trade in and
out of their own harbours under penalty of a pirate's ransom to
satiate the inexorable maw of Canada. . . .

When it became known that the British North America Act,
concocted behind closed doors in Downing Street, had been
thrust upon Nova Scotia without her knowledge or consent, the
anger of her people flamed out. The British flag was torn down
and trampled upon. The papers were issued with black borders.
The regimental commanders of the Nova Scotia militia—of
whom my father was one—waited and prayed for word to come
that revolt was afoot. The bayonets of the Halifax garrison were
doubled up to intimidate the people. Under these sweet and
benign influences Nova Scotia was ushered into a ramshackle
confederacy. . . .

Of all the arrogant edicts issued by Canada against Nova
Scotia citizens, that which forbids them buying or bringing
home a used car from any American port, smacks the most of
the air of the Boston tea-party. . . . These cars can be bought
at half the price of the Canadian, and brought here in our own
bottoms at one-fifth the freight from Canada. These edicts are
issued at the command of Canadian manufacturing juntas, who
hold the government in the hollow of their hand. . . .

There is a limit to a long-suffering people's submission to
tyranny. . . . Canadian propaganda tells us that as the blind
must not dream of sunrise, Nova Scotia must not dream of

liberty. To pluck the wild flowers of hope in our hands to warm
our hearts, is not for a conquered province. . . . Where in all
history did the domination of a maritime people by an inland
horde breed other than strife?

That was written by Mr. William Rand and presented to a
Royal Commission in Nova Scotia on Economic Enquiry, in 1934.
The people of the Maritimes have long memories.

Andrew Bonar Law and Max Aitken, first Lord Beaverbrook,
were both born in New Brunswick, and both took their talents
elsewhere to give them full play. For two men of the Maritimes
who left Canada to fulfil their ambitions, thousands have left for
other parts of Canada. From Ontario westwards they are everywhere, sober, capable, hard-working, trustworthy and trusted.
Both New Brunswick and Nova Scotia, like Scotland, have been a
reservoir of talent on which the rest of the country has drawn.
That form of bleeding is a bad thing.

If that is an explanation for the Magnetic Hill, then time will
help to settle the problem. The Maritimes lose their best people
now because the pull from the west is so strong. As the west itself
fills, the drain on the Maritimes will slacken and its people will
remain, to develop their own resources. The change may come
very soon. In the last year or so considerable deposits of metal
ores have been found in the east coast, particularly in New Brunswick and the Gaspé Peninsula, and their development may well
provide the stimulus these provinces need.

Now, the Magnetic Hill is something of a tambourine beaten by
a showman uneasy over the quality of the acts he has to offer.
When New Brunswick is holding its own people, pulling in others
to a new spurt of growth, Moncton may cease to make a noise
over a spurious gravity-defying hill and come to be more content,
maybe, with the longer view from the same spot.

4. Newfoundland

On 1 April 1949, Newfoundland joined the Confederation of
Canada and became its tenth province. The accession presented
Canada with a problem of a kind which the Federal Government
had never before encountered; that of bringing into an existing

federation a people who had experienced almost a century of independence and self-government followed by some fifteen years of Government by Commission, directed from London, unanimously accepted at its start but experiencing a descending curve of popular esteem.

Newfoundland brought no problem of immediate urgency with her. Her basic interests had always been largely parallel to those of Canada herself. The standards of living of her people were lower than those of Canadians; since confederation would almost certainly produce some improvement in them, the Federal Government could count on receiving some credit for that. Yet the Newfoundlanders were, and are, a proud and independent people. They did not ask for charity when they voted, by a tiny majority, for union with Canada; they could, and can still, be hurt by clumsiness or tactlessness in Ottawa. It would have been quite possible for Canada to build up in Newfoundland the kind of resentment that lingers in Nova Scotia from all that followed her decision to join the original confederation.

The people of Newfoundland are North Americans, not yet Canadians, another and a different ingredient in Canada in growth. The province includes both the island of Newfoundland and the territory of Labrador on the adjacent mainland. The island contains 42,734 square miles, about the same land area as Ireland, 6,000 miles of coastline, and some 360,000 people. Parts of it have been inhabited by settlers from Europe (the first permanent settlers were mainly from the West of England and Ireland) for as long as any part of the North American continent. Labrador, as defined by the Privy Council decision of 1927 which settled its boundary with Quebec, is 112,630 square miles in extent but has a permanent population of no more that 7,890 people, of whom 2,400 are at Goose Bay; politically it is part of a single Newfoundland constituency. Newfoundland is self-supporting, in the sense that its people could, if put to it, maintain life on what they can grow from the land and catch in the surrounding seas. In Labrador that is probably true only of the Eskimos. Yet Labrador contains a vast and as yet not fully known store of minerals. It has forests and it has water power. The day may yet come, as a Newfoundlander once said, when Newfoundland is known as the island off the south-east coast of Labrador.

Geologically, Newfoundland, like the Maritimes, is a part of the

Appalachian chain of mountains on the North American coast, but, so far north, only the tops of the mountain chains are above water, and they have been ground down by glacial ice into undulations rather than peaks. The main ridges run roughly north-east, south-west, and the highest point is only some 2,600 feet above sea-level. Part of the surface is bare rock. Almost all the remainder is forest, of spruce, birch and pine. About one two-hundredth of the surface is cleared and is cultivated; this is mostly in the south-east corner, the Avalon Peninsula. It is possible that greater areas could usefully be brought into cultivation, in the sense that the soil is sufficiently good, but it would need capital to clear and drain it and establish the individual settlements. Communications are a great problem. There is one trans-island railway, from St. John's in the east to Port-aux-Basques in the south-west, and that passes through Gander, Grand Falls and Corner Brook. These towns are linked by road, but there are gaps between Gander and Shoal Harbour (nearly half-way to St. John's, travelling eastwards) and between Corner Brook and Port-aux-Basques in the south-west.

The climate is not severe, by North American standards. The period of warm weather is comparatively short, from the end of May until October, but it is long enough for all root crops to mature and to provide fodder for the animals. In the winter the northern coasts are closed by ice, but it is still possible to fish to the south. To live in reasonable comfort, Newfoundland must import cereals, and sugar. For most of its history it has been able to import tobacco and alcohol as well. But before 1939 it never really earned sufficient both to pay for its immediate needs and for capital improvements such as railways, roads and public services. That cost was borrowed and added to the public debt and the public debt grew year by year.

Newfoundland's economy has always been dangerously simple, and it has not changed very much with time. Even today, of its adult working population, 18,073 describe themselves as fishermen, 9,146 work in the forests and 3,532 in mining, at the lead-zinc mine at Buchans or the iron-ore mine at Bell Island, in Conception Bay, just west of St. John's. The earnings from these industries have been:

	1935–6	1952–3
	$	$
Fishing	8,287,000	15,356,000
Timber, wood pulp and newsprint	12,826,000	39,661,000
Mining	4,655,000	12,168,000

On a basis of saleable output per man employed, the mining industry and the timber, wood-pulp and newsprint industries are each four times more valuable to Newfoundland than its fisheries. Yet the Amulree Commission, appointed in 1933 by the United Kingdom Government to investigate the history and prospects of the country, said in its report: "The codfishery has been, and must continue to be, the mainstay of the island", and certainly the whole of Newfoundland's history until 1939 was based on the belief that this sentence is true. Was it true in 1933? Is it true now?

The principal catch off Newfoundland is cod and traditionally the bulk of that catch was salted and dried, for a market in the Roman Catholic countries of Europe. There is also a market for fresh cod along the eastern seaboard of the United States as far south as New York, and that is now being augmented by an expanding trade in frozen fish. Cod is caught on the Grand Banks of Newfoundland, which stretch from 50 to 300 miles south-eastward of the mainland, and by inshore fishing around the immediate coasts of Newfoundland and Labrador. The Grand Banks are fished from early spring onwards by small schooners which carry some twenty men and the dories from which the crews actually shoot their lines. The coastal waters are fished from June to the fall, from small boats manned by two or three men. For the past seventy-five years the average yearly sale of cod from Newfoundland has been about a million and a quarter quintals a year, and before 1939 the average price realised was just over $4½ a quintal. That was sufficient to give the individual fisherman a cash income of no more than $125 a year. The other products of the sea are seal-skin, and limited salmon, lobster and herring catches which together added perhaps another million dollars a year to Newfoundland's earnings from her fisheries.

Even before the war a cash income of $125 a year could not keep a man, let alone a family, alive. Mr. Thomas Lodge, in his book *Dictatorship in Newfoundland*, published in 1939, quotes the result of an investigation, made in 1934, by a group of private individuals at St. John's. This showed that, if the head of a family were to rely solely on the cash produced by fishing for the support of his family, he could not maintain it unless the price realised for the fish caught was $10 a quintal or better. The gap between that figure and the pre-war average of $4½ a quintal was one of the frightening things in Newfoundland life. In fact, it showed that the Newfoundland fisherman could not have been living from the produce of his fishing to the extent he thought he did. He was part-time smallholder as well.

There are some 1,300 fishing villages, or "outports" as they are called around the coastline. In all of them there is some cleared land, and all of them are within reach of timber. In other words, the fisherman, when not fishing for a saleable catch, could build his house, provide himself with fish and milk and possibly some poultry, all from the land on which he lived, without spending anything very much in the way of actual currency. The cash earnings of a Newfoundland fisherman were not a true guide to his standard of living, low as that might be.

But, whatever can be said on the economics of fishing, in fact the pattern of life in Newfoundland from the beginning of the settlements there 300 years ago has been built on the produce of the sea. Almost all the outports, particularly those in the north, have no other reason for existence. Equally, the community of St. John's lives on the maintenance of these outports and the disposal of their catches. Indeed, the whole character of the Newfoundlander, his courage and his endurance as well as his individuality and intolerance of discipline, even of co-operation, in anything but the unison that must exist among a crew at sea, comes from that way of life. It is ingrained. The sea is in his blood, and for once that stock phrase is true. To him, Newfoundland is the Island, the rest of North America the Mainland. The one daily train from St. John's to Port-aux-Basques that connects with the ship across the St. Lawrence to the mainland, is called "Foreign".

The changes made by the coming of the mining and the newsprint industries were limited in their effect. The iron-ore mines at Bell Island, working a very large ore body, were opened in 1895. They are owned by the Dominion Steel and Coal Corporation of Nova Scotia and most of their output goes there. The lead-zinc mines at Buchans belong to the Anglo-Newfoundland Development Company, are operated by the American Smelting Company, and their products are exported. The Grand Falls newsprint undertaking, that of the Anglo-Newfoundland Development Corporation, was established by Lord Northcliffe in 1905, primarily to supply his English newspapers with newsprint from non-European sources (for reasons of currency, it now sells its output almost exclusively to the United States and Mexico, shipping it by sea down the Atlantic seaboard and into the Caribbean). The paper plant at Corner Brook was established in 1923, mainly by the then Armstrong Whitworth interests with United Kingdom Treasury assistance, but, after early financial vicissitudes, in 1938 became a part of the English Bowater-Lloyd organisation. These industries have grown into first place in Newfoundland's exports, but they are not, of themselves, capable of transforming Newfoundland's economy.

In that country, each industrial centre is bound to remain very much a self-contained community. None of the operating companies is owned by the people of Newfoundland, either as a community or as individual shareholders. Each has its own port; they do not use St. John's directly. Each ships out of the island all its output: virtually none is used in or by Newfoundland itself. Each has a big wage bill, but these wages, again, are either spent locally or upon products that must be imported into Newfoundland, and, of course, the profits are exported as dividends. In short, these industries support the men and women living in the four centres where their activities are. They contribute their quota of taxes. They give some business to the importing agents in St. John's. Otherwise they leave the life of other Newfoundlanders largely unaffected. Apart from seasonal work in the forests, they did not even provide anything to supplement the earnings of the fishermen. The Newfoundland fisherman, for instance, if he once works regularly in a mine, will thereafter look for mining employment, rather than go back to the precariousness of his former work.

In 1933–4, the last year of independent government in Newfoundland, State revenue was $8,906,204 and expenditure $10,427,724. Of that revenue $6,406,000 came from Customs and Excise; any increase in duties for the purpose of meeting the deficit would have resulted in a direct increase in the cost of living, equivalent, in these circumstances, to a reduction in the standard

5. New Brunswick: Fredericton

6. Labrador: The Iron Ore Enterprise, Ungava

of living. In the same year some two-thirds (65 per cent) of the actual revenues of the country were needed to pay the interest on the national debt. How, in these circumstances, had Newfoundland preserved her independence?

Newfoundland became a self-governing colony in 1854 and until the First World War, whilst rarely peaceful in its internal politics, was reasonably prosperous. With a much smaller population it bought and sold about the same quantity of fish. Immigration to the United States and Canada was unrestricted, and provided an economic safety-valve. In 1869 the country had voted against confederation with Canada by seventeen seats to five in a General Election fought on that issue. In 1895 it had asked Canada to be allowed to join the confederation but the financial terms Canada offered were not good enough, and nothing came of the proposal. In the same year, Canadian bankers refused a loan of $2,500,000 to the Newfoundland Government and stood aloof whilst the State Savings Bank was in difficulties. The Government was only saved from default at the last minute by the London money market, and the two episodes left something of a bitter taste in Newfoundlanders' mouths.

Newfoundland was a self-governing colony; she could not claim full authority over her external relations. As Canada found over the Alaska boundary dispute, so Newfoundland found over the fishing rights enjoyed by both France and the United States; in the nineteenth century Britain regarded her relations with other countries as of greater importance than the interests of these peoples living in these sparsely populated sections of the Empire. The fishing rights of France had dated back to the Treaty of Utrecht in 1713. They gave French fishermen the right to land and dry their fish on all the western and long stretches of the northern coast of Newfoundland. From this clause in the treaty France claimed that her nationals were entitled to use these lands for curing their fish in their natural state for ever and that no permanent erection might be built on any of these shores, a claim which would have prevented any permanent settlement at all. It was not until 1905, when good relations with France in Europe had become important, that the United Kingdom Government met the French with a compensation offer of other territorial concessions in Africa sufficient to persuade them to surrender their hold on Newfoundland. The fishing disputes with the United States

F

were equally complicated and were marked by a series of clashes and retaliations that extended over most of the nineteenth century. They were finally settled in 1910 by an arbitration before the International Court at The Hague. Despite this neglect of their vital interests, the Newfoundlanders, perhaps with the logic of their Irish blood, threw themselves into the First World War with enthusiasm, raised the Royal Newfoundland Regiment, (whose men won one V.C., 38 M.C.s, 32 D.C.M.s and 105 M.M.s and which has Neuve Chapelle, the Somme, Ypres and Cambrai 1917, and Gallipoli among its battle honours) and increased their external debt by one-third, by some $10 million, in the process. (The Royal Newfoundland Regiment is now a unit in the Canadian Army).

After the relative prosperity of the First World War, Newfoundland's economy returned to its state of deferred crisis, but by 1933 the crisis had reached a decisive point. Newfoundland had not the money with which to meet the annual interest on its external loans, then of some $101 million. It faced default. The depression had cut Europe's demand for cod, wood pulp and iron ore, and Italy's Abyssinian adventure and Spain's Civil War were to continue to limit two vital markets for fish. The value of exports fell from $39 million in 1930 to $22 million in 1933, and imports fell in the same proportion. Only the burden of interest on the external debt remained unchanged. In 1933, the revenues of the Government left $3 million with which to pay for all public services and keep some 90,000 unemployed from starvation. Newfoundland could not hope to pay the debt interest due on 1 January 1934, and she came to the United Kingdom for assistance.

The United Kingdom Government appointed a Royal Commission of investigation, under Lord Amulree. The Commission in a remarkably short time produced an exhaustive report, the effect of which was to advocate the giving of aid, but only on the condition that Newfoundland surrendered her right to self-government. Drastic as these proposals were, they were approved by both Parliaments and in 1934 an Act of the Imperial Government set up a Commission of Government for Newfoundland and Labrador consisting of the Governor-General and six members, all appointed from London, three from the United Kingdom and three normally resident in Newfoundland, and responsible to the Dominions Office in London.

"Our Government and our finances", one Newfoundlander said to me "were no worse than those of many of the provincial Governments in Canada, yet we were the only part of the Empire ever asked to give up independence as the price for receiving aid. And the Commissioners could balance their budget no better than we could, despite the fact that they were able to cut $2,000,000 from our yearly liability for interest by debt funding operations."

What did balance Newfoundland's budget was the Second World War. In 1939 and 1940, her budget showed a deficit of some $3 million. In 1942, there was a surplus of $8 million.

The war gave employment to some 3,000 loggers who enlisted in an Army forestry unit, to fishermen as seamen in the merchant navies, and to those who remained on the island in the construction of air and sea bases by Britain and Canada, and later by the United States. Three major land air bases were built and a seaplane base, at Botwood at the mouth of the Exploits River, St. John's harbour was improved, and various other defence works constructed. At the peak of the construction period, in 1942, over 19,000 men were so employed. And when that peak passed, the situation in the North Atlantic eased and fishing became both more possible and more prosperous. Compared with an estimated total national income of $46 million in 1935, the estimate for 1945 was $110 million, while the cost of living itself had only increased by some 60 per cent over the same period.

The Commission of Government had originally been given no specific length of life. Before the war, the Dominions Secretary had spoken as though it must last at least a generation. By the end of the war the reason for its appointment had gone; Newfoundland was once again solvent. In 1943, the Under-Secretary of State for the Dominions had said, if the people of Newfoundland wanted to return to full responsible government and if the island were then self-supporting, the United Kingdom would be very ready to facilitate such a change. In what direction?

Newfoundlanders are realists. What the average Newfoundlander in 1945 would have wished to find was an economic future which would provide the least restricted market for his fish, wood pulp, newsprint and minerals, and the cheapest source for his essential imports of cereals, sugar, tobacco, alcohol and manufactured goods. He would also have looked for someone who would, if possible, accept responsibility for defence, and for his existing external debt, and who would provide for the maintenance of such undertakings as the new airports, the railways, posts and telegraphs, lighthouses and navigational aids, and be both wealthy and interested enough to venture new capital on fresh development. He would be interested in the new wave of social security benefits, from old-age pensions to children's allowances, which seemed to be emerging from the war (and which Canada had already in operation). But, as a realist, the Newfoundlander would also have at the back of his mind the fact that before the war one-half of the population could not follow their customary calling during the winter, and that on past experience about half of them would need some cash assistance from the Government or else face starvation. He would want as much self-government as possible under these economic conditions. Most of those who favoured a return to responsible government were thinking in terms of responsible government plus a subvention of some kind from some other government.

The possibilities were:

1. A return to responsible government.
2. A continuance of government by commission appointed by the United Kingdom Government.
3. Union with the United Kingdom.
4. Union with the Confederation of Canada.
5. Union with the United States.

A straw vote taken in Corner Brook early in 1945 gave this result: for responsible government, 450; for union with the United States, 190; for confederation with Canada, 150; for a continuance of government by commission, 80.

Political union with the United Kingdom itself was never a likely proposal, from either side. Britain had no tradition of semi-autonomous provinces. The Newfoundlanders had experienced a fair measure of earlier neglect and had seen rule from Whitehall at first hand. They belonged to the dollar world, and could not leave it for the sterling area. What was to be said for and against continuance of rule by the Commission?

The Commission of Government was government by civil servants, with the advantages and disadvantages of that system. It was honest, disinterested, and when it did make up its mind, it had no public assembly that it needed to persuade into agreement. Health and Education services had benefited during its rule. In 1933–4, expenditure on education was only a half ($500,000) of of what it had been five years before. The Commission restored the expenditure to what it had been, by 1940–1 it had increased to over a million and a half dollars, and in 1944–5 the total for the year was nearly three million. But when it came to originating policy, to breaking fresh ground, the Commission was controlled from Whitehall, and dominated by the intense desire of all civil servants to avoid awkward public debates in Parliament. There was always the Treasury in the background.

Every civil service appointment in Newfoundland carrying a salary of more than £250 a year had to be approved by London first. When the Commission granted to Canada a ninety-nine-year lease of land for the Goose Bay air base, the news first broke in a Canadian newspaper and newspapers in St. John's were forbidden to print photographs that had already appeared in Canada. The British system of government by civil servants did not enhance its appeal to Newfoundlanders during the last five years of the Commission's rule.

Union with the United States was by no means a prospect distasteful to all Newfoundlanders, even though it meant severing the British connection. Ties with that country were real and varied. New York and the New England States contained a large population of Newfoundland descent. Many Newfoundlanders had lived and worked in those parts as fishermen, in bad times on shore. Newfoundland's fresh fish was sold there. One-third of her imports came from there. United States troops had been stationed in Newfoundland during the war and relations with them had been good. There was no clash in ways of life, and no public sentiment capable of building up the inevitable incident into a general xenophobic feeling. The one practical difficulty in the way of that union was the fact that the Federal Government of the United States gave no indication that it would, or would be allowed by Congress to take over the burden of Newfoundland's existing debt and her deficit-producing public undertakings.

In theory, federation with Canada should have looked more attractive. It was more logical, since both countries were British in nationality and their boundaries in Labrador marched together. Canada's progress in social welfare had already begun. Its federal system was based upon the giving of federal aid to individual provinces, and the country had a tradition of government ownership of, and subsidy to, railways, airlines, hotels and steamships that would rid Newfoundland's finances of the deficits on the Newfoundland Railway and Gander airport (Gander Airport was already costing over half a million dollars a year to maintain). But, if finance favoured Canada, sentiment did not. The earlier failures over Confederation had not been forgotten. There was still a political tradition of hostility to the very idea of joining the Mainlanders.

On the whole, the inhabitants of St. John's and its dependent districts were for a return to complete independence, for that would at once restore to them their importance as a seat of government. They had never felt the effects of a financial set-back to the fishing industry quite as harshly as had the fishermen themselves, since Newfoundland fisheries had been, and are, an industry in which the remuneration of the capitalist and manager is a first charge on all the takings. For the merchants of Newfoundland, for those who imported Newfoundland's needs, union with Canada had positive disadvantages. They were accustomed to drawing the full commission allowed by American manufacturers. Entry into the Canadian Confederation would mean that imports from the United States would be liable to federal import duties and be sold through the regular Canadian agents of the United States manufacturers. Another argument in St. John's against any form of federation was the certainty that federation would raise the level of direct taxation. In 1945, a married man with an income of $5,000 a year paid $743 a year in income tax in the United Kingdom, $584 in Canada and only $86 in Newfoundland. But the majority of Newfoundlanders were not payers of income tax. For 3,500 railway workers, for 2,500 civil servants, for 2,000 men at the airports, federation would mean higher wages, once they came within Canadian terms and conditions of work. For the people in the outports, federation would mean old-age pensions and children's allowances, possibly a larger cash income on retirement than ever they had earned during their working lives.

In July 1943, Mr. Mackenzie King had said at Ottawa: "If the people of Newfoundland should ever decide that they wish to enter federation and should make the decision clear beyond all possibility of misunderstanding, Canada would give most sympathetic consideration to the proposal." Given Mr. Mackenzie King's caution in words, that looked like a reasonable approach.

Towards the end of 1945, the United Kingdom Government announced that Newfoundland would vote the following year to elect a national convention of forty-five members to decide what Newfoundland itself considered should be the future shape of its government. The members for the Convention were elected by popular vote in June 1946 and a majority of them were in favour of a return to responsible government. After a long debate, the Convention decided to send a delegation to London in 1947 to negotiate with the United Kingdom Government on the terms on which responsible government could be restored.

In their proper time, the stories of the negotiations and the conversations in the years between 1945 and 1947 on the subject of the future of Newfoundland between the United Kingdom, the delegation and the Government of Canada will make interesting reading. It is clear that the United Kingdom Government must have come to the conclusion during the war that, when the war was over, Newfoundland unaided would not be able to sustain a standard of life comparable with that enjoyed in Canada and the United Kingdom, nor, indeed, comparable with that which many Newfoundlanders had themselves seen during the war. Somebody would have to supplement the island's income. It is equally clear that the United Kingdom Government did not intend to foot that bill. The dollar shortage was already a factor in British life and the United Kingdom Government had no intention, even if it had the resources, of guaranteeing to spend dollars on Newfoundland fish or newsprint when it could obtain both from Europe for sterling. When the delegation from Newfoundland arrived in London in the summer, it was told that independence in responsible government must also mean independence in finance. For some of its members this was a sobering thought. In the years of the Commission of Government, Newfoundland had drawn from the British taxpayer, mostly via the Colonial Development Fund, a total subvention of £3,800,000 towards Budget deficits. It seemed that day was never to return.

Having decided to cast Newfoundland off, as it were, and convinced that she would, in the future no less than in the past, need a patron, the United Kingdom Government must have thought very hard about Canada. By some means, Newfoundland had to be shepherded away from responsible government in the direction of confederation with Canada, not in the direction of the United States. Equally, Canada had to be convinced that Newfoundland must be taken on, despite the immediate burden. A strong argument must have come from the occasion, the ending of the Commission of Government, but an even stronger one was certainly Labrador, its immense resources, its extremely inconvenient boundary with Quebec, its essential part in Canadian defence, including the existing Canadian base at Goose Bay. It was of vital importance to Canada that Labrador should become a part of Canada rather than a part of the United States. It is to be assumed that Mr. Attlee's government pointed that out to Mr. Mackenzie King, and it is even more certain that Mr. Mackenzie King must have looked at that horribly inconvenient boundary line drawn between Quebec and Labrador by the Privy Council and thought that was really the final argument. To escape a boundary dispute with the United States over land that was said to be almost solid iron ore would be worth quite a price.

But besides boundaries and ore bodies there are also personalities, and it will be even more interesting to learn of the part played by the Hon. Mr. J. R. Smallwood, the present Premier of Newfoundland, in those discussions. One thing is certain; more than any one other individual, Mr. Smallwood brought about the union of Newfoundland with Canada. In the Convention he was always in a minority. When the London delegation, of which he was a member, returned to St. John's the full convention still voted 28 to 12 in favour of a return to responsible government. He led the fight for Canada into the country itself. As he had said to a journalist in London in the summer of 1947: "Union with Canada is the only thing for us. It's got to be. I'm gambling my life on it."

The Hon, J. R. Smallwood, in size, is a small man, of considerable eloquence, and possessed by a daemon that only brought him into politics comparatively late in life. He had been a journalist and a trade-union organiser; once he walked the width of the island organising men as and when he found them. At one time, he ran a daily feature on the Newfoundland radio called "The Barrel Man", named after the look-out man who was stationed in a barrel up the foremast of the old whaling ships to spot for the blows from the whale's spout, the first indication of the whaler's quarry. His hour was a miscellany of stories, true and improved, of memories of Newfoundland, contributed by listeners and put into shape by Smallwood. If the supply ran out, or, as on one occasion during the war, if it were cut short by a censor, Smallwood just talked. That did not fill his time. He was also interested in chicken-farming, goat-breeding and pig-rearing in turn, on a part-time basis, until finally the pig-breeding swallowed up the radio work. He finished the war as the very successful organiser of a scheme by which he distributed the swill from Gander Air Station among the pig-breeders of the area, including himself. When the question of Newfoundland's future became immediate politics, Smallwood lost interest in both swill and pigs.

"What shall I do about the pigs?" his brother-in-law and partner asked him a little later, when he was getting well into his campaign. "What pigs?" Smallwood replied.

After the London mission, the convention decided to send another delegation to Ottawa, to negotiate there. This delegation was in Ottawa for three months. It returned in October 1947, with a formal proposal from the Canadian Government for membership of the Confederation as its tenth province. The response of its parent, the convention, was a vote against even including confederation with Canada as one of the issues to be submitted to the electorate in the forthcoming plebiscite, but public opinion forced its hand. The plebiscite put before the voters what had become the three practical questions: continuance of the Commission of Government for another five years; responsible government as it had existed before the Commission was established; confederation with Canada. On 3 June 1949, after a winter of strenuous campaigning on all sides, Newfoundland voted, with this result:

For Responsible Government	69,400
For Confederation	64,066
For the Commission	22,311

This was followed by a second plebiscite, dropping the now plainly discarded Government by Commission; 78,323 voted for Confederation and 71,334 against. Joe Smallwood had beaten St. John's; he had carried the whole island with the exception of St. John's. A delegation of seven men, including Smallwood, left for Ottawa and began the final negotiations for the Terms of Union.

At the time the negotiations began Newfoundland had gone back to its pre-war pattern of a deficit on external trade. Its

revenues were $40·6 million, its expenditure $40·9 million, the first
deficit for seven years. But its net public debt was down and it
had liquid assets, including an interest-free loan to the United
Kingdom of $10 million, of $27·2 million. It must have been the
only country in the world to have reduced its national debt during
the war, and the real burden of all that remained was much less
than it had been in pre-war currency. Newfoundland could maintain in Ottawa that she was far less of a liability, to any government, than she had been at any time before in the preceding fifty
years. On 11 December 1948, the agreement constituting the
Terms of Union with Canada was signed in Ottawa, and the
financial provisions embodied in it were a considerable advance
on those Canada had offered the previous year.

Newfoundland became a province in the Confederation, returning for provincial purposes to the same legislative machine as
had existed before the creation of the Commission of Government. In the Federal Parliament the representation of the new
province was to be six Senators and seven members in a House of
Commons of 262. By custom, it has now become entitled to one
member in the Cabinet. Denominational rights in the schools were
protected. Its fisheries remained subject to existing Newfoundland
legislation. It retained its existing credit balances (accepting some
limitations on how they should be spent) and after union it would
receive both subsidies and grants.[1]

Canada took over the public services, including post and tele-
communications, the railway, Gander Airport and the Newfoundland Broadcasting Corporation, and her liabilities to veterans,
public servants and merchant seamen. "Now," Mr. Smallwood
could say, in a speech to the Provincial Legislature in March 1952,
"70 per cent of the entire revenue of the Government is paid over
to us by Ottawa."

I read all these provisions in the leather-bound copy of the
Terms of Union presented to each of the Newfoundland signatories and of course I asked the man who had lent it to me what
he thought of it all now. He was silent for a moment.

[1] The subsidies were a fixed sum of $180,000 a year, plus 80 cents per
head of population (agreed at 325,000) plus an additional subsidy of
$1,100,000 on terms comparable to those payable to the existing Maritime
provinces. The grants began as a sum of $6,500,000 for the first year after
Union, falling to $350,000 in the tenth, with a provision for a general (up-
ward) review of financial aid from the Federal Authorities within eight years.

"When we walked up to the Centre Block on Parliament Hill in Ottawa for the ceremony of signing this," he said at last, "one of the others said to me: 'D'you think we've done the right thing?' and I said, 'Yes,' although I felt sick in my stomach and would gladly have walked out on it even then."

"Joining the Confederation was a good thing and an inevitable thing," he went on, "but this feeling we call patriotism has deep roots and produces strange reactions. I cannot get out of my mind the thought that the day may come when a delegation from the Canadian Government at Ottawa will walk down some long path in Washington, D.C., heading for a signing ceremony that will bring into being a Federal Union of North America. I'm sure the terms will be fair and that everyone will sign, as I did. And I'm equally sure that some of them will have the same sick feeling in their stomachs that I had in Ottawa on that December day in 1948."

But that is a feeling very different from that left in the Maritimes some seventy years before, at the time of the original Confederation. The Federal Government of Canada, in 1948, could afford to be more generous than could the new Federal Government in 1870, but power to be generous and generosity do not always go together. The approach from Canada to Newfoundland in 1948, the acceptance by the Canadian people of the immediate burdens that Newfoundland (and, at one remove, Great Britain) shifted on to their shoulders, are some measure of the growth towards maturity in Canadian political thought over these seventy years.

Mr. Smallwood's Liberal Party won the first provincial election after Confederation, and the responsibility for the island was then fairly on his shoulders. Mr. Smallwood had no doubts over the action his Government should take. The economy of Newfoundland must be expanded, he believed. The island must be made more attractive to its inhabitants, it must be made more attractive to the investor. Whilst Newfoundland was still outside the Confederation and Canadian immigration laws were severe, some 2,500 or so of its population, each year, managed to cross into Canada and settle there. Once all Newfoundlanders had become Canadian citizens, the flood of emigrants might well increase. What could be done to find them more and better-paid employment at home? Mr. Smallwood's answer was that the Government should set out to attract new secondary, or light, industries into the island, and that it should use some of its accumulated surplus to help do so. With the aid of a Director-General of Economic Welfare the Government set about the task, and, by 1953, had succeeded in establishing eleven new activities, most of them industries which were quite new to the island, many of them attracted across the Atlantic from among concerns in Europe that felt the hot breath already on their neck, as one man put it to me, by a scheme under which the Government matched the tangible assets they brought with a cash advance of an equal amount, by way of loan. The largest concern that has come on these terms, from Germany, is now incorporated as a Canadian company, Canadian Machinery and Industrial Construction, Ltd., with a capital of $2 million. It has now a first-class building outside St. John's and an array of the most modern German heavy machine tools. Others include a cotton mill, a leather-tanning plant and factories making rubber garments and boots, optical goods and electric storage batteries. The total commitment accepted by the Government to the end of 1952 under this section of the scheme was $10 million.

In 1931, Mr. Smallwood in his book *The New Newfoundland*, wrote: "Newfoundland . . . has entered upon a new march that is destined to place her, within the next dozen years in the front rank of the great small nations of the world. That new march is towards modern large-scale industrialisation." People may have laughed at him then, and maybe he deserved it, for any journalist should know better than to launch so desperately vulnerable a prophecy. But Mr. Smallwood not only has the courage of his convictions; he has kept his convictions. Not all politicians when they gain office set out to fulfil the plans they cherished when they were journalists. These new enterprises, Mr. Smallwood believes today, will add $10 million to Newfoundland's yearly wage bill.

Other observers are unpersuaded. Any light industries in Newfoundland must face the problems of training unskilled labour, the handicaps that come from the high cost of the materials they must import, the difficulties in selling that come from their distance from the right markets and their unfamiliarity with them. Those are not arguments against the attempts. In the last thirty years Newfoundland's deficits have come more from using money to give men without work enough to keep alive while they remained without work than from using money to back ventures intended in the first place to give them work. But it is too soon to say that the experiment is successful, and it would be quite wrong to attribute Newfoundland's increased prosperity now to the new enterprises in their present shape.

The second line of Mr. Smallwood's attack was an attempt to make the world outside Newfoundland realise what the country's natural resources are and may be. The provincial government began with its own specialised surveys of the more likely areas for new mineral development, and it followed that up by persuading others to use their money on surveys as well; it has even induced Americans to prospect for oil. Two development corporations have been formed, the Newfoundland and Labrador Corporation ("Nalco"), partly government-owned and partly financed from New York, and the British and Newfoundland Corporation ("Brinco"), promoted by a syndicate headed by Rothschilds and including practically every well-known London financial group with the exception of Uncle Tom Cobley, Ltd. Now, taking into account the existing grants and leases held by the mining and lumbering companies, virtually the whole of Newfoundland and Labrador is included in one concession or another. All that Mr. Smallwood needs to do for the future is to negotiate the final terms on which development shall proceed when something to develop is found.

Mr. Smallwood is planning for an industrial future. In the meantime? In the meantime, Newfoundland has two important sources of revenue that she did not possess before the war. One is the United States Government, the other the Federal Government of Canada. The three United States air bases in the island at Argentia, Stephensville and Torbay, outside St. John's, are a considerable source of revenue in themselves. The United States Military and Air Force authorities are spending in Newfoundland some $24 million a year, six-sevenths of their total expenditure in Canada, which makes this the second largest item (the first was the $39 million from the wood, pulp and paper industries) in the income of the islanders. The Federal Government is another fairy godmother. In addition to its direct subsidies to the province, of $13 million, it provides another $11 million in family allowances, and old-age pensions, mother and dependant allowances. Veterans and old-age assistance add another $14 million from mixed federal and provincial sources. All in all, about two out of every five dollars going in Newfoundland pockets come from a government source. Newfoundland has become that modern phenomenon, a welfare state with a vested interest in military expenditure.

There is another man in St. John's with an importance almost equal to that of Mr. Smallwood; he is Mr. Gerald Doyle. Mr. Doyle is the importer and distributor of most of the patent medicines sold in the island. For the last twenty years he has also bought two periods of time on the air each day (save Sunday), fifteen minutes in the afternoon and half an hour in the evenings, and he has used this time to provide his own news programme.

Mr. Doyle does not concern himself with news coming in from the rest of the world. His interests are domestic. His news periods begin with local news from the island, continue with news for each region—almost for each community—and then each becomes the equivalent of a message centre for the island. "Tell Father the operation was successful and I should be out of hospital in two weeks"; "Tom has been posted to the R.C.A.F. Station at Halifax —he should get a long leave before Christmas"; "How is Uncle Joseph?"; "Please send ——"; "Where is ——?"; and so on, the personal correspondence of an island community, all by courtesy of Mr. Doyle, and with a reminder about patent medicines at the end.

Mr. Doyle maintains a correspondent in every village. In Grand Falls, his agent has spent as much as four hundred dollars in a month on telegraphed and telephoned messages from his district to Mr. Doyle's news-room in St. John's: "Not a penny of it do I grudge," said Mr. Doyle.

Mr. Doyle is also a man of power. He circumnavigates the island in his yacht each year and is met in each outport with greetings fit for an uncle from Australia. If you want an appointment with a dentist in St. John's, for which you would normally wait at least a week, Mr. Doyle will call the dentist and tell him to see you at once. He will. When Newfoundland joined the Confederation and the Newfoundland Broadcasting Corporation passed over to C.B.C., Mr. Doyle's sponsored news went with it, intact. It is the only sponsored news programme in Canada.

The success of Mr. Doyle's message centre, which no Newfoundlander would willingly miss, is instructive. Many of the messages could be telephoned or telegraphed over the island, but that would cost money, and for generations the Newfoundlander in an outport has been so desperately short of cash that he dare not indulge in what to him would be a gross extravagance. Many more of the messages literally could not be sent in any other way. They come from the schooners at sea, from men roaming the island in search for work or in seasonal jobs in the lumber camps or the seal fisheries. They go to the outports, and many of these have only the sea in summer, and the dog-sleigh in winter, to bring anything in from the outside world (for what individual in Newfoundland can afford to charter a plane?). For them, Mr. Doyle is their link with home. He is a permanent institution. To save their batteries, towards the end of winter many will switch on their radio only for Mr. Doyle's news. And, of course, Newfoundlanders are devoted to patent medicines.

St. John's is on the eastern coast and contains about a sixth of Newfoundland's people. A ridge of hills runs north and south along the coast and is broken at one point by a narrow channel, known as "the Narrows", leading in to a natural landlocked harbour, a good anchorage, perfect in its day although now too small for many ocean-going freight ships. To the north of the entrance is Signal Hill and on the summit of the hill is Cabot Tower, both a memorial to John Cabot, who discovered Newfoundland in 1497, and the place at which the first wireless signal sent across the Atlantic was received in 1901. The town itself spreads along the western side of the harbour and a great deal of its history is written in the appearance of its streets. St. John's, for instance, has never had much money to spend on its improvement.

It is old, the oldest city in North America, but there is now very little to show of its past. A great deal of the centre of the town was burnt in 1892, and that, for any town, was a bad year in which to start afresh. The business centre of St. John's, Water Street, is only too late Victorian in style, and a good English equivalent to its architectural merit is Slough, Bucks. Westwards from Water Street the streets of terraced houses climb sharply up the slope to the Roman Catholic Cathedral. Many of the houses are timber-built and yet St. John's, alone in Canada, has preserved the bow-fronted window and contrived to marry it to the flat-roofed frame building. It is a seaport but it has few of the quiet, pleasant houses found in, say Plymouth, to which the sea captain came home up the hill in the dusk, his heavy boots hard on the footwalk, his hands in the pockets of his reefer jacket and his cap pushed away from his forehead. There were fewer ships in St. John's of the size to enable their captains to earn enough to build that kind of house.

St. John's should be seen, as I saw it, from Signal Hill on a summer evening. Below me, on the seaward side, I could still trace the last remains of the baled paper they had salvaged during the war from a ship torpedoed almost as soon as it had left the Narrows. Beyond, the water was dark blue and almost still. To the south-west, the town itself was blurred with a slight haze, and all that stood out were the Newfoundland Hotel and the Roman Catholic Cathedral, the hotel a solid brick cube diagonally across the harbour, the Cathedral on higher ground beyond it, its two towers ornamented like those from a child's box of bricks. Just below me was an old battery, its muzzle-loaders still in a half-moon facing the entrance to the Narrows. An old print of about 1840 shows the battery in the same position and in very much the same state, save that a uniformed soldier is lying in the foreground on his side, reading a book.

Over to my right I could see the great expanse of barracks and store buildings of the U.S. Air Base, and just below me, beyond Dead Woman's Pond, was a shanty town, clean, with tidy gardens and the washing out in the breeze, but looking as though each house had been modelled from a freight car and built from a packing-case. The taxi-driver who had brought me up lived in one of these houses.

"I wish I was back in the war again," he said, with the faint Irish accent that so many from St. John's have. "I made good money in the harbour then. There was plenty of shipping in, damaged, or waiting for convoys, and all needing men to handle them. See the buoys stretching down the harbour? Little gold-mines to me they were.

"Now——" He paused. "Where've all the ships gone? Nothing from Boston, not much from Liverpool. We don't seem to matter no more."

Perhaps that is one of the penalties for becoming a province, but, again, how thin a shadow of the complaint of Mr. William Rand, of Nova Scotia.

4

The West

1. The Prairies

THE prairie lands are a vast sea that has become solid, and above them is the sky. The black soil still holds the mile-long crests and troughs of the faint swell that once seemed to have rumpled the surface of this sea, and the dome of the sky rests on the horizons. It seems useless to walk, for to move would change nothing, underfoot or overhead. The winds and the sky still belong to the oceans of the world.

Two pictures of this sea and this sky will never leave my mind.

I was driving by night to Regina, Saskatchewan, from a farm some forty miles to the south-east. At sunset the sun had slid down from behind the clouds that had hidden it all afternoon and for half an hour its light made the west a band of scarlet. It had sunk below the horizon as the sun sets at sea, visible to the last instant, so that one almost expected the green flash. When it had gone there were no stars in the sky, no light, only darkness. The road ran along a slight causeway, with two shallow ditches on either side. For the last thirty miles into Regina it was dead straight.

On the far horizon was the loom of the lights of the city, infinitely remote. I was at sea again. The headlights of the car changed the road into the grey wake of invisible ships ahead in the darkness and I skimmed over its fleckered surface as would a motor-boat on a calm night sea. For a time the car was isolated in this void, without movement in time or space, but the lights of the city far ahead were gradually changing, from a faint loom into a line of twinkling points. Slowly the points multiplied and separated and became more steady, until at last, from ten miles away, the pattern became fixed and identifiable, the pale green from a vapour lamp, yellow from a house, faint touches of red or blue from a neon sign. We were nearing port.

And all around us was still the same prairie, the same sea; no variation, not even the deeper blackness of a clump of trees, nor the changes in sound that come from breaks in a hedgerow alongside the road.

The other drive was from MacLeod northwards to Calgary, with the Rockies forty miles away to the west, an unreal band of picture mountains in miniature painted along the horizon to separate land from sky. It was late afternoon. We were at the centre of a vast arch of two hundred miles of sky.

Beyond the whole length of the Rockies the sky was piled with cloud, and at one point, a little to our north, a grey mass, low down, had broken through and trailed a veil of rain below it. Behind us the sky was clear and blue and the peaks of the mountains far to the south in the State of Mantana were a bright yellowish-white in sunshine. The clouds began about a third of the way up the southern half of the sky and their southern limit stretched eastwards in almost a straight line. At its edge the cloud bank was an armada of single ships, too many to count but leaving more blue than white in the sky. There were the ships of the line, the first-raters, and the frigates and the despatch vessels, sailing on in their set formation. But northwards they merged into one solid roof overhead, and as the eye followed that away to the north-east, to where the vortex of that mass of air and moisture seemed to be, the colour darkened to grey and blue-black. Only in one spot in the north had this roof of cloud an end above the horizon and there, beyond this northern eave, were the giant tops of cumulus, lit by sunlight.

That was the pattern of the Southern Alberta sky. The gusts from the west that had shaken the car as we crossed the Crow's Nest Pass from British Columbia had been bringing this air from the Pacific. Perhaps the rain to our left was the forerunner of more. Perhaps it was not too late in the year for snow. Perhaps——

All the questions in my mind that afternoon came from the sky, not from the hundred miles of land we were covering. The land of the prairies is fertile but passive. It needs moisture and warmth and they can only come from the sky. It is the sky that decides what can grow, and where, and for how long. It is from the sky that the summer hail can fall and flatten the whole of a season's crop in ten minutes; and leave that of a neighbour a mile or so away untouched. In 1946, a group of ex-service veterans decided to begin farming co-operatively on some newly drained land, and pooled all their money and their grants to make this start. In their second season a summer hailstorm destroyed the whole of their year's crop of wheat in an afternoon.

I have not seen the prairies in winter, when the wind is in the north and sweeps the snow in white arrows across the hard ground and the black background of the sky. Then the sky must be terrifying. In spring it can be aloof, carrying out its own vast campaign above the surface of a whole province, in which a mere square mile of land is of no importance whatever. In summer it can be a blazing furnace, as merciless in its way as is the winter. The sky can never be ignored.

In Saskatoon they have one of the most active training centres of the Royal Canadian Navy Reserve, H.M.C.S. *Unicorn*, a drill hall for seamen a thousand miles from the nearest salt water. I was not surprised. There cannot be that much difference between the sky of the prairies and the sky of the sea.

I drove out from the Bessborough Hotel, in Saskatoon, to the airport north of the town, late in a day towards the end of April. The sun was bright and the sky clear, although there was a sharp wind blowing from the west. Gradually we cleared the town itself, climbing upwards away from the river, and between one characteristic signpost of civilisation, the drive-in open-air cinema, and the next, the airport buildings a mile away on the horizon, there was a plain grass field. The taxi was travelling slowly, behind a battered van, and I looked out of the side window at the dry, pliable soil, at the grass shrunken and brittle with roots of pale yellow, as though all its life was still in the ground. To our left there was a narrow lake, like a flash in a mining area, and a causeway of rough stone and gravel had been built across it carrying a new road to the airport. A car came down the road across the causeway, and a cloud of light yellow dust slowly followed it. Suddenly I knew that I had seen all this before. This was in Iceland in early summer; this was a country with the same landscape, grass and dust. I had spent two years on that island and I was not likely to forget them. So the people of Saskatoon had the same kind of winter as I had known then. It was a sobering thought, and I felt a wave of sympathy for everyone I had already met on the way west.

The people of the prairie provinces are cheerful and interested in their visitors. They had been full of concern to satisfy my curiosity and answer my childish questions. They had been solicitous over London's fogs, over the East Coast floods, over the mantle of rain which, they remembered, masked the British Isles for most of the year. They had even been sympathetic over our lack of central heating, as though it was some natural phenomenon we could not remedy. If it had not been for the grass at Saskatoon I might never have thought seriously of their winter, of what it meant when the thermometer went to 20° below, or worse. In Winnipeg, one of the hoarding advertisements displayed the vast dial of a thermometer, which pointed to 40° F. when I saw it. At first I wondered what this dial, and the numbers on it, were intended to show. When I was told that it was nothing but a thermometer, and that people were sufficiently concerned with the daily temperature to welcome public announcements of where the thermometer stood, I was incredulous. Where in London is there a public indicator of our daily rainfall, for instance, or of the degree of cloud in the sky? How many people go up to the Air Ministry roof to find out?

All the prairie provinces have that kind of winter. Spring, which is when the day temperature reaches 42° F., comes to Winnipeg, to Saskatoon and to Edmonton at about the same time, the end of April. Spring comes as early far north down the Mackenzie River as it does in most of Manitoba, for the cold mass of water in Hudson's Bay holds it back. Some day, Canada will build a causeway across the mouth of Hudson's Bay (a useless stretch of water; it does not even produce many fish) as the Dutch have done with what was once the Zuider Zee, and they will plant sufficient atomic piles in the new lake to raise its temperature five or ten degrees; then the whole of Northern Canada will be transformed. But, until they do——

The maps of Western Canada are not a great help to the imagination. They suggest the western half of the Canadian shield, its broad ribbon encircling Hudson's Bay, because they show the lakes that rim its southern edge. They show the long, northwestwards line of the Rockies, and the vast Mackenzie River flowing out to the north into the Arctic at Aklavik, which has a ninety-day summer, as warm as that of Newfoundland. They hint at the flat prairie lands because they show a fine network of rivers, like veins, across Saskatchewan. They cannot show the wilderness of the woods nor the silver of the innumerable lakes. They cannot show that the Peace River has extraordinary patches of cultivable ground far to the north of where one would expect cultivable land to be. They cannot show how the prairie rivers, the North and South Saskatchewan, Bow River, High River and Milk River, wind through their shrub-lined channels, how they can provide, in the south, water for irrigation schemes that transform Southern Alberta. On the maps the prairie lands look featureless, and in a sense they are, as a plain woman may seem to be, until she speaks, or moves.

In 1931, the population of the three prairie provinces together was 2,353,529, in 1941, 2,421,905, and in 1951, 2,547,770; only in Saskatchewan did the population fall in the twenty-year period covered by the three censuses. Alberta made the largest gain, between 1941 and 1951, of 207,896, and most of that increase can be attributed to mining developments, not farming (incidentally, the population of British Columbia increased from 694,263 to 1,165,210 between 1931 and 1951). Broadly speaking, in 1931 the majority of people in the three provinces were living by growing wheat or living on the people who did grow wheat. The fall of nearly 100,000 in the population of Saskatchewan represents, first, the desperate results of the great depressions and droughts of the thirties and, secondly, the difference that mechanisation has made in the numbers needed to produce the same amount of wheat from the prairies themselves; it is a reduction from about ten to two. Yet even today, in the three provinces only one man out of every six works in a non-agricultural industry.

It is nearly 700 miles from Winnipeg to Lethbridge, where the foothills of the Rockies begin, and from Lethbridge northwards to Edmonton another 250, and from there back to Winnipeg 750, and within that triangle are the wheat-growing lands of Western Canada. Twenty-five million acres of land under wheat in 1952/53 and in that crop year they raised 520 million bushels. To Canada, to the farmer, the broker, the insurer, and the owners of the railways, the elevators and the steamships, that was worth over $1,000 million. If that wheat moves east, it must pass through Winnipeg on its way to the ports on the Great Lakes, or travel eastwards to Churchill, on Hudson's Bay. If it flows west, it must pass through the ports of British Columbia.

The prairies begin at Winnipeg. In point of time, the settlement at Winnipeg was preceeded by that at its neighbouring town, St. Boniface, but St. Boniface was a post of the fur-trappers and traders, not of settlers. When the Hudson's Bay Company established its post at Fort Garry, at the junction of the Red and the Assiniboine Rivers where Winnipeg is today, St. Boniface already had 500 inhabitants, mostly French-speaking. The hostility of the traders to the settlers, to the whole conception of a permanently settled West, drove the settlers to the shelter of Fort Garry. They made Winnipeg and today Winnipeg has 235,000 people, St. Boniface 26,000.

There are three ways by water to Winnipeg from the East, and water, until the CPR came, was the best method of transportation. The first is direct, from Ontario across the Great Lakes and on westwards by portages over the 350 miles that lie between the western shores of Lake Superior and the Red River. That was, then, a reasonable route for traffic light enough to travel by canoe. The second route was by sea into Hudson's Bay, up the river from the Bay into Lake Winnipeg and on, still southwards, up the Red River to the Assiniboine. Lord Selkirk's settlers, and the Icelanders at Gimli, travelled that way. The third route lay through United States territory into Minnesota and so northwards down the Red River. After the railways reached Minnesota in the middle of the last century, this was the most convenient route for the settler, and for trade. But the people who came that way were likely to be Americans, and, as Minnesota itself became settled, the lines of trade began to flow north and south, up and down the Red River, not east and west to and from Ontario.

Confederation, the creation of the province of Manitoba, the driving of the CPR westwards, were all a part of the Canadian urge to people the West with English settlers, travelling through Canada, remaining a part of Canada. If the whole West was not to become American—and the Canadians of Ontario were even more determined that it should not than many in London—the new lands must be conquered from Winnipeg. Winnipeg was made a provincial capital before it could be said that a province existed.

Today, Winnipeg seems a city of wide and windy streets, containing the administrative headquarters of Hudson's Bay Company in Canada, the editorial offices of the *Winnipeg Free Press* and a building that once housed the Winnipeg Grain Exchange. In their several ways these three buildings are three of the landmarks in Canadian history.

Winnipeg's first boom development came between 1881 and 1882, and Stephen Leacock describes it thus in *My Discovery of the West*.

> Everyone was counted a skilled labourer till he blew himself up or broke his leg and proved that he wasn't. I recall that a young man who went out with my father and uncle, straight off an Ontario farm, got a job the first day running the engine in a steam laundry. He didn't know how to run it but that didn't matter. No one else did. He blew himself up the same day. That didn't matter either. I doubt if they even went to look for him.

> My father opened a "real-estate" office with a sign in blue and gold thirty feet long. He had with him an English partner, a Captain Desborough—the type of those drawn from the old country by the magnet of Manitoba. The captain had been a public school boy, still knew the first line of the first book of Virgil, and commanded great respect with it in the saloons on Main Street. He and my father lasted nearly a year before they blew up.

The boom of 1881 was based on the promise of the prairies. Thirty years later, eleven million acres yielded 231 million bushels of wheat, worth $148 million. Fifty years later acreage and yield had doubled; the value was six times as great.

WHEAT

The first recorded wheat-growing in Canada was on the St. Croix River in what is now New Brunswick in 1604. The French in Canada were good farmers; by the middle of the eighteenth century Quebec was producing three-quarters of a million bushels a year and exporting some to France. But the real beginnings of the Canadian wheat-growing industry are to be found in Ontario.

It was first sown in that province in 1781 and by 1860 Ontario had a crop of some 24 million bushels a year. In the last century wheat from Canada has come to mean wheat from the prairie provinces. Before their lands could begin to supply the world with wheat it was necessary to find a grain that would complete its cycle of life to maturity within the hundred days between the thaws in spring and the first frosts of the fall. That grain, so the story goes, was found by chance.

In 1841, David Fife, a Scotsman farming near Peterborough, Ontario, asked a neighbour who was going back to Britain to send him some samples of northern European wheat. The neighbour was given, in Glasgow, a sample from a shipment from Danzig, in Poland, and in the spring of 1842 Fife planted that sample. Only one kernel sprouted, sending up five—some say no more than three—heads of wheat. Fife put a fence around the experimental crop, for protection; even that did not save it all. A cow from the farm put its head over the fence and began to eat the heads of wheat. Then came the classic twist of fate; David Fife's wife saw the cow and chased it away in time to save two of the heads. These heads matured ten days earlier than any wheat Fife had yet encountered. By the third season he had half a bushel of seed from the original heads and he named it Red Fife. Its use spread though Ontario and that was the seed wheat the settlers from Ontario took with them when they began to move out into the West.

The next steps forward came from experimentation, at first by Dr. W. S. Saunders on the Government's experimental farm, later by his son Charles, who became Sir Charles Saunders, the government cerealist. The father established that the original Red Fife sample must have come from Galicia, in Eastern Poland. Under Canadian conditions Red Fife was excellent in vigour and yield but it still matured dangerously late for the early onset of the prairie frosts. The son, among his innumerable experiments, thought to cross it with an Indian wheat, Hard Red Calcutta, and the resulting strain he named "Marquis". Marquis matured six to ten days earlier than Red Fife and was resistant to rust. It is on Marquis that the later fortunes of the prairie provinces have been built. The two most popular strains of wheat sown in Canada to-day are "Thatcher" and "Saunders". Thatcher was developed in the University of Minnesota in 1935 and Saunders at the Dominion

Rust Research Laboratory at Winnipeg in 1947; both have blood-
lines from Marquis in their pedigrees.

Wheat is still the vital element in the Canadian economy. Over
the ten years to 1952 the average yearly value to Canadian farmers
of the grain crop was $800 million, whereas the yearly average of
Canada's output of metals was $445 million, of the products of her
forests $455 million. But there are a great many elements in the
price paid by the ultimate consumer that do not go to the grower.
The grain must be collected, graded, transported by rail to a port
shipped and perhaps transhipped, and stored again at the country
of its destination. It costs 12 cents a bushel to freight wheat to
Vancouver from Calgary, and 34 cents to ship it from Vancouver
to Britain. It costs 15 cents a bushel to freight it from Calgary
to Fort William, on Lake Superior, and 37 cents to ship it
from there, via the St. Lawrence Ports, to Britain. To the farmer,
all these charges appear as deductions from the ultimate selling
price. They must be, and they are, paid before he can receive what
is left, and from the start the farmer has tended to regard the vast
marketing organisation, as parasitical on him. Half his battles have
been to free himself from those whom he regarded as profiteering
at his expense.

The other half of his battle must of necessity be with the other
wheat producers of the world. Despite the percentage of his crop
that the Canadian producer exports, he can never hope to dominate the world market. Even in a bumper year such as 1952, with
a crop not far short of 700 million bushels, Canada contributed no
more than 10 per cent of the world's crop of wheat. The Canadian
farmer must either compete with, or combine with, the farmers of
the United States, Argentina and Australia.

During the seventy years that have passed since the railways
first opened up Western Canada the wheat farmer has changed
from an individualistic producer and seller into a man who
believes that collective action is essential to his financial health
and that the responsibility for that action must rest ultimately on
the Federal Government. The movement towards collective action
began in protest against the policy of the C.P.R. in granting what
were in effect private monopolies to those who put up and operated grain storage elevators along its lines in the prairie provinces.
Where an operator had erected his elevator with the agreement of
the C.P.R., the C.P.R. refused to handle any grain from that district

which did not pass through that operator's hands. On their side, the wheat growers accused some of the owners of these local monopolies of under-weighing and under-grading the wheat they delivered to them, allegations which found some support in the findings of a Royal Commision published in 1899. Co-operation between the farmers began, about the beginning of this century, as a move to counter this situation and took the shape of district co-operatives to handle and ship the grain; by the start of the First World War each of the three provinces had a provincial co-operative in operation. In 1912, the Federal Government passed a comprehensive Grain Act and by 1914 the grain trade was working under government regulation as regards handling, grading, storage and transportation. But the final market in the grain remained absolutely free. Grain was offered and sold on the three great grain-exchanges of the world, at Winnipeg, Chicago and Liverpool, and the price of wheat depended entirely on what individuals on those exchanges bid for the quantities on offer.

The circumstances of the First World War inevitably resulted in an extension of Federal Government action and for three years, between 1917 and 1920, the Federal Government controlled the buying and selling of Canadian wheat (the Winnipeg Grain Exchange itself was closed during those three years). But political sentiment regarded this as no more than a wartime expedient and in August, 1920, the Wheat Board was dissolved and the Winnipeg Exchange reopened. For the next few months the price of wheat continued to rise but in 1921 it began to fall and then the experiences of the wartime organisation produced their reaction. As the price fell, the farmers pressed for a restoration of the Wheat Board. The Federal Government was willing; not the Manitoba Provincial Government. It threw out the necessary Bill and by doing so set the pattern for the next ten years. The farmers returned to their co-operatives, to provincial wheat-pools, and by the end of 1923 farmers controlling about 45 per cent of the wheat acreage in Alberta had agreed to sell all their crop to the new pool-organisation for the succeeding five years. Pools were formed in Saskatchewan and Manitoba in the following year and the three pools jointly set up a Canadian Wheat Pool, to sell all wheat delivered to it by the three provincial organisations. The Wheat Pool was basically a farmers' co-operative, independent of the Federal Government. The pool made an initial payment to the

farmer on delivery and allotted each farmer a quota based on a fair
share of the market it had itself secured for all it handled.

That pattern was broken by the slump of 1929 and it was the
initial payment made by the pool that wrecked the scheme.

The pool made an initial payment of $1 a bushel in the summer of
1929. The slump came in the October and the world price of wheat
fell disastrously. In the end, the average price realised by the pool
on that year's crop was more than 85 cents a bushel. The pool
sustained a loss of $22 million, and this time some form of govern-
ment help was essential. The loss was met by the banks and by
guarantees from the three provincial governments to the banks
that had made it good. Faced with the chance that the same
might happen in the following season, the Federal Government
decided to support an alternative organisation, a central selling
agency, managed by one man, Mr. J. I. McFarland, who was
given the promise of Federal backing both to assist in financing
the marketing of the 1930 crop (and the carry-over from the 1929
crop) and to support the price of wheat itself. The provincial
farmers' co-operatives reverted to their grain handling and storage
operations, but ceased to engage in selling.

McFarland's activities were successful. Over the five years of
his appointment his agency obtained better prices for the Canadian farmer than those realised by Argentina and Australia and he
finished his operations with a net surplus of $9 million. But his
agency could not, unaided, fight a way back to prosperity for the
prairie farmer, for by then the depression was accompanied by
drought and the drought by reduced yields. The next stage was
the Board set up by the Canadian Wheat Board Act of 1935. That
was something more than a selling agency. It was, in effect, a
government agency for supporting the Canadian farmer by guaranteeing him a minimum price for his wheat. At the beginning of
each season the Board fixed its buying price; the farmer was
free to sell to the Board at that price or not. But between
1935 and 1938, the Board's buying price was above that obtain-
able by the farmer on the open market and the Board in fact
handled most of Canada's wheat. The crops from the drought
years were so poor—in 1937 the total crop was only half of what it
had been five years before—that some authority in Canada had
to subsidise the farmer, either in this way or by direct aid, or see
him starve.

The final phase came with the last war. The droughts ended and the yields per acre increased. The war improved the price of wheat but German occupation of Europe in 1940 limited the market. By 1943 Canada was in the paradoxical position of having a heavy carry-over of wheat but of seeing the beginnings of a speculative boom in the grain. The Government's decision was to convert the existing Wheat Board into an agency which bought compulsorily all Canadian wheat and to close the Winnipeg Exchange (it has not re-opened since). Now, the Board handles all supplies of wheat, oats and barley coming forward into commercial channels from the three prairie provinces, and two districts in British Columbia. Over the course of the five-year pool from 1945 to 1949 the Board sold 1,435 million bushels of wheat and paid the farmer for No. 1 Northern wheat at the terminal (the recognised standard) a steady $1.85½ per bushel.

In 1951, the Manitoba Government held a plebiscite of its farmers on the issue of whether they favoured a continuance of the Wheat Pool organisation or wished to return to speculative selling. Some two-thirds of those entitled to vote did vote, and of these nine out of every ten favoured the continuance of the Wheat Board. In November 1952, Mr. C. D. Howe, Federal Minister for Trade and Commerce, and no lover of government trading activities for their own sake, said: "We must face the fact that practically all buyers of Canadian wheat are governments or government agencies.... In the circumstances of the war and post-war periods the judgment of the Western farmer in favour of the present Wheat Board system of marketing grain has my full support."

Yet no Board or International Wheat Agreement can wipe out all the gamble from wheat farming. I stayed with a farmer not far from Regina. He farms three-quarters of a section, 480 acres, and his sole crop is wheat. Normally, with two hired men, he can sow and reap his land within the five summer months and produce a crop large and valuable enough to give him a full year's income. His land is rich but poorly drained; not that that mattered in the drought years for there was nothing to drain. Last year the spring rains were heavy and only eighty acres of his land dried quickly enough for wheat to be planted. Eighty acres; one-sixth of his normal acreage and so yielding no more than one-sixth of the income he had had the year before. The dicebox in which his gamble is made is in the sky.

This seventy-year battle by the prairie farmer to produce wheat and to sell it has been a grim enough struggle on occasions. The disasters of the 'thirties threw up the Social Credit Party in Alberta and gave it an impetus that has kept it in office ever since. It produced a hunger march and a fatal riot in Regina and in that province gave birth to the Commonwealth Co-operative Federation. the CCF, now Canada's main left-wing party. It was a fight with hunger and despair in it, for if the prairie farmer might not grow wheat he could grow nothing else. It left the farmer of the depression years, who found that his land could grow little wheat and who faced immense difficulties in selling what little his land did yield, cursing the city men of Toronto and Montreal who collected their loan interests and maintained a tariff which added to the cost of everything he bought. It left so strong an emotional legacy that, even in 1953, a farmer could still say to me: "Why shouldn't we join the United States? Then at least I should be able to buy my machines for what they're sold at a hundred miles south of here."

THE JOURNALIST

In 1901, a journalist named John W. Dafoe was appointed editor of the *Winnipeg Free Press* by its owner Mr. (later Sir) Clifford Sifton. Dafoe had first worked for the paper in 1886. He was a Liberal and the paper was a Liberal paper and his first political campaign, in 1889, was that of the Manitoba Schools question, a defence of the action of the Liberal Government of Manitoba in abolishing the denominational system of education in the province which, so the French-speaking Roman Catholics claimed, had been guaranteed to them by the Federal Government's Manitoba Act of 1870 when the province was established. His last campaign as editor of the paper was between 1932 and 1939, and it was to convince his country that isolationism in world affairs was foredoomed to failure and that collective security based on the League of Nations was the only honourable, sane and safe policy for the democracies of the world. The gulf between the two battles was a measure of the growth of both the man and his country during these forty years.

Dafoe fought many battles between 1901 and 1944, when he

died. He fought for fairer railway rates for the prairie farmer. He fought both the proprietor of his paper and the Conservative Party for the proposed reciprocity treaty with the United States in 1911, believing that reciprocity in trade was good for the West. He was the sole official representative of the Canadian Press at the Peace Conference in 1919. He was in the thick of the battle between Mr. Mackenzie King, the Liberal Leader, and the Conservatives that revolved around the actions of Lord Byng as Governor-General in 1926. He fought to preserve the Canadian National Railways system from dissolution in 1935 when it was under indirect attack from the C.P.R. His last public activity was as a member of the Royal Commission on Dominion-Provincial financial relations in 1937, and during this time he made the *Winnipeg Free Press* one of the great newspapers of the world.

There is a great parallel between Winnipeg and the *Winnipeg Free Press* and Manchester and the *Manchester Guardian,* just as there is between the editors, Dafoe and C. P. Scott (although Scott's editorship began some fifteen years earlier). Both cities were dominated by one trade, and, since that trade was international in its scope, however much the citizens of each might disagree with the policies advocated by their leading papers, they could never be wholly indifferent to the issues and policies discussed in the editorial columns. Both Dafoe and Scott became public consciences rather than mirrors of public opinion. They told their cities, and their countries, how they should reason and what they should do, and when their contemporaries failed to heed their advice they never lost heart. They wrote all the more strongly on what happened in consequence. So, in this process of battering the heads of governments from the distance of provincial capitals, both men raised their provincial capitals to become cities of the world.

Dafoe began as a Liberal and ended as a liberal. He held to the principles he thought applicable to government; he did not hold that theories were essential to government. As Scott understood the workings of politics in Britain, and knew the importance of personality, so Dafoe could say to George Ferguson, then his assistant, that "He had never known an important issue in Canadian politics which had not been deeply influenced and sometimes determined in its result by factors of the most purely personal kind."

In his sketch of Dafoe, Ferguson wrote: "Dafoe did not make Winnipeg. The town, on the other hand, was an ideal environment for him. It brought out and emphasised the qualities which later became so notable in him; a refusal to feel himself beaten, a sturdy unquenchable faith in the future. The pioneer's present is always so rough that he quickly learns to live for tomorrow. Dafoe did that all his life."

The pioneer's life is always so rough. In that, Dafoe exemplifies both the Winnipeg and the prairies of his day, and their development. Just as he changed from a Liberal believing in the strict theories of free trade and *laisser-faire* to a Liberal who saw that some circumstances can only be met by actions that cut across these theories, so did the prairie farmer. In the end, the prairie farmer asks one question: "What is the best way to market my crop at the best price?" and no veto based on any political theory will turn him away from action that may provide him, at that moment and in those circumstances, with an answer. A country's prosperity, he believes, depends on what its people have to spend; in Canada that means that there must be at least a floor to the price of wheat.

ALBERTA

As between Calgary and Edmonton, only Edmonton can claim today any trace of the old days of the frontier on the prairies. The policemen of Calgary are all Scotsmen and they have long since rid the city of any of that kind of nonsense. Calgary is neat, prosperous and bourgeois, if that word can be used by anyone from Europe with no underlying sneer. The new streets of little bungalows built all around it are for people whose connection with horses is now so remote that they do not even bet on them; if they bet at all it is on oil stocks. Once a year, Calgary stages its Stampede, a cowboy rodeo, and it is now as artificial a show as any Hollywood could contrive. The arena stands in the centre of the city, and seems to resemble all other sports arenas in Canada, save that its boundary fence is a solid log stockade, so beautifully painted and varnished that it looks like a plastic substitute for wood. Only late at night, in the square facing the station, can one see visitors from another and an older world, sad little groups of men, sometimes three or more together, who are obviously attachments for riding horses. They alone wear their high-heeled boots and their rather soiled check shirts as though these were their normal working clothes, and they are mostly silent. They seem as out of place in the Calgary of today as a centaur would do on board ship.

The real Calgary of today belongs to the Ranchers Club, the Golf and Country Club and the summer ball of the Calgary Highlands at the Hotel Palliser. The Ranchers Club is a solid brick mansion in a solid brick suburb. It is the place for luncheon of the men in oil and the stockbrokers and lawyers who look after the men in oil. Its walls carry photographs of Calgary and its saloons, as they were sixty years ago, and now the photographs are brown and faded. The Calgary Golf and Country Club is smart and modern, with a shiny bar and a lounge full of steel furniture. Its ladies are elegant and modish and play a good hand of bridge. They are at home against the background of the Calgary Highlanders Ball, with its kilts and its parade of pipers in the street outside, and its general air of being something arranged by the Duchess of Richmond. In some indefinable way they suggest a childhood spent in Texas.

I met one Englishwoman in Calgary. She served tea, real tea, in what is called a coffee shop at the airport. She was blonde, about thirty-five, and she would have been equally at home in any of the night cafés along the main roads out of London. "I am sorry to miss the Coronation, dear," she said, "but it can't be helped. It wouldn't be right to be flipping off just when you felt like it, would it, dear? But I'd love to see her dress." She leaned on the counter and casually wiped down its plastic top. "There's something that puzzles me out here, I must say. How does everyone know I am English as soon as I open my mouth?"

Calgary brims over with activity and adventure and friendliness. Its climate and its future are equally stimulating. It likes to be a little sentimental at the graveside of the last buffalo killed on the range but its people do not really look backwards over their shoulders into time. Why on earth should they?

Calgary is in business, in oil, in cattle, in packing and canning, in all the industries that its sources of power are bringing to it. Yet the medal ribbons that the officers and men of the Calgary Highlanders wear on their blue undress uniforms are equally real. They have served their time and they have no illusions over what may follow any ball.

Calgary and Edmonton have long been rivals for the position of leading city in Alberta. Edmonton has had the provincial seat of government but, over oil, Calgary had one great advantage. The first oilfield in Alberta was discovered at Turner Valley in 1914 and Turner Valley is no more than thirty miles south of Calgary. As that came into production, the oil companies made Calgary their centre in Western Canada, and by doing so gave Calgary a lead in the administration of the industry that it is not likely to lose. The Turner Valley field now yields some 10,000 barrels a day and Calgary is the terminus of a pipe-line for natural gas that connects the Jumping Pound field twenty miles to the west with the Bow Island field 140 miles to the south-east. Calgary has electric power, oil and natural gas. It has the water of the Bow River. All these things mean that it can offer industrial facilities to any industry searching for a new site in the west.

Nonetheless, in the race to attract industry Edmonton is leading and is likely to pull ahead. Calgary may become a Philadelphia; if so, Edmonton will be the Pittsburg of the province. And Edmonton—

I know I am likely to be self-deceived about Edmonton, for on my first evening in the city I saw the fire brigade go by, on duty, and no one could be indifferent to a city that provided that display.

Far down the main street, to the south, I heard the faint wail of a siren. It grew louder and louder and as it did, the cars and the trucks that filled the roadway in front of me seemed to cower in towards the kerb and stop, some at once, some daringly using the occasion to gain a yard or so in the stream of traffic. And then I saw a rapidly advancing cloud of dust. At its head was a police motor-cyclist travelling at full speed. Immediately behind was a fire engine with its warning lights flashing an angry orange and its siren now a wail that filled the whole air. The roadway ahead of them was quite empty and they swept past at a good sixty miles an hour. Another vehicle followed, indistinct in the dust, and another; in all five, and each with its siren shrieking at full strength, each pounding along as though it was a race for a gold cup and that by superb driving it might gain the lead. The only ingredients missing from the spectacle were the revolver shots, and these may have been drowned by the sirens. Even these five did not complete the column. Fifteen seconds behind the last

H

wagon came the fire chief's own red car, with the fire chief still
wrestling with the buttons at the neck of his tunic. The wails grew
fainter and fainter away to the north, and gradually the stunned
traffic began to flow again. It was the one occasion in my life on
which I found I had no urge to follow the turnout to the outbreak
itself. I knew that would surely be an anti-climax.

Edmonton is an oil town. The best vantage point from which
to see it all is the eighteenth floor of the annexe to the Macdonald
Hotel, opened in 1953 and so urgently needed that, so it is said,
the first guests were occupying one end of a floor while the
painters were finishing the rooms at the other. If one looks southwards from the Macdonald, half left is an oil refinery and alongside it is a tall metal chimney from which, day and night, springs
a plume of red flame. Further away on the horizon there will be,
by day, two or three lazy colums of black smoke, reminiscent, if
one is morbidly minded, of the funeral pyres of crashed bombers.
There is virtually no waste from an oilfield today. The natural
gas may not be burnt; no well may be brought into production
until there is a market for its natural gas. The plume of fire and
the columns of smoke are no more than an infinitely small proportion of the wealth and power that lie under the farm lands around
Edmonton.

The virtual certainty that oil existed in Alberta and Saskatchewan
has been known at least since the discovery of the Turner Valley
field nearly thirty years ago. Another indication was the Mc-
Murray Tar lands in the north of Alberta, a vast bed of sand and
rock impregnated with the residual products left when a deposit
of oil is exposed to the air and the more volatile compounds
evaporate. The strata of sedimentary rocks in which oil may well
be found spread northwards along the whole belt of land east of
the Rockies. They extend under the States of Montana and
Wyoming and North and South Dakota, under all of Alberta and
the southern half of Saskatchewan and they stretch northwards
in a narrower band under the bed of the Mackenzie River to the
Arctic. In Canada these beds cover three times the area of Texas.
For years past the oil companies have been prospecting and of
course their problem has always been to locate the particular spots
in which an accumulation of oil exists. In the Albertan fields the
oil is frequently found confined in a limestone reef bed, a forma-

tion which is a coral reef of centuries ago and which therefore still has the irregular and unpredictable shape of the shore line of some ancient sea. The first big find anywhere in the west, after that in the Turner Valley field, was at Leduc, south of Edmonton, in 1947. That was followed by the Redwater field, in 1948, and the largest yet charted. Golden Spike in 1949, and a chain of finds with names like racehorses, Wizard Lake, Bonnie Glen, Pigeon Lake and Wetaskiwin, followed later still. All these are within fifty miles of Edmonton, and the number of these smaller fields is still increasing. Natural gas has been known to exist in the province since a bore-hole sunk near Medicine Hat to find coal in 1890 produced natural gas instead.

The biggest challenge of all remains the tarsands at McMurray. Estimates of the quantity of oil that these contain vary from 100,000 million barrels upwards to twice as much. The tarsands have been known for at least thirty years, but so far they have defeated all attempts at development. They set the chemist and the engineer an array of problems, the one to devise a process which will separate oil from waste, the other to devise machinery which will carry the process into operation on a commercial basis. A Canadian Government scientist has reported that the oil could be separated, distilled and transported at a cost of $3.10 a barrel.

Canada now ranks tenth among oil producing countries, with a present estimated production of some 400,000 barrels daily. Between 1946 and 1952 consumption of oil in Canada doubled; at the same time, Canada's own output of oil enabled her to supply four-tenths of her total consumption, instead of no more than one-tenth in 1946. There is in Canada all the oil that Canada needs, and, although questions of transportation make it unlikely that all Canada will use only Canadian oil, some 4,000 miles of oil pipeline already bring the oil from the prairies to the Great Lakes and to Vancouver. The essential fact is that the Western oil and gas fields can provide now all that industry west of Winnipeg can use, and can offer to fresh industries a remarkable range of both power and natural products. The Consolidated Mining and Smelting Company's plant at Calgary makes agricultural fertilisers from natural gas, air and water, plus power; nothing else.

Edmonton is at the centre of this vast unassembled power house. It is base camp for the whole of this activity, ranging all over Alberta and northwards through the Peace River to the Mackenzie (in Alberta alone over 2,000 wells are drilled a year). It is a city at the centre of a network of railway systems, and a staging point for the Alaska Highway. It is the airfield from which both the scheduled lines and the individual bush aircraft fly north, east and west. It is a place to which a man may fly five hundred miles to have a tooth fixed

It is not, of course, a town which would suit everyone. There is a great deal of beauty left in the valley of the North Saskatchewan River that winds through it. It will have a fine University quarter, and it will have an increasing number of individually fine buildings. It has now appointed a town planning expert from Britain, but it will probably not begin to tidy up its extraordinarily haphazard and sordid outgrowths for at least a generation; it will think itself too busy to do so, and on that account the final bill will be all the heavier. It is unlikely that Edmonton will ever organise the equivalent of the Calgary Highlanders; its local unit will be called cavalry and will be fully mechanised. It is a masculine city, impatient, and active. The kitchen is untidy and there are no flowers in the living-room, but the bank balance swells.

SASKATCHEWAN

By contrast with Alberta and its bustling rival cities, Saskatchewan and the cities of Regina and Saskatoon are quiet; they are waiting. Alberta jumped at the chance to exploit its oil. Saskatchewan was more hesitant. Alberta has a Social Credit government, which believed that it should do no more than lay down the rules, set up the ropes and let the cannier fighter win. Saskatchewan has a Co-operative Commonwealth Federation, or C.C.F., government and it considered that the oil situation required considerable thought before any action was permitted. At one stage it even toyed with the idea that it might take part in the operation itself. The province produces some 60 per cent of the whole of the western wheat crop and, although mining is developing, it has very little industry which is entirely independent from farming. The Saskatchewan farmer is of Scandinavian habit of mind. He was inclined to view the smooth gentlemen from the oil companies as sharks in wolf's clothing, on principle. The smooth gentlemen were not impatient; a great deal of their training has been in the Middle East. They moved on to Edmonton instead. Saskatchewan is taking oil far more seriously today. Virtually the

whole of the southern half of the province is shared out among
the prospecting teams of the major oil companies, yet Regina and
Saskatoon are still primarily and in appearance two cities of a
farming community.

Regina can never hope to be more than a collection of houses
in the middle of a vast field. It has its provincial legislature buildings, facing an artificial lake, its C.P.R. hotel, the Saskatchewan,
and a population of 71,000, but they do not make it any the less a
small town. It is the kind of place in which one feels that when
the inhabitants are good they are very, very good and that when
they are bad they can do nothing else but get drunk. I liked all the
people I met in Regina, and they were all very good and I was left
with the uneasy certainty that if I lived there myself I should get
drunk once a month.

Saskatoon is different. It stands on the banks of the South
Saskatchewan River and I was conscious at once of how much
easier it is to remain sane when there is moving water in views.
Saskatoon has a population of 53,000 and the University of Saskatchewan, and the proportions of the two are in harmony.
Edmonton pushes its university to one side; it may be useful as a
technical college but Edmonton is too busy to pay full attention
to anything else it may have to say. The university at Saskatoon is,
by some British standards, equally a technical college, for its main
faculties are science, medicine and agriculture and forestry, but
the people of Saskatoon are not brash enough to take the material
aid and ignore everything else the university represents. The
liberals in the University of Alberta have that faint spiritual
anaemia that clouds the life of their fellows in the Middle West
of the United States. They brood over such theories as Civil Liberty and read the *New Statesman* assiduously. In Saskatoon I
doubt if they do, in quite the same spirit.

It is fortunate for Canada that the two provinces are so different, for it would be a pity if the partial industrialisation of the
west had only one pattern to follow. The impact of oil on Saskatchewan will not be identical with that it is having on Alberta,
and perhaps more lessons are learnt by contrast than in any other
way.

BANFF

If Winnipeg is at one end of the prairies, Banff must be taken as the other limit. Banff is in Alberta. Both Banff and Calgary are on the Bow River as it flows eastwards to join the South Saskatchewan and find its way ultimately to Lake Winnipeg and Hudson Bay. Calgary is 3,000 ft. above sea level. From there the land slopes gradually upwards until, forty miles beyond Calgary, it breaks into foothills at the base of the Rockies themselves. The Rockies, the eastern mountain barrier in the 600 miles between Alberta and sea, are of comparatively recent origin, in terms of the time scale of the development of the earth's surface. For age after age the sedimentary rocks under the prairies drifted westwards, pressing harder against the older, more solid, rocks of the Selkirks beyond, as ice-floes pile up against a rocky shore, with the result that their shattered slabs now climb another 5,000 ft. into the air, like gigantic paving stones along the rim of a bomb crater. The C.P.R. chose this wild confusion of cliff and peak and outcrop as the site for its Banff Springs Hotel. In this edifice, I feel, the C.P.R. has its finest achievement.

Admittedly, the actual line by which the line travels from Calgary westwards to Vancouver is impressive, as a feat of engineering construction. The track through Kicking Horse Pass and on down the Fraser River involved, no doubt, a great many engineering problems, much harder to solve seventy years ago than today. But what had to be done was obvious enough, and in the end the engineers produced no more than some hundreds of miles of narrow level pathway along which they had just room enough to lay a single railway track. But when it comes to planning a hotel, the man who builds has an infinitely freer hand and so is required to meet a far more serious challenge to his imagination. He must choose the site, he must decide upon the outer casing that will contain the essential fittings for a modern haunt of pleasure, he must settle every detail and proportion. Whether he can provide sufficient imagination or not, he will be judged by the standards of those who can. He may produce a structure such as Grosvenor House, London, W.1., or a vision of no known world, such as the Banff Springs Hotel, Alta. I know which I prefer. The basis of the architectural style at Banff is Scottish baronial, but the architect to the C.P.R. suffered from no timid hesitations in the adaptation of that style to the needs of the company and the challenge of the landscape.

The hotel stands, a mile above sea level, at the junction of the Bow and Spray rivers, some two hundred feet above the valley floor, built into the wooded slopes of a mountain. A vast terrace, complete with swimming pool, looks eastwards down the river gorge, a setting theatrically perfect. Across the valley is a golf course, to the south a ski-lift to the snow, north, the road to Jasper and the icefields. Inside, to quote from the brochure, the furniture resembles many periods, Elizabethan, Gothic, Flemish, Jacobean and Queen Anne. The regally appointed lounges, dining-rooms and suites, the brochure continues, almost rival the grandeur of nature herself, and the word "almost" is a rare example of under-statement in an advertising hand-out. Each of the six hundred bedrooms must have a view of some mountain or other, or at least of a mounted policeman on horseback, for, if ever the R.C.M.P. do ride horses in Canada, it will be at Banff. The main building was finished in 1913, at a time, no doubt, when the C.P.R. hoped that thousands of Canadians would buy railway tickets to visit it. It is in fact mainly used by Americans, none of whom would dream of arriving otherwise than by automobile. But that is the kind of circumstance that Banff can take in its stride. Here is a hotel that turns the peaks and valleys around it into no more than a backcloth. One has the feeling that it must have sprung complete from the earth in some vast convulsion of nature.

From the year 1885, when the C.P.R. line went west, the company has made certain that the Rockies are the best known natural feature in Canada. It would be hard to blame it on that account. The mountains and forests and lakes photograph well. The sight of a double-headed train winding through a forest of spruce with a blue lake and a snow-covered peak in the background has all the romance of the nineteenth century in it, and, when the C.P.R. was largely British owned, if ever dividends were disappointing, to send romance across the Atlantic instead was extremely intelli-gent. But, having seen the reality, I feel that perhaps the C.P.R. has overplayed its hand. One could never say the Rockies are a disappointment. They have grandeur. They are deeply impressive, but they seem to lack some of the essence of beauty. Beauty must have proportion in time as well as in space; something is lost if a piece of music is played in endless repetition. The truth is the Rockies go on for far too long.

They are at their best on a summer evening; dusk can limit their extent and the changing tones and colours of the twilight give each of the surrounding peaks a stronger personality than it has by day. The glare of the snow is no longer harsh, and the shadows cast by the now almost horizontal light change continually the forms and relationships of the upper slopes. The greens in the valleys blacken and those of the high eastern faces grow brighter by contrast. Against the oyster-pale northern sky individual trees on a skyline ten miles away become a pencilled frieze of fantastic delicacy. The summits are clear of cloud and in the fading light they seem to come more closely together so that, when the sun is gone, and there is only the afterglow, the skyline hangs above the valley at the end of the town like cardboard. The only sound is that of a far-away train until, for the first time all day, one becomes aware of the perpetual rustle of the river water over its stones and reefs. Then the mountains have their greatest enchantment.

2. British Columbia

To me, British Columbia is the most attractive country in the world. There may be others more beautiful that I have not yet seen but British Columbia has a power to draw one's mind back to it that in my experience is unique.

The province of British Columbia is a part of Canada, of course, but—. Why does the "but" slip in so very easily? What exactly is the qualification it is intended to hint at?—for there always has been a qualification of some kind. The line of the watershed along the whole length of the Rockies has been known from the first as the Great Divide, and the men who chose that word "Divide" used their words in a blunt enough way. They were conscious of some deep difference between what lay to their east and what lay to their west.

I left Banff just after midday on a fine morning in May. The air was clear and cold and the only green to be seen was that of the spruce and firs lining the track by the station. Their greens are perpetual. Not a new leaf showed itself anywhere; the birches were silver stems holding up their network of fine black branches. The train ran fast through the forests in the valley to Lake Louise and the lakes and swamps beside the track were yellow and brown, and the dead timber grey. From that point the track started to climb alongside a river running fast over shallows of stone and gravel and still lined with banks of ice and snow. There was snow under the trees and when we reached the final pass to the west and the road joined us its surface, too, was grey and yellow with dirty ice. Beyond the watershed the sky darkened with clouds and we climbed down a spiral of tunnels to the upper reaches of the Columbia River and up the Albert Canyon to the Connaught Tunnel and by evening we had reached Revelstoke.

And then I saw something that I had not seen before in all Canada; a lawn of grass that had already had its first mowing of the year. When I awoke next morning we were in the valley of the Thompson River, the sun was shining, the cuttings beside the tracks were dotted with ferns, the grass in the fields was thick and each tree carried its full plumage of leaf. I had skipped almost a whole chapter of the coming of spring, for three days later a gardener in Vancouver said to me, as gardeners always do: "You should have seen the place last week. The tulips were at their best then."

In the end I did see more than one spring in Canada. As I went eastwards by road through the Rockies up to the Crow's Nest Pass we seemed to be travelling backwards in time. At noon the leaves on the trees alongside the road were fully unfurled. By mid-afternoon they were no more than buds breaking through their coatings of the winter. And I saw a display of tulips at their best; in St. John's, Newfoundland, a month later.

That is one part of the Divide. Physically, British Columbia lives in another world from that which the remaining nine provinces of Canada must tolerate, but the divide is not only a matter of climate. British Columbia is the only part of Canada in which men landed from the west and pushed their settlement eastwards. For many, the first of Canada they saw was the coast of Vancouver Island as they sailed up the Straits of Juan de Fuca, or the islands to the north on the journey to Prince Rupert.

In 1790, England and Spain agreed on the Nootka Convention, so named from the village on the seaward coast of Vancouver Island used by the Spaniards as a base, and by that agreement

Spain relinquished all her claims to control of the Pacific coast from California northwards to where the Russian territory in Alaska began. In 1825 England concluded a treaty with Russia that defined the British possessions along that coast more exactly (but still not exactly enough, for that treaty was at the bottom of the Alaskan boundary dispute with the United States in 1903). In the meantime, the fur traders of the North West Company had crossed the Rockies and were making their way down the rivers to the Pacific, but they were not settlers. The first settlers came from the south, to Victoria first and later, with the rush to pan out the gold from the sands of the Fraser River, into the mainland itself. British Columbia came into existence as a union of the Crown Colony of Vancouver Island and the mainland colony in 1866. It entered the Confederation in 1871, induced partly by the promise of a railway across Canada to the Pacific within ten years but even more because it was British in sentiment and feared the pressure towards annexation from the United States, strong in the years immediately after the Civil War. The creation of British Columbia was not a purely political gesture, like the setting up of the first prairie province. The settlers of British Columbia, small as the settlements were, existed as a separate community from the start. They are Canadians, but Canadians with a different orientation from those in the east. They have always been more conscious of the Pacific than of the Atlantic.

It is hard to realise, until one has been there, how real a barrier the mass of rocks and valleys of British Columbia are, even to one's thoughts. One knows that, six hundred miles away, the mountains and the land dip down to the foothills of Alberta, no more than ripples around the base of a reef of rocks. From there the land slopes gently away eastwards and northwards, a totally different landscape and a totally different climate. If one travels far enough and crosses the thousand miles of woods and lakes north of Lake Superior, one reaches Ontario, the valley of the Ottawa, and Ottawa itself. To go beyond that is to reach the land where people speak French, and the Maritimes, of which one read at school. Still further is an island in the Atlantic called Newfoundland. All that is Canada, but it is difficult when in Vancouver to accept that anything east of, say, Regina is of vital interest to British Columbia. The nearer prairies send their wheat through Vancouver's elevators and over her quays. Other parts of Canada buy British Columbian timber, door frames and window fittings, but so do the West American States. Neither Canada nor the United States buy anything like enough of British Columbia's canned salmon, to British Columbians' way of thinking, and it is hard for them not to think of both the rest of Canada and the United States as "they" when they say that. True, it is possible now to leave Vancouver Airport at an hour before midnight and to be in Toronto by two o'clock, local time, the following afternoon. The air in fact is breaking down the barrier, which is in itself a confession of what the barrier has been.

But are the British Columbians Canadians? Of course they are, with one possible qualification. That concerns the inhabitants of the area on Vancouver Island known as Victoria. I have doubts over whether Victoria is a part of Canada. It may well be a detached part of New Zealand. It has the same lush woodlands and forests, lakes, and the same tree-clad shores, the same unmistakable extrusions of lava rock, swelling up from out of the grass like the rounded backs of gigantic water beasts. It has the same happy provincial air, in which the village pump takes on the dimensions of a waterworks of world-wide repute, and the sporting event of the year is the local yacht race. It is not Canadian; unless, of course, the rest of Canada is untypical.

But it is certainly not English.

All the way across Canada I had been told: "Wait until you reach Victoria; that is an oasis of old England. You must go to the Empress Hotel for afternoon tea. You'll find them all there." It was a dismaying prospect. I had not come to Canada to take tea with people who would probably, I thought, be thinking of Sir Winston Churchill as the hero of the Sidney Street siege, and who would talk about the servant problem and mutter "Ninepence for Fourpence" under their breath. I did see the Empress Hotel; it can only be described as, externally, an inflated version of the kind of structure the old Great Western Railway would have put up at Windsor had American tourists been at all plentiful in Queen Victoria's reign. I had a meal there; supper. It was taken in the cafeteria in the basement and, since the American tourist season had already begun, the main feature of the meal was the spectacle of three American children lolling in their seats, so exhausted, (probably, judging from their behaviour, with the effort of being rude to their parents all day) that they had hardly energy

enough to eat the vast ice-cream concoctions in front of them. The
Empress Hotel, as shown, in the auctioneers' phrase, is about as
English as Gleneagles Hotel is Scottish. Or as the ice-cream con-
coctions were English.

Yet there must once have been some foundation for this curious
Canadian myth. One cannot be in Victoria half a day without
hearing of the grim English spinsters and widows of the pre-war
years who took their ritual tea in the lounge of the Empress every
day and who withered every new arrival through, or by means of,
their lorgnettes. There was once, it is said—it must have been
early in 1942—a small uniformed American major who arrived at
tea-time and who was compelled to walk the hundred yards of
lounge from entrance door to reception desk under this battery
of Edwardian eyes. He had almost made it when the carton of
ice-cream that he was carrying under his arm dropped and burst
on the marble floor. The silence was so long and so intense that it
was he who finally broke it with his screams. But they are all dead
now. Who, since 1939, has been able to retire to Victoria, B.C., on
a pension payable in sterling?

Victoria, ah, Victoria! "The most lovely country that can be
imagined. . . ." So Captain George Vancouver wrote in 1792. He
first saw it in 1791, although its little harbour may have been
sighted earlier by Spaniards and Russians, and he named the two
islands immediately off-shore from the names of his two ships.
The Hudson's Bay Company moved its headquarters on the Pacific
coast to Vancouver Island early in the nineteenth century and set
up Fort Camosun where Victoria now is. Vancouver Island became a Crown Colony in 1849 and for eight years between 1858
and 1866 possessed a government separate from that set up on
the mainland at the mouth of the Fraser River by the get-rich-
quick gentlemen from further south. Its people today do not talk
of the Sidney Street siege, nor of servants: they talked to me of
the places in which they had lived, of Texas, Hong Kong, Delhi,
Singapore. Several knew Ontario quite well. Perhaps they would
be happier even now with their own government, save that there
must be a certain gratification in the knowledge that Victoria
remains the provincial capital despite the rate at which Vancouver, once called Gas Town, has grown in size, importance and
wealth.

Victoria reminds me irresistibly of the unhappy spouse of the first Lord Nelson, outwardly composed and perfectly polite but brooding over the fact that her lawful husband, the province, is living with a lusty and beautiful paramour, Vancouver, on the mainland, and enjoying himself mightily in the process. But, she says to herself, whatever his preferences may be, I have the law on my side. He's legally married to me and I'll see him to hell and back before I give him a divorce.

Vancouver, as Lady Hamilton must have been, is very beautiful.

British Columbia is a land of mountains, rivers, lakes and trees. It has some of the finest agricultural land in Canada, in the Fraser Valley, but one hardly notices it for the trees. Four of its major rivers, including the Fraser and the Columbia, flow into the Pacific, two flow east and north. Twenty-five years ago its population was some 600,000; it has now doubled and its two largest cities, Vancouver and Victoria, hold half its people. It exports almost twice as much as it imports and its scenery draws over half a million tourists each year from the United States. Three-quarters of its farmers farm their own land. The British Columbian salmon is known all over the world, yet its prosperity remains based on its forests. Every second dollar is still a wooden one, they say.

Long before I ever saw British Columbia I had marvelled at the section of the Douglas fir in the Natural History Museum in London, a fir that must have been a handsome tree at the time of the Battle of Crecy. Long after I left British Columbia I remembered the forests I had seen on the flight from Penticon to Castlegar. The aircraft, a D.C.-3, spiralled upwards over the lake at Penticon and then flew into a shallow valley eastwards towards Castlegar, a hundred miles away, climbing all the time (but not, it seemed at first, as fast as the ground rose underneath us). There were the trees, square mile after square mile; remote and inaccessible, powdered more and more deeply with snow as the altitude increased, young and old, some gaunt silver skeletons from earlier fires, others massed arrays of a million Christmas trees. For a hundred miles nothing but trees, and if one had flown in any other direction it would have been the same. Almost one-third of the whole land area of the province contains marketable timber, and about 90 per cent of all the mature timber-lands are still in Crown ownership.

Then there was the logging camp at Jordan River, on Van-

couver Island. The logs, felled the previous year, were being
yarded. The base point was a colossal trunk sixty feet or so high,
and held erect by stays of steel cable. Logs from five hundred feet
around were being skidded over the ground to the base point by
steel cables drawn by a winch, dropped and immediately secured
by two other cables slung from a double boom of wood that
pivoted on the central truck, and then placed neatly on to a trailer
for haulage. The camp at Jordans has been in existence for years.

In an official enquiry into the forest resources of the province
made by the Chief Justice in 1945, the Commissioner wrote:

Looking back, however, there may be discovered a fairly consistent philosophy underlying the gradual evolution of tenures
and the terms thereof. It may be summarised under four head-
ings:

(1) All productive forest land was to remain in Crown ownership.

(2) The Crown was to receive a fair share of the wealth
produced by the exploitation of this natural resource.

(3) Speculation in timber by private interests was to be
eliminated.

(4) The export of logs in unmanufactured form was to be
reduced to a minimum.

In general, and to a degree, these objectives have been attained.
It is a guarded statement, but there are few areas in North
America which could honestly claim a very much better record.

But the forests of British Columbia are not inexhaustible; in
fact, this official enquiry (of which the 1945 Report was a result)
was made because an increasing number of British Columbians
believed that their province was, in effect, living on capital. As
the Chief Justice himself wrote later in his report:

We must change over from the present system of unmanaged
and unregulated liquidation of our forested areas to a planned
and regulated policy of forest management, leading eventually
to a programme ensuring a sustained yield from all our productive land area. . . .

I would define "sustained yield" to mean a perpetual yield of
wood of commercially usable quality from regional areas in
yearly or periodic quantities of equal or increasing volume. . . .

Has British Columbia achieved these objectives, and, if so, how?

It is too early yet to say that the objective is achieved, that the total yield is now sustained. The British Columbian Government accepted the conclusions in the 1945 Report and has strengthened its own services to the forests. It has also gone a good deal further than before to create the conditions under which the yield will be sustained, both by regulations, by its system of granting licences to fell and in the general atmosphere of development; Macmillan and Bloedel, Ltd., for instance, the biggest concern in the timber business in the province, now consider it desirable to advertise that they operate on this principle of sustained yield. The Government's own services include forest surveys, forest research, re-afforestation (which includes forest nurseries and re-planting programmes), forest protection against fire, insects and disease, and the maintenance of schools for forest rangers.

Over commercial development, the main changes were made by the Forest Act of 1948. This set up two schemes, the forest management licence and the public working circle. It had been a complaint of the man developing the timber that the old licensing system, based on a grant for a fixed period, gave him no incentive to replant; he cut the timber on the land covered by his licence and returned the denuded land to the Crown. Under the forest management licence, he first applies for a licence to take a stated quantity of timber from a designated area on a sustained yield basis. If the licence is granted, he is given exclusive possession of the land, but the licence is non-transferable. He is under obligation to cut no more than the stated quantity and to keep all potentially productive forest land stocked in accordance with standards laid down by the Forest Service. The public working circle is essentially the same plan, but directly managed by the Service, and those who join pay a higher royalty since the Service bears most of the cost of re-afforestation.

Between them, and in almost equal proportions, western hemlock, spruce, Douglas fir (which is not a true fir at all, merely a *pseudotsuga*) and western red cedar make up four-fifths of British Columbia's timber. On the coast where the rainfall is heavy and the climate equable, the cedars and Douglas firs grow to a height of 200 feet and a diameter of ten feet. In the colder or drier parts of the province firs and larches replace the cedars and hemlock. Water is the means of transportation. The timber is floated down the rivers to the mills dotted along their length. It is floated to the sea down the streams along the coast and assembled in vast rafts, to be towed along the coast to the nearest mill or factory. The shorter the haul by any means but water the better, for trucks wear out more quickly than tugs and no one need spend money on the maintenance of the surface of the sea.

British Columbia timber is exported in the round. It is cut into planks and boards and exported in that way. It is processed into furniture, boxes, doors, sashes and windows ready for use, and again shipped to the United States, by far the largest market now. It can become veneer or plywood or flooring blocks, or be treated and turned into paper or pure cellulose. In the last fifteen years British Columbia has learnt that none of it should or need be wasted. Walter Koerner, of Alaska Pine and Cellulose, Ltd., was almost apologetic when he showed me in his Vancouver plant a kiln in which some remnants of the intake were burnt. Despite the mining and industrial developments in British Columbia, its oil and coal and its salmon fisheries, no one there yet believes that any of these will replace for a very long time the wooden dollar from the forests as the main support of the province.

Nonetheless, the Kitimat undertaking of the Aluminum Company of Canada, Ltd., is the show-place of the new industrial development in the province since the war.

KITIMAT

The Kitimat plan might have been designed to capture the imagination, for can anyone who has built a sand wall on a beach to hold back the tide fail to respond to a project that is reversing the flow of 125 miles of river and leading its waters ten miles under the mountains to fall nearly three thousand feet in one drop to the sea? Of course the directors of the Aluminum Company are not wholly romantics.

In choosing Kitimat as the location for its newest aluminium smelter the company was moved by two major considerations. Aluminium can only be produced economically where there is cheap power, and water still gives the cheapest power in the world. Further, since the capital expenditure involved could only be remunerative on a long-term basis, the site must be in an area of political stability. British Columbia met both these requirements. It is more economical, in the long run, to bring the concentrate of bauxite, alumina, to the source of power than to take

7. N.W. Territories: Weather Station on Cornwallis Island

8. British Columbia: The Kootenay River at Nelson

the power to the concentrate. The alumina for Kitimat will be shipped from Jamaica, a haul of nearly 6,000 miles. The metal itself will be shipped from Kitimat all over the world.

The operations at Kitimat are in four sections: the creation of a sufficient head of water to provide the power needed, the provision of the generating station, the transmission of the power over the fifty miles that separate the power station at Kemano from Kitimat and the construction at Kitimat itself of the smelters, port facilities and a township for the workers. The total cost of the undertaking will be of the order of $600 million.

Topography is all important in the whole project. Kitimat, until 1951, was the name of a small Indian village about 400 miles north of Vancouver in a direct line and on the shore of the northern arm of a deep water fiord known as the Douglas Channel. The fiord runs inland from the sea for some seventy miles and at its head there is an open and level valley divided into two by the Kitimat River. That is the site for the new Kitimat, chosen because of the area available for building and for its deep-water access. The valley itself leads northwards and gives comparatively easy access to Terrace, on the Skeena River, some forty miles to the north, and the C.N.R. line which has its terminus at Prince Rupert. A branch of the C.N.R. is being built from Terrace to Kitimat now.

Along this part of the coast the coastal range of British Columbia rises sharply from sea level to about 9,000 feet. Eastwards the land falls gently away in a plateau broken with lakes and the river systems drain into the Fraser River at Prince George, some 250 miles from the coast. Among these rivers is the Nechako, which drains an area of about 5,400 square miles through a series of lakes, the highest of which is Tahtsa Lake. Tahtsa Lake is 2,800 feet above sea level and its western end is no more than ten miles from the Gardner Canal, the arm of the Douglas Channel running south-eastwards. If the flow of the Nechako River could be reversed and the ten miles of mountain tunnelled, a generating station on the Gardner Canal would have available the power coming from a very great head of water 2,800 feet high, which is some eighteen times the height of Niagara. That is the essence of the Kitimat project. By building a dam across the Nechako River 115 miles east of the head of Tahtsa Lake, and by cutting a ten-mile long tunnel through the coastal range, enough water can be sent down to the turbines of a power station to develop

I

2,240,000 horse power in the shape of electric current. To have given the plan an ideal neatness it should have been possible to have built the smelters at the power station site itself, but that was not feasible. The valley is steep and narrow; its floor is not large enough for power station, smelters and town. The power station is a quarter of a mile inside the seaward flank of the Coastal range, in a cavern blasted out of the rock.

The first site chosen for the dam across the Nechako River failed to provide on both banks a solid foundation for the dam. A new site was chosen further downstream, just above the Grand Canyon, and on 8 October 1952, the Kenney Dam was finished, the diversion tunnel closed, and the flow of the Nechako above it ceased. Work on the first buildings in Kitimat began in April, 1952, and in that summer about 1,600 men were living and working on the site in temporary buildings. The number in the summer of 1953 had doubled. The first two hot-lines of an eventual twelve are due to come into operation this year and will produce 80,000 tons of aluminium metal per annum. An output of this size needs a labour force of about 1,200 men, so that direct employees of the Aluminum Company will give Kitimat an initial population of from 6,000 to 7,000 people. The public statement by Aluminium Ltd., the parent company, published in July 1953, stated that an additional 182,000 tons of metal could be produced at Kitimat without substantial alteration to the hydraulic works or the transmission lines and that the ultimate limit of power available could produce 500,000 tons of metal in a year. That remains a possibility, but it does foreshadow the growth of Kitimat into a town of some 50,000 people.

The creation of Kitimat itself is a fascinating experiment in town planning. It is a virgin site in virgin territory. The area of land chosen for the township is about four miles long on a ridge of ground at the head of the seaway, bounded on the south and west by water and the flood plain of the river, on the north by a tributary of the Kitimat flowing west and on the east by the sharply rising mountain slop. The ridge contains three terraces of comparatively level land. The north-western corner of the site is cut by a gully; that is the area reserved for a golf course. The plan for the town is based upon a single city centre with six major and three minor neighbourhood centres. Each section of the town will be completed in a settled sequence and the various facilities and amenities will be "phased in" as the town grows. In addition, the City Centre will have a theatre and a hotel.

Each neighbourhood area will have two elementary schools, some with community facilities, and a junior high school. The two senior high schools for the whole town, with playing fields, will be centrally placed. The general pattern of the town is the now familiar one, with a limited number of main traffic roads encircling each neighbourhood centre and the houses grouped together in closes. Those the company builds, and lets, will have the minimum of amenities and low rents. The company does not desire Kitimat to be a company town and men will be encouraged to build and own their own houses (since Kitimat rates as a defence project, they will be able to obtain a 90 per cent mortgage from the federal mortgage corporation). So far as social life is concerned, two things should help to create a community; the churches and sport.

To anyone from Europe, Kitimat seems horribly isolated. All around are the wooded mountains, evergreen, and so changing little in colour over the year, snow-buried in winter and masked in fog and drifting cloud in the spring and the fall. It is a long way down the Douglas Channel to the openness of the sea. The railway from Terrace should be completed by the end of the year. Not so the road, and that, the one road out of town, will lead still further north. But, to the Canadian, distance is not, of itself, isolation. There are two regular steamship services, weekly, to Vancouver, and air services that run southwards down the coast, west to Prince Rupert, and, soon, eastwards through Terrace to the north of the province and on to Edmonton and Alberta. If the facilities for travel are there, they will be used.

The undertakings centred on Kitimat have already had a considerable influence on the economy of British Columbia. At the height of the construction work they were employing some 10,000 men for the summer season and paying them high wages. There was a general rise in wages throughout the province in consequence and the repercussions of that are certainly not fully exhausted. But the long-term influences of Kitimat on British Columbia are an interesting speculation. The smelters produce one product only. British Columbia neither supplies the raw material nor can its existing industries absorb more than a fraction of the resulting product. The aluminium is for export. Alcan itself will have a big payroll in Kitimat and it will contribute to the provincial revenues in taxation. It can do little more, directly. What will, perhaps, in the end be more important is the use that others may make of Kitimat and its facilities. It will have people, economic power, a deep-water port, and the shortest rail link with the north of two provinces, British Columbia and Alberta. It will also have on the doorstep all the aluminium that any industry could ever want, without appreciable freight cost. Those are the new opportunities that Kitimat presents to the rest of British Columbia, and to the rest of Canada. It may yet rival Vancouver as a Pacific port, and as a manufacturing centre for the interior.

Whatever Kitimat may ultimately become, it is to me already one of the triumphs of this century, one of the reasons for my profound admiration for the spirit that moves in Canada. It is at once an act of faith, an essay of the imagination and a monument of skill, courage and experience. It was an act of faith to believe that the world will need this additional aluminium. It was an act of imagination to site the smelters at Kitimat. To plan and execute each step in the operation in conformity with such a strict time-table demanded the highest practical qualities of which man is capable. And, I suppose, to some, all that would be damned because Aluminium, Ltd., is a company that makes a profit and pays a dividend.

THE SALMON

The development of the Kitimat project has already had a direct and physical effect on one of British Columbia's chief industries. The Kenney Dam was closed and began to fill on 8 October 1952. Within a month the flow of water in the Nechako River at Fort Fraser, about fifty miles downstream from the dam, had fallen from 4,680 cubic feet per second to 70 cubic feet per second. What difference will that make to the salmon fisheries of British Columbia?

The Pacific salmon is a remarkable fish. It is spawned in fresh water, in the rivers and lakes that flow into the Northern Pacific, in the late summer and early fall and has an incubation period of from 60 to 120 days, depending upon the temperature of the water in which the eggs are lying. It has a life cycle of between three and five years; the normal, for the Fraser River "sockeye" salmon, is four. In its second year the Fraser River fingerling swims down to the sea and its movements for the next two years are not accurately known. At the beginning of the fourth year it starts its journey back to its spawning ground, which is always the exact spot in which it was itself spawned. It will not spawn anywhere else. This may be 700 miles from the sea, perhaps in a lake 4,000 ft. above sea level (the king salmon of the Yukon River may travel 2,000 miles inland), and each salmon so times the start and the duration of its journey that it reaches the spawning ground almost exactly on the anniversary of its own appearance there as an egg. And, having spawned, it dies. From the moment when it leaves the salt water of the sea and enters the fresh water of the river, it ceases to eat; in fact, its stomach and digestive organs atrophy. It lives on itself and as its substance diminishes on its way up-stream so does its capacity to withstand a rise in the temperature of the water. In the Fraser River, at the start of its journey up-stream, a salmon can live in water with a temperature of 70°F. On the spawning beds themselves, the salmon may die, without spawning, if the mean water temperature is above 63°F.

The effect of the Kenney Dam, and the danger it presents to the salmon, is this: No salmon ever entered the water area now en-closed by the dam to spawn; the rapids of the Grand Canyon just below the dam were and always have been too great an obstacle. But many thousands of salmon pass up the stretch of the Nechako River between Prince George, where the Nechako joins the Fraser, and its tributary, the Stuart River, and many more swim on up the Nechako to the François and Endako Lakes, which drain into it. That stretch of river received the water now enclosed by the Kenney Dam and the existence of the dam has now re-duced the volume of water in the Nechako between the Stuart River and Prince George by some 40 per cent and, higher up, between the Stuart and Fort Fraser, a stretch of 58 miles, by some 80 per cent. The reduced volume of water uses the same wide river bed and, in consequence, that section of the Nechako will be more shallow and will move more slowly. The water will therefore retain more heat from the sun in summer. If its mean temperature rises above 68°F. the salmon travelling up the Nechako to the Stuart River and to François Lake may die before spawning, and the salmon fisheries of British Columbia may lose, so the International Pacific Salmon Fisheries Commission esti-mates, as much as two million dollars a year in consequence. That

worries the Commission. It also worries the Federal Ministry of
Fisheries in Ottawa. It has not disturbed the British Columbia
Government quite so much; at least, the possibility did not induce them to insert any conditions governing this point in the
water licence granted to the Aluminum Company of Canada
under which the Kenney Dam was built.

The sockeye salmon that spawn in the lakes and creeks of the
Fraser River system, the area, some 90,000 square miles, super-
vised by the International Commission, travel in a number of
separate runs, depending on their ultimate spawning grounds.
These runs have differing characteristics and the salmon may
almost be said to belong to separate tribes. The Indians, who
depended on them for food, have known all about their habits
and timings, and records started by some of the factors of the
Hudson's Bay Company go back over a hundred years. Each
separate run seems to have one major year, for numbers, in every
four and the pattern of the four-year cycle did not vary much from
period to period until there happened what the fishermen call
the Hell's Gate disaster in 1913 and 1914. Hell's Gate is a narrows
in the Fraser River and in 1913 and 1914, as a result of railway
construction work, followed by a landslide, part of the river
channel was blocked, which vastly increased the rate of flow of
water through the remainder. The salmon is capable of an immense burst of energy but it cannot sustain its effort for long.
From 1914 onwards, at certain times in the early summer when
the river was running fast, few salmon could make the sustained
effort needed to pass through the Hell's Gate rapids. They fought
for days in vain, and, unable to reach their spawning grounds,
they died in their thousands without spawning. The runs most
directly affected, that is, those that normally passed through
Hell's Gate at this time of year, began to fall in numbers and
fewer and fewer salmon returned to the upper waters of the
Fraser.

The International Pacific Salmon Fisheries Commission was set
up by a convention between Canada and the United States, made
in 1930 and ratified in 1937, for "the protection, preservation and
extension of the sockeye salmon fisheries in the Fraser River
system" and its jurisdiction covers the whole of the river and a
portion of the high seas from the river mouths to the Straits of
Juan de Fuca. For the first eight years after 1937 the Commission

was authorised to conduct research. It came into full operation in 1945. Now it fixes the periods during which fishing is permitted in the salt waters and it adjusts its closed periods from time to time to ensure as far as possible that the catch for the season is divided equally between Canadian and American fishermen. Its other function is to make recommendations to the two governments. The Commission has six members, three appointed by each country, and a permanent staff, and its expenses, including the cost of all works it promotes, are borne equally by Canada and the United States. One of its first and major tasks was to investigate the Hell's Gate section of the Fraser. Its answer was to recommend the construction of fishways, to enable the salmon to avoid the direct current where it flowed most powerfully. Two were completed in 1945, a third a year later and the fourth fishway, cut through a higher section of the rock for use when the river was in flood, was finished in 1951.

The effect on the number of fish returning to the old and virtually deserted spawning grounds up-river was immediate. So far as possible, the commercial catch at sea, made before the salmon enter the Fraser, is limited to about three-quarters of the estimated total; the remainder are known as the "escapement". In 1940, the total escapement was 467,000, in 1944, 431,000, in 1948, 998,000 and in 1952, 852,000. In some areas, virtually barren between 1913 and 1945, the rise in numbers was phenomenal; in the Birkenhead River, the number rose from 27,000 in 1940 to 120,000 in 1948. The value (at wholesale level) of the salmon fisheries to British Columbia rose from $20 million in 1941 to $44 million in 1951.

With the interests of the salmon fisheries in mind, the Commission keeps an eye on all developments within the Fraser River system that may in any way affect the purity, volume or temperature of the river water. It brings pressure to bear on municipalities to deal effectively with sewage effluent, on wood pulp plants to keep their sulphide wastes out of the river, on logging companies to refrain from making log-retaining dams that will damage spawning grounds. All the natural resources of British Columbia can be developed, the Commission holds, without injury to the salmon fisheries, provided there is foresight used in the initial plans and in the way the resources are handled. The Commission is an unobtrusive body. It has an Advisory Council to assist it in its contacts with the trades interested directly in the salmon, on both sides of the frontier. It must reason and persuade rather than order, and probably that makes its educational effect all the more potent. But the Aluminum Company has deprived the Nechako River of some 9,000 cubic feet a second of water by building the Kenney Dam, and the Commission has not yet solved the problem of keeping in the channel of the Nechako enough water at the right temperature to enable the salmon making for the Stuart River and the François Lake to reach their destinations and spawn before they die.

COMINCO

The largest single mining undertaking in operation in British Columbia today is that of the Consolidated Mining and Smelting Company, based primarily on the fabulous Sullivan mine at Kimberley and its attendant smelting and refining plant at Trail a hundred miles or so away as the crow flies (two hundred by rail) to the west. The Company turns out some 90 per cent of all the lead produced in Canada, approximately 460 tons a day. Its daily output of zinc is 500 tons, of silver 35,000 ounces. The ore body at Kimberley also yields tin, cadmium, mercury, bismuth and indium and enough gold to make, once a month, a solitary gold brick. In addition the plant at Kimberley piles up a vast reserve of iron ore for which the Company has no immediate use.

Mining spread into British Columbia from the south, up the Columbia River. In 1890 two prospectors, by name Bourgeois and Moria, struck a payable deposit of copper-gold at Rossland, in the hills seven miles to the south of the spot on the Columbia River where the town of Trail now stands. Within five years some 2,000 claims had been staked out. In no time at all Rossland became a mining camp, complete with saloons, dancing girls, all the paraphernalia for the extraction of metal both from the ground and the pocket. Its heyday lasted perhaps twenty years. Then production waned and mines petered out like candles. It was Trail that grew and flourished and, with polite indifference to such a romantic past, it turned Rossland into a residential suburb of itself. The track for the pack trains from Rossland down to Trail End Creek, Trail's first name, is now a paved road home from the works for supper. Halfway up is Trail golf course and, a little further on, the cemetery. Rossland itself lies in a cup in the mountains where the valley widens out. The ski-ing enthusiasts have cut their own run through the woods and built a ski-lift and a week-end hotel. In its day Rossland was a kind of apprentice school through which most of its generation of mining engineers in Canada passed.

Among the earlier inhabitants of Rossland was a Mr. F. A. Heinze of Butte, Montana. Mr. Heinze believed that there was more money to be made in dealing with ore after it had been mined than in digging for it. The route by which the wealth of Rossland travelled to the outer world was by pack train to the river, by river boat down the Columbia into Montana, and from there on to a smelter. Heinze thought it would be desirable for all, and profitable to him, if he built a railway track from Rossland to the river and a small copper smelter at Trail. This he had done by 1896. He also obtained a railway franchise which entitled him to build a line from Trail to Vancouver and by 1897 he had constructed a standard gauge track up the Columbia River valley from Trail as far as Castlegar, some twenty miles to the north. In the following year the C.P.R. appeared on the scene. That Company was intent on building its southerly line from Alberta into British Columbia, over the Crow's Nest Pass and on to the coast. To complete it it needed control of Heinze's railway franchise and to obtain Heinze's franchise it was compelled to buy from him his smelter at Trail as well. That was the start of what is now the Consolidated Mining and Smelting Company. Heinze is also immortalised in the name given to the peak immediately to the north of Trail, Mount Heinze.

The Consolidated Mining and Smelting Company of Canada, Limited (it adopted its present name in 1906, and that is now officially shortened to "Cominco") is a unification of the originally C.P.R.-owned Canadian Smelting Works at Trail with a number of other mines at Rossland and Moyie. It acquired the Sullivan mine at Kimberley in 1910. The Sullivan mine is on the site of one of the largest single deposits of metal ore in the world; its only serious rival is at Broken Hill in Australia. It was discovered by four prospectors in 1892; one of them lived to see it blossom into its present fullness, and he died a pensioner of the Company. For thirty years little use could be made of its ore body because the metals were too closely mixed; Sullivan ore contains about 4½ per cent of lead, 5½ per cent of zinc, 20 per cent of iron and

18 per cent of sulphur, in the form of sulphides, and even as late as 1910 the lead ore had to be separated by hand. In 1920 the present vice-president of Cominco solved the problems of successfully separating the ores on a commercial basis—the method he he perfected was flotation, the floating out of waste rock from the ore and of one sulphide from another—and by doing so allowed the mine to expand. It now yields 11,000 tons of ore a day.

The ore is delivered to the concentrator at Kimberley in the form of crushed rock. In the first stage the waste rock is floated off; mixed with a proportion of the iron suphide recovered later, it goes back into the mine to fill the excavated sections and in fact sets again as rock. The metal sulphides are next dried and ground to a fine powder and are themselves in their turn separated by flotation. The lead goes first, followed by the zinc, leaving the iron. The lead and zinc concentrates are sent on to the plant at Trail for refining, approximately 1,550 tons of them a day.

The country around the entrance to the Sullivan mine is not unlike that of a Welsh mining valley, save that the main entrance is horizontal, not vertical, and is at the 3,900 foot level, that being its height above sea level. The thickness of the vein is from five to three hundred feet and it is worked down to 4,000 ft. below surface level from two main horizontal galleries. The ore body is blasted, crushed by machines within the mine and dropped by gravity chutes into the waiting trains for a journey to the concentrator. In the mine offices they have a three-dimensional model of the mine, with the galleries and shafts shown in coloured wire and the worked-out sections, or stopes, represented by coloured plaster casts (disturbingly like medical models of corroded livers). The mine superintendent who took me below ground was a former R.C.A.F. navigator, which was reassuring. No one in Kimberley will venture on any estimate of when the mine will be worked out. A bad fault ends the lateral extension of the mine on one side, but towards the east the ore body seems to run down and down and down. It is now worked for nearly a mile horizontally.

Cominco is also in the fertiliser business.

It is, of course, notorious that disasters stimulate human ingenuity. The original electrolytic plant at Trail was built in 1916 to produce zinc at the urgent request of the United Kingdom Munitions Board of that war. By the end of the 1920's it was faced with another problem. The ores it was treating were sulphides of the metals. In treating the metal the sulphur was released and Cominco allowed it to disappear up the factory chimney in the form of sulphur dioxide, a gas. The prevailing winds at Trail are westerly. They blow down the valley of the Columbia and, at that time, after leaving Trail they carried a considerable charge of sulphur dioxide, powerful enough to destroy very effectively the vegetation on either side of the valley. If Trail had been further north it is possible that little would have been done about it, at least for quite a time.

But ten miles downstream from Trail the Columbia crosses the United States border and the sulphur concentration crossed with it, to continue its work of destruction among the crops of American agriculturalists as well. The invasion was not relished. The farmers spoke to their Senators and the Senators spoke to Washington and Washington could speak only to Ottawa. The result was an international convention between Canada and the United States, the setting up of an international arbitration tribunal, and a series of awards of damages to the farmers, all payable by Cominco. Cominco might well have believed that some of the American farmers planted their crop each year solely to harvest an award of damages from Cominco at the end of the season, but it could hardly hope to convince an international tribunal of that. It was, therefore, compelled to find some way of keeping its sulphur dioxide from United States territory, and that meant that it was compelled to find some way of using it commercially. It did. The sulphur now becomes ammonium sulphate, an agricultural fertiliser of established repute, and contributing to the profits of Cominco, particularly when the prices of base metals are depressed. It was this experience that gave Cominco the wartime management of the Calgary plant for the production of explosives (chemically akin to fertilisers) and its subsequent opportunity to purchase the plant outright. Cominco now produces a total of 1,700 tons of fertiliser a day, ammonium phosphate, ammonium sulphate and ammonium nitrate. It is also, of course, a producer of sulphuric acid, but in carboys.

Mining, in all its processes, needs power. The Trail plant has a load of 270,000 h.p. a day, three-quarters of which is for the electrolytic processes on the metals. So far, Cominco has drawn all its power from a series of five dams across the Kootenay River, in the stretch between Kootenay Lake and the point at which the Kootenay joins the Columbia at Castlegar. These dams were built between 1898 and 1944, and in 1952 they were linked with Kimberley as well, 86 miles of transmission line across the mountains, including a two-mile unsupported cable across Kootenay Lake. This year these will be supplemented, and to some extent replaced, by a new hydro-electric plant, with a dam, on the Pend-d'Oreille River south of Trail. This is the Waneta project. The Pend-d'Oreille River spends only some fifteen miles within Canada. It rises in Montana and joins the Columbia River a few hundred yards above the frontier. During that distance it will provide Canada with another 420,000 h.p. of electric power at Waneta, with the possibility of yet another dam higher up. This is one of the instances in which the entirely arbitrary frontier along the 49th parallel has worked to Canada's advantage.

The story of Cominco is far from unique. A company begins as a small venture, a one-man enterprise. It transpires that it has a nuisance value to a larger concern; it is absorbed, with the result that capital resources needed to carry it into a second phase are available. A war comes and places a premium on its products. It hires a technician who develops the new methods it then needs and so opens a third phase of expansion. It is driven by circumstances to branch into a new field, to make use of a by-product, and that in its turn leads on to fresh developments during another war. Now it extends still further, to new mines and new metals, in Northern British Columbia and at Yellowknife in the North-West Territories. All that activity is spread over nearly fifty years, and it has been accomplished by a balancing of all the forces present in industry, from the need to make a profit to the personal desires of executives to utilise their skills and judgment to the full. That is how the Canadian mining industry has grown and these are the forces still at work in it.

The Columbia River at Trail is wide and powerful, flowing in a fairly narrow valley along the floor of which are terraces, of different heights of gravel and moraine brought down long ago from the surrounding hills. Trail itself came into existence because there the stream, and valley, from Rossland met the river, and left on the southern bank three tiers of flat gravel terraces on which man could easily build. The town occupies the lowest tier, the smelter is on the middle tier and the fertiliser plant on the third. On the northern bank there is a long narrow stretch of gravel with two smaller isolated terraces rising above it, one of which contains the new school, the other the hospital. Trail is spread out along the river banks, a homely town, oddly Italian in parts, for many of the early workers at the plant were Italian immigrants and they in time set up their own shops and still speak but little English.

The river sweeps away to the east, bearing gradually south. The road to Salmo (where there is another lead-zinc mine) leaves its northern bank and climbs over a spur above the valley. Along the valley floor, a few feet above the river level runs the new road to the Waneta dam, wide, gravelled and dusty. The trees that are beginning to climb the slopes again grow singly or in small groves, where they can find soil, and the grass on the gravel beds by the river is coarse. Only occasionally is there anything that looks like good pasture. It is an arid country and deserted. Its colours are yellow and brown and olive green, and it is very beautiful. At Waneta, when I saw it, one of the two centre sections of the dam had still to be built and the late spring flood water swept through that gap in an arch of immense power. The generating plant is housed on the northern bank below the dam, and when it is complete the shield of natural rock left to protect it during construction will be shattered by a hundred separate explosions and its component boulders will be swept away in the race of water. It will be a lonely, fascinating place in which to live, for the Columbia River will always be a changeable companion, and in times of flood frightening.

The road from Trail up the river follows the right bank and the river bends away to the north. Very little grows in the valley but there are one or two little villages of wooden houses where man can make something of a garden. At Castlegar the road crosses the river by ferry and turns right up the Kootenay River eastwards. Nelson, the next town, is twenty miles on and the river valley that leads to it is wooded and green. It is wide and the trees grow thickly up its sides. There are farmlands along the valley bottom, and the great dams of the power company make waterfalls of white, foaming water. It seems as peaceful as any in central Wales.

But this is the country of the Doukhobors. Their farmhouses, ugly square wooden buildings, with a chimney stack in the centre, like a suburban house, are always built in pairs, one house for the men, the other for the women. In their moments of exultation they set fire to their buildings, their schools, even their own houses, which increases the dismay of the British Columbians over the problem they still present. The Doukhobors in Saskatchewan are the most settled and assimilated, those in British Columbia the most difficult.

By the cynical, the story of the Doukhobors could be used as an object lesson in the wisdom of non-interference. Originally they were a sect of Russians persecuted by the Tsar and his Cossacks because they refused to undertake any kind of military service. The Liberals of the world, headed by Count Tolstoy and assisted by Aylmer Maude and the Society of Friends of Philadelphia, round about 1899 organised a mass emigration programme for these unfortunates. Some 8,000 of them were extracted from Russia and settled first in Cyprus and, when that settlement failed, in Western Canada. They were regarded, then, as harmless anarchists—no doubt the men of Philadelphia thought that Canada was big enough and empty enough to assimilate them all. Some have been. The sect in British Columbia, the Sons of Freedom, have not. They are still anarchists, fighting every form of government regulation, from military service to the registration of births, marriages and deaths.

Their extremists remain incomprehensible to the Western mind, secretive, feudal, hating and fearing external authority, unable even to come to terms with themselves. The newspaper I read that day said that the leader of one sect in British Columbia was calling on his flock to emigrate. "And what country," the man who was driving me said, "would be fools enough to take them in?" Only time will break down their extreme exclusiveness for time is the only weapon a democracy may use. For those left in Russia, the problem has already been solved, in one way or another. The Soviet authorities report that they are all now either Orthodox Christians or Baptists.

At Nelson the river broadens into one arm of the Kootenay Lake. The road eastwards crosses on another ferry and follows the shore through woods to the village of Balfour where there is yet another ferry across the two miles of the main lake. Once across the lake the road travels south, cut into the steep side of the hill, winding through woods almost all the way to Creston. All this is part of the Trans-Canada Highway. "Vancouver" was the destination plate of the buses coming towards us and the snack bar at Creston gave the times of those going on to Lethbridge and away into Alberta.

Creston is a fruit- and wheat-growing centre. The southern end of Kootenay Lake becomes increasingly shallow so that it is possible to dam and drain it and add more acres to the flat rich lands at the valley bottom. The main road eastwards crosses the hills and wanders along minor valleys on its way to Cranbrook and beyond, to Fernie and the Crow's Nest Pass. The land is largely empty save for trees and all the motorist sees is the chipmunk playing by the roadside. Everywhere along the valleys the soil is the same, gravel and silt and boulders washed down from the mountains in the past. It is good pasture land. There are streams to irrigate it. It still needs people. When one compares it with the country lands around Zurich, in Switzerland, which it resembles very closely, one sees how much can be done, and how much will be done, in time. These mountains—the Selkirks— are less pretentious than the Rockies and easy to live with. It is a quiet country, and its beauty is cumulative.

VANCOUVER

To me, Vancouver is a beautiful city.

That sentiment, expressed in that way, can, I know, mean very little. It does not explain itself and it certainly does not describe Vancouver. There are a great many beautiful cities in the world, from Salzburg to Sydney, and they are not identical. Nor are the reasons why man calls them beautiful. In one it is the setting, in another the architecture, in another the whole relationship between city, people and activity. London is beautiful by chance, Paris by design, Venice because it is a reflection in which time has altered both the image and the mirror. None are perfect; there is some ugliness in them all. Vancouver is not perfect. Like most western Canadian cities it has grown too fast. It has slums. It is untidy. It contains a great sprawl of suburbs and suburbs do not happen by natural circumstances. More often than not they are an expression of an indifference to order and shape, and order and shape are the only two concepts able to give coherence to the material aspect of any civilisation. Without them, North American civilisa-

tion is an uncontrolled growth, like cancer. Why, then, do I find
Vancouver beautiful?

First, there is the setting. Vancouver lies on the mainland, on
the southern shore of an arm of the sea, Burrard Inlet, on the
east of the Straits of Georgia which separate Vancouver Island
from mainland, and so is possessed of a lovely land-locked harbour. North-westwards is Howe Sound, another deep-water inlet.
Originally the whole area was forest, and the forest has been
preserved in Stanley Park, a mile to the west of the centre of Vancouver and with the sea on three of its sides. Wherever you are in
Vancouver, the mountains to the north are a frieze against the sky.

When the air is clear before rain, they are sharp in outline and
close across the water. When the rain comes in from the south-
west, they are the pedestals on which the clouds rest. When the
evening is still and warm, they are blurred and distant and the
smoke from some fire may wash a band of lighter blue across their
darkening faces. At night, the lights along the ski-lift are a stair-
way to the stars, but, like the Tower of Babel, too short to reach
them, while Vancouver itself, from those mountains, is a formal
garden of light and darkness, surrounded by a lighter sea. The
only prospect I know of mountains so positioned, mountains beyond an arm of the sea and fretting the base of the northern sky
so that they face the sun and change with every alteration in his
light, is from Reykjavik, in Iceland, looking across to the mass of
Esja. Esja is a clearer canvas for the sun to use, for its rock is
bare, but neither in Reykjavik nor Vancouver does the sun shine
all the time.

Then there is the fact that Vancouver is a port. That is a personal idiosyncrasy. Maybe it is because I was born in a city that
is a port. Maybe it is because, when I worked in the City of
London, I would gain comfort from the ships that came upstream
to berth just below London Bridge, bringing with them, so I
thought, some powerful emanation of the places from which they
had come. I remember one hot summer afternoon in Cherbourg, in
July 1944, when I sat on the ruins of a defence wall in the ruins
of a town and watched a Liberty ship discharge overside into a
fleet of attendant D.U.K.W.s and she seemed to lead the mind outwards across a fresh and living sea away from the looking-glass
distortions of life in Normandy at that time. Bayeux was intact
but overwhelmed by the invasion. Cherbourg was half destroyed

9.   British Columbia: Building the Waneta Dam

10.   British Columbia: The Kitimat Enterprise

but living, drawing its life from the unchanged sea, as it always had. Life comes naturally to a city with the salt water. The ships at Vancouver's quays and in the harbour carry such place-names as "Kobe", "Köbnhavn" and "Karachi" on their sterns. Does not that make a city beautiful, or is it only an imagining? I do not know, except that there is a magic in the journeyings of ships that has not faded yet.

Then there are the people. Perhaps it is carrying a subjective approach too far to say that the beauty of a city depends upon the people who live in it, and yet cannot the ugliness of a people destroy the illusion of beauty that setting and buildings if seen alone might be capable of creating? And do not the activities of the people of a city stamp something on the impression of the place that the traveller carries away? Take, for example, the complicated pattern of Genoa: its antiquity, and so both its assurance and its indifference; its extremes of wealth and poverty, which break up the mirror of beauty as a rifle shot stars a glass. Can one admire the villas and the gardens overlooking the Mediterranean without reservation when one has walked through the slums to reach them? Did not the beauty of Karlsbad, in Czechoslovakia, fade like that of a cut flower when the artificial but intense life that built it up was killed, and that without an alteration to a single building?

Vancouver is, I felt, the most relaxed city in Canada, using the word "relaxed" in the North American sense, and finding it hard to translate as I do. Quebec is inward looking, Montreal is very aware of itself, Toronto is harassed, and Edmonton is thinking of next year. Vancouver is like a man walking to his office on a warm spring morning, in step with a distant military band playing Elgar's "Pomp and Circumstance" March, and facing a day which he feels will go as planned. It is a masculine city. It has few doubts and hesitations. It will grant that it has made mistakes in the past but it is sure that the future will give ample time and opportunity to put them right. It has many insensitivities, but at least that is matched with a certain tolerance for more uneasy creatures. Vancouver is not a place for those who feel that human beings are at their most interesting when they are depressed and frustrated. It sees no glamour in the death-wish, and existentialism is not likely to reach it for some time.

Vancouver is the last home in Canada for the tycoons of the

K

earlier part of the century. Most of its men of fortune made their wealth by prodigious labour and the hard driving of men. Their relations with those whom they pay every week are harsh and un-compromising, and the accepted mode of settlement for disputes is the direct clash in which victory goes to the side possessing the greater strength and endurance. But, whereas in the east one feels that industrial conflict is a game of chess in which both sides will try to alter the rules whilst the game is in progress, and where the ultimate prize money will in any event be found by the consumer, in Vancouver it is Jacob wrestling with the Angel (which is which I do not know), titanic, not immediately decisive, but honest and profoundly important. In Vancouver it is possible to believe that a process of synthesis in the relations between capital and labour is actually at work. Heaven knows what Vancouver may not build in the end.

The standards that determine whether a city is beautiful are not those applied to a statue, for a community should be dynamic and cannot be wholly beautiful if it is not. There is a beauty of youth and a beauty of maturity. Vancouver is young. It is restless but not impatient.

5

Ten Provinces in Search
of a Metropolis

TEN provinces in search of a metropolis?

Of course they have some centres for some of their activities. They take their politics to Ottawa and the malicious would say that they have no need to take their money to Toronto because Toronto will find its own ways of collecting it. The pictorial arts go to Montreal, learning to McGill—but that is unfair, because the universities of Canada are much closer to being a true democracy in every way than that would imply. But a metropolis?

Is Ottawa any more than a small town with a strip of public buildings along the bank of the river and a suburb of odd, alien characters, the corps diplomatique, a source of gossip but hardly a part of the normal life of any town? Has Toronto ever thought of being a metropolis? It seems almost absent-minded, like a man standing at the door of a bank, inquisitive over the goings on outside but listening with half an ear to the rustle of the notes over the counter behind him.

Montreal? The city has handicaps; one, a city constitution that was once dictated by a bondholders' council and which has in consequence as cunningly devised a voting pattern as any thought up by a corporation lawyer intent on ensuring that voting control remains in the hands of his clients and no one else. Two, the curious phantasy in the minds of so many of the two peoples of differing speech that the other does not exist. But Montreal has certain advantages (of which the fact that it is a port I would include as one). Its vitality, not surpassed, if equalled, anywhere else in Canada. And vitality itself is too plain a word to use. There is vitality in Edmonton, more in Vancouver. In Montreal its texture is richer. The girls and young men that take the air on a summer's evening along the eastern half of St. Catherine's Street are not all duplicates of some set 'teen-age style. They have individuality. They are capable of surprise. They are not lost by themselves, not afraid of themselves. Has not Montreal the consciousness of prestige, and a plain, vulgar satisfaction with it, that are almost the full answer to the question what is and what is not a metropolis?

Then there is Winnipeg. Winnipeg ought to be the metropolis, if one goes by the map. Was it John Dafoe, or the Siftons, who created its greatness, but only for a limited time? Was it the Grain Exchange? Surely not—that would be far too reactionary a view, and yet—. And yet the days of greatness of my own native city were based on the West African slave trade and set with grim finality when the Cotton Exchange closed its doors, leaving the city given over to the Chinese, the Lascars and the Irish. Or is it that Winnipeg is waiting, waiting for the time when there is a surge within itself, waiting for an occasion to synthesise east and west?

Or is there no answer to the question at all?

The fact is that this search for a metropolis may not be any part of Canada. Metropolis: chief city. London, the capital of a country in which all trains go up to London and their counterparts go down to—it doesn't really matter where, for one has always bought a return ticket. Is this search for a metropolis in Canada merely an extension to another country of a pattern that has grown in England over the centuries and will, fortunately, not be repeated elsewhere? Did the men of Plymouth or Bideford ever give a thought to London in the first Elizabeth's day, except as the place where the Court happened to be? Why should these provinces need a metropolis? Is not St. John's as good as Saskatoon, and Kingston as good as Victoria? Are they not each themselves and all a part of Canada?

Perhaps metropolises are tribal burying grounds.

6

The Threads in the Necklace

IF CANADA is a chain of ten provinces slung like a necklace above the opulent figure of the United States, what are the threads, immaterial as well as material, that hold them together? Of the immaterial links, the most important are, of course, the government, the political system, a common history as a people mainly of European origin, a common basis to their education, and those are hardly to be described as devices for maintaining unity. They are part of a wider subject; what makes a Canadian? Why is he different from the other North Americans, the citizens of the United States?

Here let me deal with two only of the others, broadcasting and the films of the National Film Board of Canada, for they have this much in common. The institutions responsible for them were set up deliberately to foster this integration of a people. They are instruments of a national policy, and whilst they may, and do, have other functions as well, it is important to keep in mind their original and still basic purpose.

1. Broadcasting

In the Report of the Royal Commission on Arts, Letters and Sciences, commonly known as the Massey Report, the Commission drew a broad distinction between two kinds of broadcasting systems. "Radio," it said, "may be regarded primarily as a means of entertainment, a by-product of the advertising business. . . . The

second view of radio operation assumes that this medium of communication is a public trust to be used for the benefit of society,
in the education and enlightenment as well as for the entertainment of its members." Broadcasting in Canada began as the first
of these, and very much as an annexe of the American advertising
business.

The turning point was the Royal Commission of 1928, under the
chairmanship of Sir John Aird, appointed because of the unease
felt at the American invasion, almost monopoly, of the air. When
the Commission published its report there were 62 broadcasting
stations in Canada, with a total of 296,000 licence holders. They
were basically advertising stations, the bulk of their programmes
came from outside Canada, and their coverage and programmes
were concentrated on the urban areas. The Aird Commission's
advice was drastic. It recommended that a national corporation
should be set up to be responsible for all Canadian broadcasting,
that all private stations should be either taken over or closed
down, and that the coverage to be given by the new corporation
should be extended to the whole country. The majority of the conclusions of the Commission were accepted but there were two
obstacles in the way of immediate action on the Report. The first
was that, not unnaturally, the British North America Act was
silent on whether radio was a federal or a provincial responsibility
and some of the provinces claimed that control and operation
should be their business. The second was that no international
agreement existed governing radio channels in the North American
continent and it was difficult, then, to find sufficient wavelengths
free from interference to allow of proper coverage for the whole
country. The first problem was settled by legal action which
reached the Privy Council; the decision was that radio was a
federal matter. The second was finally settled at a conference in
Havana in 1937, which allocated the available places on the North
American wavelengths among the North American countries.

The Canadian Broadcasting Corporation, C.B.C., was set up by
Federal Act of Parliament in 1936 and opened in the November
of that year. It has a Board of nine, with a full-time chairman,
general manager and assistant general manager all appointed by
the Government. It broadcasts, in the words of the Aird Report,
"in the interests of Canadian listeners, and in the national interests
of Canada". It is a legal monopoly. It alone can license transmit-

ting stations, but it did not take over all the private stations that existed in 1936 and it has licensed new private stations since. In fact, there has grown up in Canada since 1936 a complicated mixture of publicly and privately owned broadcasting which is not easy to unravel.

The C.B.C. puts out three sound programmes each day, Trans-Canada, Radio Canada and Dominion, and, in the year that ended on 31 March 1953, of their time on the air four-fifths were "commercial" and one-fifth non-commercial. To complete this set of figures, 83 per cent (in time) of the programmes, commercial and non-commercial, originated in C.B.C. studios, 14 per cent came from either American networks or the B.B.C. and 2 per cent came from private stations in Canada. Trans-Canada, English-speaking, and Radio Canada, French-speaking, are the main networks, and Trans-Canada carried about two-thirds of the total of the year's broadcasting. The Dominion network is an evening programme, generally lighter in content than the other two, and carried 11 per cent of the year's broadcasting. The programmes originating from C.B.C. are broadcast both by the transmitters of C.B.C. and privately owned stations. At 31 March 1953, there were 111 stations in Canada owned by C.B.C. or affiliated to the C.B.C. networks; of these C.B.C. owned 20.

The affiliated stations fall into three groups, Basic stations and Supplementary A and Supplementary B stations. Basic stations receive all C.B.C. programmes and must reserve time for and transmit a certain number of hours weekly from these programmes, including newscasts. These are stations in areas in which the C.B.C. itself has no station. Supplementary A stations may use all C.B.C. non-sponsored programmes, must put out a smaller section of them but may not use C.B.C. sponsored programmes without the consent of the sponsor. Supplementary B stations do not receive any C.B.C. programmes as of right, but may receive C.B.C. sponsored programmes with the consent of the sponsor and may be brought in for a national hook-up if so required by C.B.C.

It requires 15,000 miles of land line to maintain these links over Canada but the result is that virtually the whole of the population of Canada can receive a Canadian programme. There are, in addition, 48 non-affiliated, completely independent stations with their own transmitters.

Radio Canada, the French-speaking network uses twenty-five transmitters, the majority in Quebec, but with three in Ontario and one each in New Brunswick, Manitoba and Saskatchewan. It is administratively separate from the English-speaking networks, has its own Director, and news service, and claims credit for introducing to Canada both schools broadcasts (in 1938) and farm broadcasts (in 1941). The general level of its programmes is slightly above those of the English-speaking networks—for instance, it broadcasts more serious music—and of course most of its live broadcasts must originate in its own studios. It takes a certain number of recordings and transcriptions from R.D.F., France. Where the French-speaking public is in a minority, it sometimes claims that C.B.C. stations that serve the area do not give the French language a fair proportion of time on the air, but inside the C.B.C. itself there is no serious friction between the two language programmes. Fair minded English-speaking C.B.C. producers will admit that, on the whole, the French-speaking can provide a fraction more liveliness and originality in their programme contents (the French-speaking, ever courteous, would, of course, return the compliment).

The common justification for the continued existence of the private stations in Canada is that they serve a useful purpose in their own localities. They have a transmission range of perhaps fifty miles. They are freer to advertise, and to seek local advertisements, and the station, and the advertiser, can claim that they give a service to the family out of town by telling them where to buy what. They can collect and broadcast local news and they can find and encourage local talent. There is no reason why they need to be privately owned to be able to do this, but to replace them the C.B.C. would be compelled to set up a corresponding number of virtually autonomous units, and to carry an additional weight of criticism for every local mistake. Immediately after the publication of the Aird Report, the private stations feared for their lives and were humble in consequence. After nearly twenty-five years of continued existence, they have acquired, in their minds at least, squatters' rights on the Canadian air, and they have come to resent the fact that it is the C.B.C. that grants their licences to operate. Judge and jury in its own cause, they say, and subsidised by public money as well. The proprietors of the private stations are American in outlook. To them radio is an industry, and, on the terms of that approach, the C.B.C. is a subsidised, Government controlled, monopolistic competitor.

The same mixed pattern is growing in television. Television began with the Montreal station, C.B.F.T., in September 1952. The Toronto station opened the same year, a relay station at Ottawa last year, and the next stations planned were for Winnipeg, Vancouver and Halifax. By the end of last year some fifteen privately owned stations had also been licensed. In its first year, about 60 per cent of the programmes transmitted from Montreal C.B.F.T. were produced in C.B.C. studios, the remainder came from American networks. At Toronto the proportions were about half and half.

Financially, sound broadcasting at the moment provides C.B.C. with a surplus sufficiently large to carry the initial deficit on television. In round figures, out of C.B.C.'s total income, for 1952–3, of $15 million, the Government provided $6¼ million, by way of grant, the public $5¾ million, in licence fees (now being replaced by a tax on certain components) and advertising revenues $3 million. After covering interest on capital loans and depreciation, the year's operations resulted in an operating surplus of $376,000, but the surplus on sound broadcasting was nearly $3 million, the deficit on television $2½ million. In addition, the Federal Government carries the full cost of the International Services put out by the C.B.C.

Canadian broadcasting, then, presents a totally different picture from that of the United Kingdom. There is no monopoly. There is no station without some advertising during the day. How does it compare in operation?

So far as the C.B.C.'s own programmes are concerned, its control over advertising is very great. Internally, that is in the hands of a Commercial Acceptance and Production Department, which both fixes all advertising rates for all C.B.C. stations and supervises the contents of all programmes. In sound radio, sponsored programmes may be produced by the C.B.C., on payment, by freelance producers or by commercial agencies. They must be approved before being transmitted. In television, all programmes are produced by C.B.C. studios. Supervision over the contents of the programmes is concerned with both the subject matter to be advertised and the method of presentation. The C.B.C. maintains a list of "unacceptable accounts" (laxatives, mouth-washes, reducing agents and the like are among them), and may forbid the broadcasting of certain aspects of a product accepted for advertising: e.g. a toothpaste proprietor may not claim that his product eliminates bad breath.

In addition, the C.B.C., as licensing authority, has power to lay down statutory regulations governing all licensed stations, including those privately owned. Its present regulations, which came into force on 1 July 1953, contain general rules for the conduct of public broadcasting. The maximum advertising content of any advertising programme is specified; it ranges from two-and-a-half minutes in a ten-minute programme to seven minutes in an hour's programme (less during the peak listening period, from 6 p.m. to midnight). Certain types of advertising are absolutely prohibited (among them bond-selling and the matter encouraging the purchase of alcoholic liquor). Others are conditionally permitted; e.g. no food, drug or medicine may be advertised unless it has been approved by the Government Department of National Health and Welfare. Is this the species of debased radio that justifies the so many gasps of horror in Britain?

It seemed to me in Canada, and when I returned to the United Kingdom, that the gasps of horror were curiously conventional. There is a parallel in Britain to the commercial radio in Canada; it is to be found in those cinemas that display short advertising films. The audience comes to see a feature film. In its moments of waiting for that it sees perhaps three or four one or two-minute advertising films. In exchange for its tolerance in submitting to them, it pays rather less for its seat than it otherwise would. The advertising shorts are not offensive. They are a feature of an activity that must, after all, be paid for in one way or another.

If there exists an individual whose enjoyment of a Beethoven symphony would be ruined if an announcer were to say at the start: "This performance comes to you by courtesy of Spratt's Dog Biscuits", then the burden of reading *The Times* must for that man be well-nigh intolerable. If he argues that dog biscuits are never likely to be linked with a performance of Beethoven, he ignores the evidence available in Canada. If he finds the spoken advertisement too excruciating to be borne, can he prefer the hypocrisy of the B.B.C., which never advertises, of course, save for the personal puffs in practically every variety and light entertainment programme it puts on the air?

Radio in most of Canada, and particularly in Ontario, is in direct competition, in its standards, with American radio. The majority verdict in Canada would be that the C.B.C.'s programmes, both sound and vision, are respectable but dull. My own verdict, based on what I did see of each, would be that C.B.C.'s programmes show some signs of lacking the money at the disposal of the Americans but that they escape the incredible monotony in so much of what the American stations put out. In music, Canada has not the reserves of talent on which the B.B.C. can draw; otherwise its programmes are comparable. In drama, it is as well placed. In its talks it avoids the B.B.C.'s almost obsessional desire to eliminate controversy (despite the fact that most of the baby, personality, then disappears with the bath water), and is rather more lively in consequence. In the United States radio stations assume that they must plug away on the lowest level of intelligence of the assumed audience, and in both those activities they succeed admirably. The C.B.C. accepts the responsibility of maintaining a balance among the interests it knows exist among its audiences. It is not an example that may be quoted by anyone who believes that advertising must inevitably debase a programme; on the contrary, I was left with the feeling that the contribution the advertiser makes in money and the presence of advertising matter in a programme are matters largely irrelevant to the issue of whether the general level of programmes will be good or bad. What matters is the standard the administration sets for itself.

2. Films

Canada claims that the first exhibition of motion pictures anywhere in the world was made by two Canadians named Holland in New York in 1894, and that the first theatre specifically designed for the showing of motion picture films was opened by Ernest Ouimet in Montreal in 1907. It is a considerable responsibility to accept, and perhaps the debt to humanity is being paid by the National Film Board of Canada.

Production of films by the Canadian Government began in 1921 with a Motion Picture Bureau set up under the Department of Trade and Commerce. The Bureau achieved a satisfactory reputation as a producer of scenic and travel pictures but virtually perished of financial starvation during the middle 'thirties. The Canadian Government then asked John Grierson to make an investigation and his report, completed in 1938, formed the basis on which the National Film Board was set up by Act of Parliament in 1939, with the duty of producing and distributing films intended to "interpret Canada to Canadians and to other nations". John Grierson became the first Film Commissioner under the Board and remained in Canada until 1946.

For the war years the new Board's productions were as might have been expected. It won an "Oscar" from the Academy of Motion Picture Arts and Sciences, for "Churchill's Island" as the best documentary of 1941. It produced a scoop in the shape of "Zero Hour" the first picture of the Normandy landings to reach Canada in 1944. It ended the war with twelve production units, and a production schedule of 308 separate films for the year. The momentum of its wartime work carried it over until 1946 and it was in that year that it laid the foundations for its post-war productive life by a successful change from aspects of the war and Canada to aspects of the Canadian people and their problems at home. The tide in favour of reduced expenditure was bound to set in, but the National Film Board had established its reputation in time to escape being loosed from its moorings.

The most important achievement of the National Film Board during the war years was its success in building up an organisation for the distribution and exhibition of non-entertainment films throughout Canada flexibly designed to make use of the existing patterns of Canadian life. This organisation rested mainly on voluntary work and it escaped two serious disadvantages in consequence. An organisation built up and maintained solely by a federal staff would inevitably, sooner or later, have attracted the criticism that it was an infringement of provincial freedom and a step in the direction of a totalitarian state, thrusting state propaganda down the population's throat. It would also have been the type of organisation only too easily hamstrung by the budget cut that was, some day, bound to come.

Distribution and exhibition during the war were primarily intended to take the films out of the towns into the country. The Board's operations were based on the rural circuit, the area that could be covered by one man in four weeks of constant travelling.

Each circuit had one full-time field representative, organiser, transporter and projectionist. It was to his interest to build up local committees and a reserve of competent projectionists in each area, and gradually these people themselves became interested in and responsible for the whole organisation in their area, and for the cost of the equipment; equally the field representative gradually became a film adviser and salesman of ideas rather than an operative. There are now some 343 local film councils over the whole of Canada, all voluntary bodies and representing nearly 8,000 voluntary organisations of every description. In 1952 the Film Board's audiences totalled 11,610,232 people.

The Board now produces some 200 films a year, about half of which are one reel in length. They cover every side of Canadian activity, from mental health to soil composition; from a biography of a Canadian painter to the training of N.A.T.O. airmen by the Royal Canadian Air Force. One third of its main projects in 1952 were in the French language and a quarter were in colour. It had a budget of $3,500,000, of which about two-thirds was Government subsidy and the remainder earned. It can look forward to an expanding market in production for showing on television.

The Board is established. It has good relations with all provincial governments, save that of Quebec. It sold abroad nearly 6,000 prints of its colour film "Royal Journey", of the tour of Canada by the Queen, then Princess Elizabeth, and the Duke of Edinburgh. A seven-year-old girl in Ontario remembered from a film a method of saving life in a fire and applied the lesson in her own home, to the advantage of herself and her two-year-old brother.

3. The Railways

And now for the material links.

The history of the railways of Canada is a remarkable compound of enterprise, optimism, national strategy, political opportunism, technical skill and plain dishonesty; in that, of course, save for the element of national strategy, it resembles the history of the railways of the British Isles. Likewise the major problems of the railways today, rising costs, government control over freight rates, civil service time-lag in the disposal of applications for their increase, and the loss of the most remunerative classes of traffic to road transport, can be duplicated on this side of the Atlantic. Passages from the President's last address to the shareholders of the Canadian Pacific Railway could be switched with paragraphs in the latest report of the British Transport Commission and no one would notice the exchange.

The two main railway systems of Canada are the Canadian Pacific Railway and the Canadian National Railways. The ordinary stock of the Canadian Pacific Railway is still privately owned, 49 per cent by individuals in the United States, 26 per cent in the United Kingdom and 16 per cent by Canadians. The Canadian National Railways is an amalgamation, established by Federal Act in 1919 and operating as a unified system since 1923. Of its capital, some $4½ million of what might be called equity stock is privately owned. The public are also interested in some of the preferred stock, which is now a quasi-government security; the remainder of the equity is government owned. Over traffic, it can hardly be said that the two companies are in competition; in fact, the Canadian National-Canadian Pacific Act of 1933 directs both to agree on such co-operative measures as will produce economies in each of the two systems. They are, however, competitive in prestige and performance and, because of the different natures of their ownerships, they cannot ever reach a fundamental alliance.

THE CANADIAN PACIFIC RAILWAY

Pride of place in rail transportation must go to the Canadian Pacific Railway; and it has been more than a mere railway. In inception, in construction and in operation, it has played a great part in the history of Canada. The promise of a railway to the Pacific was an element in the compact under which British Columbia entered the Confederation, and the method, and the financing, of its construction is a part of the political history of both Sir John Macdonald's and Alexander Mackenzie's governments. Once completed, the C.P.R. became a major immigration agency for the peopling of Canada, indirectly because it existed, directly because it needed the traffic that only the work of the immigrants would provide. This is no place to attempt a proper history of the line, but here is an outline of its inception and development.

In the summer of 1871, British Columbia joined the Confederation and the ten-year period within which the Federal Government was to promote a trans-continental railway began to run.

The Conservatives under Sir John Macdonald were in office and had made the bargain. The Liberals were in opposition and were opposed to the promise as given to British Columbia and to the railway as planned. It was, they said, both a financial and a physical impossibility. They were voted down, of course, and in the fall of the year the House of Commons at Ottawa resolved that the railway should be built by a specially incorporated company (the Canadian Pacific Railway becoming ultimately the chosen instrument). Forthwith two rival groups, one in Montreal and the other in Toronto, began to get together syndicates to undertake the contract—to become the C.P.R. in fact—whereupon the Government began its negotiations to bring the two groups together, desiring that a railway intended to bind all Canada together should not begin by dividing Quebec and Montreal still further. In the general election of 1872, although the Conservatives retained power, they lost ground. In 1873, the Pacific Scandal broke.

The Pacific Scandal was an allegation that the Conservative Party had promised the contract for what was to be the C.P.R. to Sir Hugh Allen and his associates, the Montreal group, in exchange for considerable contributions by Sir Hugh Allen and his associates to the party's election funds for the 1872 election. Sir Hugh Allen had undoubtedly subscribed to the Conservatives' party funds, but he had been told, so Sir John Macdonald protested, that his group would not be given the privilege of building the railway, that there would be an amalgamation of the Quebec and Ontario interests, and, Sir John subsequently added in his apologia to the Governor-General, only one of the thirteen directors ultimately appointed could be called a Sir Hugh Allen nominee. The verdict of history seems to be that Sir John was personally honest, that Sir Hugh certainly wanted to build the line and was prepared to pay money to advance his aims, and that the standards of Canadian politics of the day did not wholly rule out private contributions to party funds from aspiring beneficiaries under future contracts. It also remains a fact that the head office of the C.P.R. is and always has been in Montreal. A general election followed in 1874, the Conservatives were defeated and the Liberals took office, to hold it until 1878.

The Liberal Prime Minister was Alexander Mackenzie, a Scot by birth, as was Sir John Macdonald, but a dour man whereas

Macdonald was a gay and some would say feckless Highlander.
The Conservative view of the C.P.R. was that it should be built
as rapidly as possible because its building would open up the
country through which it ran. The Liberal view was that it should
be built as and when the country through which it ran did open
itself up. The Liberals, in short, did not believe in a ten-year
gallop to British Columbia. "You will see how unlikely it was that
that road, with all the power of man and all the money in Europe,
could have been completed in 1881," said Mackenzie, at Sarnia,
Ontario, in October 1875, and with that rather pessimistic view in
the mind of the Prime Minister it is hardly surprising that, when
Macdonald took office again, in 1878, only two stretches of line,
totalling 264 miles, had been finished. So, from the start, the C.P.R.
came to symbolise two opposing views on the development of
Canada.

Having won the 1878 election, Sir John Macdonald set about
redeeming his promise to British Columbia, but he had first to
find the money needed for the construction of the whole railway
in one operation. He found it, in London in 1880, but at a price.
The Canadian Government insisted that the C.P.R., once re-
launched, should accept an obligation to complete the whole line
by 1 May 1891, and that it should deposit $1,000,000, as a guaran-
tee for that performance, but those who provided the finance insisted that the company should be given a grant of $25 million
towards the cost and a free gift of 25,000,000 acres of land in
blocks along the line of the route from Winnipeg to the Rockies.
The contract was signed in Ottawa on 21 October 1880, and
ratified, after a hot debate, by Parliament with a vote of 128
to 49. The Company was incorporated in February 1881.

Construction began at once, from either end. The company
needed two loans from the Government (both later repaid) to
meet the wages needed to finish the line but, on 7 November 1885,
Donald Smith, President of the C.P.R. and later the first Lord
Strathcona, drove in the last spike to join the two sections at a
spot twenty-eight miles west of Revelstoke, in British Columbia.
On 24 July 1886, fifteen years to the day after the signing of the
agreement with British Columbia, Sir John Macdonald arrived at
the British Columbia terminus by train from Ottawa on what can
only be described as a state visit. But for an unfortunate intervention of a Liberal Government, he might well have then said, the

11.   British Columbia: Vancouver

12.   British Columbia: Timber in Honeymoon Bay

bargain with British Columbia might have been honoured to the letter.

The C.P.R. was the first Canadian line across the continent and it set about reaping what benefit it could derive from the circumstance, by extending branch lines, by building up immigration and by acquiring and developing land. Before 1896, it was comparatively easy for any company developing the prairies to acquire land from the Federal Government, in whom it was then vested. A development company might buy land at two dollars an acre, payable by instalments, on condition it provided colonists for the land at the rate of two per square mile. If it completed its settlement programme as contracted, it received a rebate on the price due for the land of $120 for each settler. The railways, particularly the C.P.R., became wholesalers, and stockists, of land right across the prairies. Over the construction of one branch line alone the C.P.R. earned 1,400,000 acres. By 1923, it had sold no less than 18,000,000 acres of agricultural land, at prices ranging from $3.20 an acre, in 1900, to $20.48 an acre, the highest figure before 1940, in the boom of 1920. After 1896 the practice of granting land to railways as part of the inducement to them to construct fresh lines was ended; thereafter a new railway project might look for support in the shape of subsidies or loans in cash, not for aid in kind.

But the C.P.R. was more than a passive agent. In its year of greatest all-round expansion, 1913, it is estimated that it spent nearly $100 million on capital works and improvements, more than the total cost of the original line. In 1912 it took over some 650,000 acres in Southern Alberta, in the Lethbridge area, and spent some $15 million on irrigation, including the construction of 3,400 miles of canal. It bent another section of activities to fostering immigration and land settlement, through the Canadian Land Settlement Association and the Colonial Finance Corporation, which was finally replaced by the Dominion Agricultural Credit Corporation. The C.P.R. was first in the field and it never lost the advantages that gave it, but, in Canada's years of greatest prairie expansion, up to 1914, while the company certainly made money, it worked for it.

THE CANADIAN NATIONAL RAILWAYS

The Canadian National Railways system is an amalgamation of five major railways originally privately owned and operated. The

L

first, the Intercolonial, was the first major Canadian railway project and largely political in conception, intended to link the Maritime provinces with Quebec and to give the St. Lawrence Valley access to the Atlantic ports that were clear of ice all the year round. The idea of such a railway was older than the Confederation and a common desire to proceed with its construction was one of the understandings that shaped the intentions of the men who brought Confederation itself into being. The Intercolonial opened for traffic between Halifax and Levis, opposite Quebec City, on 1 July 1876. The Prince Edward Island section of the Canadian National Railways came under Federal ownership in 1873. The provincial government had made a contract for the construction of a railway at a fixed rate of $25,000 a mile, but had not limited the number of miles that the contractor should be permitted to squeeze out of the province. By the time the contractor was well on the way down his serpentine track to fortune, the people of Prince Edward Island were so scared of what the final bill would be that they accepted Confederation (which they had rejected in 1867) provided the Federal Government paid for the railway.

The second, the National Transcontinental, was primarily intended to link Moncton, New Brunswick, directly with Winnipeg, across a thousand miles of then almost uninhabited country in Quebec. It was financed by the Federal Government, given the benefit of a Government built bridge across the St. Lawrence at Quebec City, and placed under the management of the Grand Trunk Railway on favourable terms to the company. The project was, at its start, of considerable benefit to the contractors who built it. It also opened up, almost by chance, the areas of Quebec and Ontario that now produce so much of Canada's timber and metals.

The third, the Grand Trunk Railway, linked Ontario and Quebec, with connections stretching south into the United States; when it became part of the C.N.R. system in 1923, about a quarter of its 4,776 miles of track were in the United States. It built the first railway line from Montreal to Toronto in 1856, the first railway bridge over the St. Lawrence at Montreal in 1859, and the first railway tunnel between Canada and the United States under the St. Clair River in 1891. By 1900 it was anxious to extend to the Pacific, with the result that, while the Government built the National Transcontinental line, the Grand Trunk formed the

Grand Trunk Pacific and set out from Winnipeg for the West. The Grand Trunk had a Government guarantee of $13,000 a mile towards the cost of the line across the prairies and of 75 per cent of the cost of the mountain section, free of interest to the company for the first seven years. The rest of the money required was subscribed by a bedazzled public, mainly in the United Kingdom. Construction began in 1905 and on 9 April 1914, the lines from Winnipeg and Prince Rupert met at a point 374 miles east of Prince Rupert. It was remarkable that they met at all, for the company was then in financial difficulties, and in 1919 the Government appointed a receiver. In the end, after the Taft arbitration in 1921, both preference and ordinary stockholders found, when the Government finally absorbed the whole undertaking, that all they had subscribed to the country's development had gone.

The Canadian Northern Railway was a very different affair. It can be described as a line put together on a shoe-string by two men, William Mackenzie and Donald Mann. They were financial geniuses of the painstaking kind. They began in 1896 by buying a charter granted seven years before to the Lake Manitoba Railway and Canal Company, and then followed a series of transactions, mergers, the acquisition of running rights, and leases, the picking up of charters, and provincial government guarantees, which built up their railway empire. They reached the Atlantic at Lunenburg, Nova Scotia, in 1903, Edmonton, Alberta, in 1905, and finally the Pacific, at Vancouver, in 1915. In 1918, in financial difficulties, their railway was dumped in the lap of the Government.

It was the Pacific that lured them all on. Like Cortez, the directors longed to stand on their peaks, and think, as probably Cortez thought, of gold. As a child, my earliest recollection of anything connected with Canada is of the name "Prince Rupert" on a brochure that must have been pressed into my small hand by some over-enthusiastic salesman of Grand Trunk Pacific scrip. If the companies had been content to stay east of the Rockies they might have remained solvent. If they had, Canada would have been that much the poorer in so many other ways. The first dozen years of the century were the days of a great wave of immigration from Europe, and of expanding wheat exports to Europe, moving eastwards only by rail, since the Panama Canal was not yet open. The C.P.R. was already across the continent. The others arrived too late to reap the full benefit of the traffic of those years.

The C.P.R. had always one great advantage. It carried through the bulk of its construction before 1910, before the time when costs, in both labour and materials, began to rise fast. It acquired its land when the prairies were empty and seemingly valueless, when the Government was disposed to give land away by the square mile. For the others, the interest-free years of the loans ended all too soon. Today, the C.P.R. enjoys an income approaching $4 million a year from the oil under 11 million acres of Government granted lands, and it still has the almost fortuitous benefit of its ownership of stock in the Consolidated Mining and Smelting Company (which, in 1951, paid a dividend of $2.20 a share on the 8,412,500 shares held by the C.P.R.). The C.N.R., until the last financial reorganisation in 1951, carried fixed interest charges of $47 million, twice its present net income.

The manner of the growth of the railways in Canada forms a rich and rewarding study in capitalist development, of the late nineteenth-century pattern. On the credit side are the railways themselves, the blossoming of the country that has followed their coming, and the fact that Canada has acquired the political ability to use and maintain such an asset to such good advantage. On the debit side are the wasted millions, the money that could have been saved had a dictatorial planner, gifted with foresight enough to read accurately forty years beyond his time, been in charge of the whole operation. Of course the answer is that no planner has that foresight and no dictator could have extracted those millions from the pockets of the people who owned them in 1900. The planner of 1900, in the United Kingdom as well as in Canada, would have had the mind of Alexander Mackenzie, and there would have been no C.P.R. at all, to prove him wrong.

OPERATIONS

Freight rates are an important element in all Canadian costs and are therefore ever present in the Canadian mind. It was a feeling that the C.P.R. was a monopoly, and the conviction therefore that its freight rates must be unfair, that supplied a great deal of the political impetus that carried the Grand Trunk Pacific and the Canadian Northern lines across Canada to the Pacific. It was the same feeling that drove the C.N.R. northwards to Churchill, on the Hudson Bay, despite great reluctance on the part of the Federal Government. Mr. W. A. Mather, President of the C.P.R., in his address to shareholders in May 1953, skated lightly over some of the difficulties of the past but put the position fairly enough when he said:

> The historic pattern (of the rates), established at a time when railways were the only effective means of overland transportation, was intended to encourage the opening up of new land areas and to develop the commerce of a young nation. It is therefore understandable that a dominant consideration should have been to insure that the products of the farm, the forest and the mine would be moved to the market-place at minimum rates. . .

> The practical application of this early policy found expression in what is known as the value of service principle. Relatively low rates were granted for low-valued and raw commodities. Higher rates governed the movement of processed commodities and those of high values. When first established, the low rates for low-value primary products covered the direct costs of rail haulage and made a relatively small contribution to overhead.

In terms of 1952 costs, the overall average freight cost was 1·3 cents per ton-mile, while the individual rates ranged from one-half a cent per ton-mile to over ten cents per ton-mile. Now, Mr. Mather continued, the situation is vastly different, and he went on to the familiar story of competition from the road haulier, based on the fact that the processed and high-value commodities are exactly those that the haulier can handle and deliver more conveniently as well as more cheaply than the railway.

The railways have not only direct competition to meet. Their road competitors are freer to fix and adjust their rates as they wish and to meet the individual customer, while the railways face the complicated procedure of an application to the Board of Transport Commissioners of Canada before their freight rates may be changed. The largest post-war application, one for a 35 per cent general increase, was filed in October 1946. The Commissioners, as they are bound to do, held public hearings and received evidence in each province, and sat for 150 days. Their final sitting was in Ottawa in December, 1947, and they did not deliver judgment until 30 March 1948, when they allowed a 21 per cent increase. By that time, of course, costs had risen further. The present battle over freight rates is complicated still further by a demand, discussed in the Report of the Royal Commission on Transport in 1951, for equalisation of rates throughout Canada.

The railways of Canada remain the basic traffic arteries of the country, and because of that they raise the common problem of transportation today. They must be kept efficient, which needs continuing capital expenditure. They must be maintained and offer reasonable conditions of work, which means that operating costs still rise. They must be competitive, which limits the amounts by which their rates can be raised. They are a political problem, in Canada as everywhere, but in Canada there is this additional complication; to what extent can the Federal Government sub-sidise the C.N.R. without subsidising the C.P.R.? If it does not discriminate between the two systems, it is open to be accused of subsidising a privately owned concern with public money. If it does discriminate in favour of its own child, it can be accused of wilfully injuring a corporation which is half owned by citizens of the United States. The 1951 Royal Commission was against unifi-cation of the Canadian railways under state ownership (only the provinces of Saskatchewan and Prince Edward Island raised the question even tentatively) but the day may come when the C.P.R. lines are transferred into public ownership and, if the terms are reasonable and the C.P.R. stockholders are left with their other assets, they may well fare better as a result.

4. Air Lines

The development of civil aviation in Canada has been a success-ful compound of private and public enterprise, and the existing shape of the national organisation owes a great deal to the drive and breadth of vision of Mr. C. D. Howe, the first Minister of Transport. The present phase in development began in 1936. At that time Canada possessed a number of small operating com-panies, a great deal of practical experience, particularly of bush flying in and out of the North, and a supply of trained men, but no scheduled transcontinental services. The years of the depres-sion had left the existing operators with inadequate equipment and few cash reserves. If Canada were to be given an adequate system of internal air communications, both Government and operators would need to spend a great deal of money on capital equipment. It would fall to the Government to provide the framework of facilities without which scheduled services could not operate with speed, regularity and safety. The operators would need to spend money on new aircraft large and fast enough to use such facilities to their full, and on maintaining those fleets in operation, probably at a loss, for long enough to establish an adequate public response. It was a situation in which the Government must take the first step, and the creation of a separate Ministry of Transport, and the appointment of the engineer, Mr. C. D. Howe, as its Minister, was that first step.

TRANS-CANADA AIR LINES

The first proposal the new Ministry evolved was that an operating corporation should be set up in which the C.P.R. and the C.N.R. and the Government would each have a third share. This the C.P.R. did not accept; it declined to supply finance to a corporation in which it would be in a perpetual minority and in which the remaining two-thirds of the capital would be controlled by the Federal Government. Equally, the Government was not prepared to finance a corporation in which a private corporation, the C.P.R., would have majority control, which was the C.P.R.'s alternative suggestion. When agreement was clearly impossible the Government decided to create its own corporation, Trans-Canada Airlines, established by Federal Act of Parliament in May 1937. This Act empowers T.C.A. to establish, operate and maintain regular services of aircraft of all kinds. The corporation has a capital of $25 million and its shares are vested in C.N.R.. Parallel with the creation of T.C.A. the Ministry of Transport began its work of preparing airfields and navigational aids across Canada.

T.C.A.'s first scheduled passenger service, from Vancouver to Seattle, began on 1 September 1937 with ten-seater Lockheed Electras. Scheduled mail services across the Rockies between Vancouver and Winnipeg began on 1 October 1938. Six months later a regular passenger service from Montreal to Vancouver was in operation and by the end of 1939 it had been extended to Moncton, New Brunswick. Canada had the framework of its transcontinental air line.

Trans-Atlantic flying had been pioneered by Imperial Airways and Pan-American Airways, and can really be said to have begun, as a commercial activity, at the conferences called by Newfoundland in 1933, and by Canada in 1935. For their initial surveys, the operating companies used flying boats, making Botwood, in Newfoundland, their staging point, and the first regular Imperial Airways flight, weekly, from Southampton to New York, began on 8 August 1939. The war killed that six weeks later. The war also killed the tentative plan that had been agreed at Ottawa, in 1935, that the North Atlantic passenger air service should be the responsibility of a single corporation, in which the governments of Canada, the United Kingdom, the United States, Newfoundland and Eire should be interested and of which Imperial Airways and Pan-American Airways should form the nucleus of the executive limbs. Aircraft development during the six war years, the improvement in meteorological information and service, the completion of airports at Gander, Goose Bay, in Labrador, and Keflavik, in Iceland, all made it clear, by 1945, that the northern route across the Atlantic had become no more difficult or hazardous than any other air route across the world.

No country saw greater development in the air during the war than did Canada. It was the training ground of the Commonwealth air forces. One hundred and forty-three new airfields across Canada, including those of the North Western staging route to Alaska and beyond, were built. The Canadian aircraft industry began. So, too, did the Canadian Government's Trans-Atlantic Air Service, which by 1945 was flying passengers to and from Europe on a regular service schedule. Tickets were sold at T.C.A. offices and a steward had become a regular member of the crew. By 1946 the civil air lines of North Atlantic countries were ready to extend across the Atlantic. T.C.A. joined them when it took over the Canadian Government's war-time service on 1 May 1947.

CANADIAN PACIFIC AIR LINES

The C.P.R. had rejected the 1936 plan for a joint airways corporation for Canada. It was not, however, uninterested in commercial air services. It had purchased a holding in Canadian Airways Limited in 1937, and in 1941 it carried through a merger of Canadian Airways with a number of smaller companies, mainly operating in the west, into a new company, Canadian Pacific Airlines, which it wholly owns. The internal services maintained in Canada by C.P.A. now run mainly north and south, in Alberta, British Columbia, Yukon and the North West, with another division in Quebec along the St. Lawrence Valley. T.C.A. has a monopoly of the full transcontinental service, and eastwards and southwards from Montreal. In 1948, C.P.A. was given a licence for the Pacific routes westwards and southwards from Vancouver. Its services to Australia, New Zealand and to Hong Kong via Tokio began in July 1949 and the services to Mexico, Peru and Brazil in 1953. T.C.A. and C.P.A. are not directly competitive in their scheduled services for passengers. They may be in the future over freight.

Two other Canadian air services should be mentioned: Maritime Central Airways Limited, operating from New Brunswick and Nova Scotia north-eastwards to Prince Edward Island, Newfoundland and the French islands of St. Pierre and Miquelon, and Queen Charlotte Airlines Limited, operating water-borne aircraft northwards up the British Columbian coast from Vancouver. There are also a vast number of non-scheduled operators, from the single civil flyer to the charter fleet. Their work and importance in the north is immense and it is significant that, in 1951, they flew 151,676 hours to the scheduled lines, 194,659.

OPERATIONS

Air transport in Canada is established. It is safe. T.C.A. had no fatal casualty between 1947 and 1954. It is becoming cheaper. In 1928, the rate from Winnipeg to Calgary was 15c. a mile; it is now 7c. a mile, which as in Europe compares with railway fares plus overnight sleeper accommodation. It is regular and punctual. It is used. The growth of traffic is shown by these figures:

COMMERCIAL AIR CARRIER TRAFFIC, 1922 to 1952

	1922	1938	1947	1952
Passenger miles	184,928	13,530,746	257,945,385	839,587,265
Freight: lbs.	14,681	19,623,133	34,241,378	12,654,572
Mail: lbs.	62,025	1,901,711	6,965,895	18,328,310

It can also be profitable; at least to T.C.A. In 1952, on operating revenues of $55 million, T.C.A. managed to make a net income of $2,757,000, out of which it paid $750,000 interest on capital,

$1,200,000 in income tax and was left with a surplus of $807,000. Nor did it receive any concealed subsidy in the shape of favourable contracts for transporting the mails. In 1943, mail revenues accounted for over 40 per cent of its receipts. In 1952, the percentage had fallen to 14 per cent.

The war aided the smaller airline companies to modernise their fleets from civil aircraft that were surplus after 1945. For all the operators it provided benefits in the shape of development work on aircraft. The longer services of T.C.A., for example, are based on the "North Star", a 48-passenger, four-engined machine produced in Canada by Canadair Limited, and powered by four Rolls-Royce Merlin engines. The North Star was designed for the R.C.A.F. as a transport aircraft and is comfortable and reliable (if noisy), with a cruising speed of 260/280 m.p.h. T.C.A. regards it as one of the most reliable and efficient four-engined transports in the world but this year it has begun to replace it on external services by eight Super Constellations and will supplement it on internal services with Vickers Viscounts, of which it has already ordered fifteen. In 1947 a North Star cost $650,000; today, a Vickers Viscount costs nearly $1,000,000, and a Super Constellation over $1,500,000 (true, this has almost twice the seating capacity of a North Star). The smaller operators face a greater relative rise in replacement costs. They could buy a war surplus D.C.-3 in 1946 for $25,000; today a new one costs some $200,000. But, by May this year, all T.C.A. North Stars had been 100 per cent depreciated; that is, their original cost had been written off completely. That fleet will then gradually be converted to freight carriers.

It is surprising that air freight has not developed faster in Canada; in 1952, T.C.A. could report that less than one half of the freight capacity in its passenger aircraft across Canada had been used, and revenue from freight has yet to reach as much as 10 per cent of its total operating revenues. C.P.A. suggest that in part that is due to T.C.A.'s monopoly position in the full trans-continental service and last year it applied for a freight licence for that route. T.C.A. disputed the allegation and the application was refused by the Air Transport Board. T.C.A. is in a curious position. It has no monopoly, of course, on routes outside Canada; in fact it meets heavy competition. It has not a complete monopoly in Canada, but it defends the position that it has there because it is a public corporation. "The people of Canada", said the President of T.C.A. in evidence before the Board on the C.P.A.'s application, "now have an investment and equity in Trans-Canada Air Lines totalling more than $31 million. In my view this investment and equity of the people of Canada is entitled to protection from the threat of duplication of service entailing economic waste"; the classic answer of the holder of a monopoly. Yet T.C.A. remains one of the most efficient, if not the most efficient, airlines in the world. It will be interesting to see how the air freight struggle develops in Canada. T.C.A. will be in a very strong position. Will it be able to make the same strides forward in air freight development as it has already in passenger traffic? Will C.P.A. succeed in convincing the Air Transport Board that competition, not duplication, is the end for which it strives?

Important and valuable as the war was to all aspects of Canadian aviation, its chief benefit must have been the men it trained and handed over to civil flying afterwards. The present President of T.C.A., Mr. Gordon McGregor, is a case in point. He was born in 1901. Before the war he was a district manager for the Bell Telephone Company Limited and a part-time flyer. He joined the R.C.A.F. reserve in 1938 and at the age of thirty-eight was a Flight Lieutenant in a fighter squadron at Northolt from which he saw the Battle of Britain and shot down five German aircraft. In 1942 he was in Alaska and is credited with the only Japanese aircraft shot down on American soil. He finished the war in command of 126 Wing, the first fighter wing to land in and operate from Normandy. On his release he was invited by the President of T.C.A. to become his special representative, or "trouble-shooter", and in 1948 he succeeded Mr. H. J. Symington as President.

It is instructive to contrast his career with that of the President of the C.P.R., Mr. W. A. Mather. Mr. Mather is twenty-six years older. He has been in the service of the C.P.R. all his life, from the time when he first worked for it in his vacations from McGill University, Montreal. He graduated as a civil engineer and he knows both the engineering and the operating sides of the line, from Montreal to Vancouver. But it was his first ten years in the company's service that he saw the peak of the railway expansion in Canada. Today, the railways may add stretches of track to their existing systems but the main pattern is set. The task of Mr. Mather is to consolidate and improve what exists, to wring a better performance out of an existing machine. In the air neither machines nor methods are settled.

Most of the men in the various Canadian airlines have seen service with the R.C.A.F., the R.A.F. or the U.S.A.F. and learnt the essential lessons of care, sharpness of mind and rapidity of decision. The problem today is their replacement, for the qualities needed are of the highest order, and these are reflected in the salaries they can earn, of up to $14,000 a year. Fortunately, the Canadian, by temperament, is well suited to the needs of civil flying. He is cautious. He believes in methods of safety to a greater extent than does his American opposite number. He is intelligent and his country leaves him with no illusions over the risks that only carefulness can avoid. Over most of the country he need only look down to see the penalty for mistake. He is stubborn, and he is not too imaginative. To fly in Canada is to learn a good deal about Canadians as well as of their country.

7

The Economics of Prosperity

OVER Canada's present-day prosperity there are three questions to be answered:

1. On what is that prosperity based?
2. What are the forces that keep the economy in balance?
3. What are the prospects for the future?

Canada's life as a nation and her present-day prosperity rest on the fact that she has the commodities and the services that other countries need, and the ability to make them available on a competitive basis. That is an obvious statement. It is equally true of all countries whose economics are dependent on their exports. It is true, too, that twenty-five years ago, not only did all Canada's present resources exist; with the exception of the oil and the uranium, they were known to exist. What has changed in the twenty-five years has been the size of the world's demands for the raw materials that Canada can provide and the skills of the world's technicians in their extraction and use.

When anyone in Canada talks of the future of his country, he will before very long refer to the Paley Report, more fully, the report to the President of the United States on "The Resources of Freedom" made by the President's Materials Policy Commission in June 1952. That report has become the flag at Canada's economic masthead. The essence of that survey is that the United States has already crossed the great industrial divide. She is no longer a supplying nation; she has become a receiving nation. She must look forward to an increasing dependency on the outside world for her supplies of iron ore, copper, lead, zinc, timber and oil. In

1900, the report says, the United States produced 15 per cent more raw materials than she herself used. By 1950, she was importing 9 per cent of her needs. In another twenty-five years the percentage of these essential imports may have risen to 25 per cent; the United States may even have to import water. Canada on the other hand is well short of that divide. Within her borders lie many of the raw materials—wood-pulp, nickel, uranium, even iron ore, that the United States has either never had or has already used up. Canada's growth began fifty years ago, because she could sell wheat in ever increasing quantities to Europe. It will continue, she hopes, because she will be able to supply ever increasing quantities of other primary commodities to the rest of the world, including the United States.

That is not the sole basis of her prosperity, nor a situation which she desires shall remain unchanged. Every ton of raw material exported unprocessed is an export of an equivalent amount of potential employment for Canadians. It is better to sell doors and door frames, for instance, than timber in the round, provided the manufactured article is itself competitive. In common with every other nation that is a source of raw materials, Canada desires to increase her own manufactures, and they do grow. Forty years ago, two-thirds of Canadian exports were raw materials wholly unprocessed. Now the proportion has fallen to less than a third. Canada cannot hoard her raw materials until she herself can use them all, but the tendency, and the incentive, to process them within Canada is there.

The rise in the general standard of living over the last twenty-five years has been impressive. Income per head, after tax, is some two-thirds higher, in terms of purchasing power, than in 1926. In the same terms, one third more is spent on food and on clothing. Excluding defence expenditure entirely, the amount spent on government services has more than doubled, and that in terms of a dollar of constant value. Hours of work in the manufacturing industries fell by ten hours a week between 1926 and 1952. In 1952 income per head was $1,257, which compared with $1,872 per head in the United States (and gave Canada the second highest standard of living, in terms of cash income, in the world). There is no doubt of the prosperity. Has it happened entirely by chance, or is it managed?

Canada has an economy based on free enterprise. "Free enterprise" is a vague expression but there is no better definition of it, in a Canadian context, than a quotation from a speech by Mr. St. Laurent, the Prime Minister, in a debate on natural resources in May 1953. He said: "We are all most happy when free enterprise does what is required to be done and public authorities do not have to intervene." That sentence, of course, begs a great many questions—what is required? when and to what extent should the public authorities intervene?—yet it describes very fairly the atmosphere in which the economy of the country functions.

A NATION IN BALANCE

A proper account of Canada's economic development over the last fifteen years would take a book in itself. The immediate question is whether Canada's growth has been balanced, and there is more than one answer to that. Is Canada balanced in the sense that she is self-sufficient? No. She produces more than she needs of some things, not enough of others, none at all of such primary products as cotton or rice. But complete self-sufficiency is not a state which she could ever attain, even if she desired. Has her industrial expansion been balanced? That, too, is a question the meaning of which depends very much on what is in the mind of the person who asks it, but at least there is one reasonably comprehensive answer. If Canada's growth, if the lines of development she has followed, had been unsound, one would have expected the mistakes to show up in terms of unemployment. Until last year, the average of unemployment since the war had not risen above 2½ per cent of the working population. In 1952 it was 130,000 out of a total labour force of some five and a half million. Only towards the end of last year were there signs of a more than seasonal rise.

The one balance that is most essential to her continued advance, that of her external trade, is the one over which she can never hope to have full control, but at least she is perfectly aware of the need for expansion. In an article "Canada's Trade Policy" by the Federal Minister of Trade and Commerce, Mr. C. D. Howe, in the spring of 1950 issue of *Public Affairs*, he wrote:

Our broad policy in Canada is to pursue measures that will strengthen our position as a major trading nation, both as a buyer and as a seller—and to do so with the maximum emphasis on positive, expansive methods and the minimum reliance upon the restrictive. We must continue to bend every effort towards keeping the door wide open to the return of multilateral trading practices throughout the world.

And, if Europe desires to buy wheat, or the United States wood-pulp, Canada is a source of supply to which each must turn.

A virtually important balance is that of the internal economy of the country. The principal danger, the most insidious risk in a dynamic and expanding society, in the conditions that Canada has experienced for almost fifteen years, is inflation. In those conditions, the defences against the dangers of inflation, the upward rising spiral of prices and wages, with wages always behind, and fixed incomes hopelessly out-distanced, depend upon the habits and propensities of the people and the ability with which their government either manages or controls those habits and propensities.

When a country is expanding its means of production fast, this is the kind of situation that arises. A company, say, employs 1,000 men at $50 a week for a year to build an aluminium smelter. Over the year, that company pays out $260,000 in wages, not a cent of which can be spent on the products of that factory; there are none. The men who receive that $260,000 must either save it or bid up for the products of other, existing factories. Repeat that situation on a grand scale and there is the risk of inflation, a country of people looking for things on which to spend their earnings. An expansion of buying power of this kind may have a damaging by-product; because of this immediate increase in available money, with a corresponding rise in demand, the manufacturers of consumable goods are encouraged to increase their plants at once, and they begin to bid for the materials that should be going into the aluminium smelter or the power station. The essential feature of every economic society is that, at any given moment, the supply of all resources is limited and cannot be increased at more than a certain, and a comparatively slow, rate. The greater the proportion of those resources devoted to the production of things not for immediate sale, the greater the pressure to buy the remaining articles that are for sale.

How did Canada escape from—or at least diminish—the difficulties of this period? In various ways, in part by adroit government action, in part by favourable circumstance. Again very broadly, the main factors at work were these:

1. The wave of increased incomes, and so of increased potential demand, brought by the war reached the farmers first; the total income of the farmer jumped from $548 million in 1941 to $1089 million in 1942, of other businesses from $587 million to no more than $671 million. But this almost doubled money came to the farmer at the end of years of depression and drought. It was used first in paying debts (which handed the money back to institutions whose business it was to save) and then it was accumulated against the day when new equipment could be bought. The farmer has less opportunity than the city dweller to spend his surplus income on consumer goods, and so a greater propensity to save. The impetus to advance in Canada after the war, and the financial resources to put behind it, first came from the large wartime savings within the country.

Further, by its dollar aid to Europe, particularly to the United Kingdom, the Canadian Government assisted very considerably the smooth transition of the economy to peace conditions. It assured the farmer of a continuing market and so gave him confidence enough in his future to induce him to spend his savings on new equipment, on what are called durable consumer goods. Equally, the demands for these helped the manufacturers in the reconversion of their factories from the manufacture of military equipment to that of farm machinery, for example.

2. A second important factor was the proximity of the United States. The United States has played two important roles in Canada's development since the war. It has supplied, and is supplying, the risk capital needed to develop the oil and the iron ore. It supplied the consumer goods that the wage-earning Canadian wished to buy with his wages.

Nineteen-forty-seven was a difficult year for Canada. The pre-war triangle of trade, by which Canada earned a surplus from her trade with Europe and ran a deficit on her trade with the United States, had been broken. Canada could still earn a surplus in Europe, but only of European currencies, and these were not good legal tender in the United States. Europe's gold and dollar reserves were running out and Marshall Aid was only a proposal, not a fact. In the fall of 1947 Canada was driven to impose restrictions on imports from the United States and on the use of the American

M

dollar. Three things brought about an improvement. Marshall Aid eased the position in Europe when dollars began to flow. The Geneva agreement on international trade (G.A.T.T.) reduced United States tariffs on direct exports from Canada and so raised their volume. The third was the discovery of the Leduc oilfield in Alberta. That altered American thinking about Canada. From then on a portion of the risk capital element in the United States began to move into Canada, bringing dollars with it, and that portion was, relative to Canada's size, large enough to carry the main burden of development in these new fields of Canadian activity.

Over the post-war period as a whole Canada has been a net exporter of capital, which is remarkable in a country expanding so fast. She has re-purchased capital previously held abroad, increased her holdings of foreign currency, met her own municipal and provincial borrowings, strengthened the structures of her established industries, and made considerable loans to other countries on government account, principally to the United Kingdom.

In short, Canada maintained a balance between the various calls on her own savings. Some have said she has been too cautious, but, if she has thereby allowed the United States to finance many of these new ventures and so establish a claim to a corresponding share in their future profits, she has benefited, and will benefit, from the increased tempo of growth. In a paper read in New York, in March 1953, Mr. Louis Rasminsky, Executive Assistant to the Governors of the Bank of Canada, made this claim:

> Our ability to pay a return on the foreign capital invested in Canada has grown more rapidly than the return we have been called upon to pay. There are two main reasons for this, both of which suggest that these large amounts of foreign capital have been put to good use in Canada. Our capacity to pay has grown rapidly because so much of the capital we invested was used to build up our export capacity, directly or indirectly, in industries in which we could compete effectively on world markets. And the foreign exchange return we have been called upon to make to foreign investors has increased slowly because many of them preferred to reinvest a portion of their Canadian earnings in further expansion of their Canadian enterprises.

Canada's other advantage was that the United States provided a source of supply of consumer goods for the Canadian market. If the Canadian people had been compelled to rely only on Canadian sources of supply for all the goods they could afford to buy, and wanted to buy, between 1949 and 1951, the risk of inflation in those years would have been severe. As it was, they shopped in the United States. For the years 1950 and 1951 Canada had again a deficit in her external trade: the Canadian people in 1951 spent $1,000 million more on imported merchandise than in the previous year, but in the changed circumstances then, this was something of a safety valve. Nor did the process reduce Canada's holdings of gold and American dollars because those were the years of the influx of American dollars, crossing into Canada partly to finance new ventures and partly because the Canadian dollar was then at a discount of 10 per cent with the American dollar. By 1952 the position had righted itself; the excess of the value of exports over that of imports was $150 million.

The table at Appendix II brings out two important facts; since the war the Canadian people as a whole have been saving about one-fifth of their gross national product, and during that time the total of these savings has kept pace with the total spent in capital development.

3. Another element has been resolute action by the Canadian Government in its financial policy. It has used the financial machine to manage rather than the dictatorial power of Defence Regulations to control. To some extent, in so doing it was making a virtue of necessity; as soon as the war ended the provincial governments clamoured for the return of the independence they had surrendered during the war, and attempts at continued control by wartime regulation would have met with great resistance. Yet governments do not always make virtues out of necessities. The Liberal Government was flexible enough in its approach to use, and use intelligently, the implements that did lie within reach of its hand.

The political differences between Canadians and British must be dealt with later, but there are great resemblances between the two systems of government. Canada, like the United Kingdom, has a government which is expected to govern. There is not in Canada the division of power, and so of responsibility, between legislature and executive there is in the United States between President and Congress. The Canadian budget is not an affair of compromises between President, Senate and House of Representatives, each with one eye on a different election date. Canada, too, resembles the United Kingdom in the relations between its central bank and the trading banks. The Bank of Canada is publicly owned, and the financial world is concentrated in Montreal, Toronto and Ottawa. When the authorities (to use a deliberately vague word) decided to restrict loans to certain classes of borrower and for certain purposes, the Bank of Canada called the chartered banks together in February 1951, and their subsequent statement on their agreed policy was as smooth, and as effective, as anything put out by the Bank of England after a cosy chat with the heads of the Big Five Joint Stock Banks in the City of London. And in Canada the directors of the Chartered Banks are themselves the presidents and directors of the large Canadian industrial corporations; it would be hard to say if the banks man industry or if industry mans the banks. And above all, Canada has an excellent civil service, and an admirable machine for the assembly of statistics. There is no excuse for any Minister, senior civil servant or banker in Canada not knowing what is happening. The figures are always there to tell him.

Such a system makes the Federal Budget, potentially, a powerful and flexible instrument in the management of the economy of Canada. The Federal Budget does not impose the whole of the taxation borne by the individual (the financial relations between Federal and provincial governments are dealt with later) but it does carry the full burden of defence expenditure, and, by 1953, the amount raised in taxation under the Federal Budget equalled one-fifth of the gross national product. Throughout the Federal Minister of Finance budgeted for a surplus and, when defence expenditure began to mount in 1951, he met those needs by decreasing civil expenditure, by adding a 20 per cent surtax to individual and corporate taxes and by raising the sales tax to 10 per cent.

4. Another factor has been selective immigration. An immigrant becomes a charge on a country's resources, in the shape of food and housing, from the moment he lands. He ceases to be a charge as soon as he is in work, but he then becomes an influence on the direction which the country's economy is taking. The immigrant will have a tendency to look for, or create, work of a kind which will use his existing skill, so, if a country's economy is to be kept

in balance, it is advisable to select in advance immigrants whose skills match the activities which it is desired to encourage. Between the end of the war and 30 June 1953, some 850,000 immigrants entered Canada and the Canadian authorities were firm and unsentimental over their selection.

At first they began by attempting to define on paper the categories of those skills which they would accept. They changed their methods, but not their ends, in 1950. By statutory order of 1 July 1950, written classifications were abolished and for them were substituted a general provision that all suitable entrants of European origin would be admitted. At the same time the authorities strengthened very considerably the administrative machine abroad which carried the duty of deciding who was "suitable". In short, immigrants to Canada are virtually hand-picked.

The result has been that immigrants have slipped into place, industrially, with remarkably little dislocation. The authorities did not find each one a job; they were not so very interested in men who would only move to a guaranteed job. But they knew, in general terms, that if, say, a hundred carpenters were reaching Canada in a certain month there would be, somewhere in Canada, approximately a hundred vacancies for carpenters. It was up to the individual to find, and choose, his place in the country. For the same reason the authorities preferred to expand immigration during the summer months, when the seasonal trades were more likely to be searching for men, although T.C.A. and the C.P.R. would have preferred to fill their aircraft and ships during the emptier winter months. Of course the Canadian authorities have been fortunate in being able to pick and choose, but, again, they made use of the opportunity.

5. A final element on the situation was the Canadian Government's attitude over housing. It set up a Central Mortgage and Housing Corporation, a Crown corporation, which both administers the Federal Housing Act and makes advances on mortgage (80 per cent in the normal case, 90 per cent if the house is connected with a defence project) provided the house is up to a minimum standard. It makes grants to veterans for the building of their own homes. But it has declined to follow the line taken by the United Kingdom Government and base its whole policy on subsidising housing built for letting or the rents of such houses when built. It therefore, left unimpaired the strongest and most

wide-spread motive the individual can have to save, the desire to own his own house. As a policy it was far harsher than that of the United Kingdom over the same period. The arguments in favour of subsidised house building and subsidised rents are full of emotion, but the result can be something the equivalent to carrying a child of twelve months everywhere, to save the poor little chap from tiring himself. He never learns to walk. There are still some grim enough slums in Canada, and plenty of new housing that is cut as near to the bone in cost as is possible, but Canada as a whole has reaped one very great advantage from this policy. The individual Canadian has put his money into savings banks and life policies, and later into the repayment of mortgages, to provide himself with his own house. By doing so he has supplied his country with a great deal of the fresh capital it so urgently needs. And Canada has, incidentally, avoided the tangle of housing subsidies, and decaying rent-controlled properties, that will plague United Kingdom politics for a generation.

But, whatever all the chances, skills and managings that went into the economy of Canada during the eight years since the end of the war, the basic cause of the country's success was the individual Canadian. If production has risen, it is because management and labour have worked that much more intelligently. If the economy has been in balance, it is because the Canadian chose a government that would and could assist him to keep it balanced. He is a hard worker. He is more flexible in his approach than his British counterpart. He is not bound to his localities as is the man in the United Kingdom. Seasonal work, and the risk of seasonal unemployment, is a part of his way of life. He is prepared to live away from home if need be, and to move if need be. He is prepared to build his own house, and the electrician, even though he may be a trade unionist, is prepared to wire a self-built house. The Canadian does not hang back because someone makes a profit; he is not naïve enough to think that, today, he can found a second Aluminum Company of Canada but he believes there is no reason at all why he should not become president of it, and he is prepared to work for that. He does not feel that the only permissible way to become a capitalist is to win a football pool. If Canada is prosperous, it is the Canadian who has made it so, and he is sharing in its prosperity.

FEDERAL AND PROVINCIAL FINANCES

In broad outline, under the 1954 Budget the Federal Government of Canada will have a revenue of $4,464 million, of which five-ninths comes from income and corporation profits taxes and three-ninths from import and excise duties. From that total, it planned to spend $2,000 million on defence, $460 million in interest on public debt, $350 million on family allowances, the principle federal social security services borne by the general budget, and $240 million on veterans. The budget also included payments out of rather under $300 million under the tax rental agreements and $20 million in subsidies to the provinces. The total expenditure as planned was $4,460 million, leaving a budget surplus of no more than $4 million for the present year. Outside the budget proper, an "under the line" payment, in terms of the United Kingdom budget, the Federal Government was due to pay over $75 million in the year to the Central Mortgage and Housing Corporation.

Since the beginning of 1952, federal payments for old age security have been taken out of the main budget. The Old Age Security Act of 1951 provides for a payment of $40 a month to all eligible persons over seventy, without a means test. Family allowances, introduced in 1944, are a general charge on revenue. They give a family an income for each child which starts at the monthly rate of $5 and rises to $8 a month when the child is between thirteen and sixteen. At sixteen the allowance ends. These allowances are now being paid to some two million families.

The pattern of taxation over Canada is inevitably complex because the Federal and the provincial governments each have the right to impose parallel forms of taxation and jealously protect their spheres of authority. Broadly speaking, the Federal Government may impose taxation on the whole of Canada by any mode or system, and the only possible limitation on that right arises from doubts (in the minds of the Judicial Committee of the Privy Council, before which the question was bound to come) as to whether the effect of the British North America Acts was not to restrict the right of that government in the disposal of the proceeds of that taxation. These doubts are the causes of the hesitations over, and provincial objections to, such projects as a complete federal unemployment insurance scheme.

Provincial governments have the right to impose "direct taxation within the province" in order to raise revenue for provincial purposes, but the expression "direct taxation" needs some explanation in the Canadian context. In the United Kingdom, now, the expression direct taxation is commonly used to describe taxation directly imposed on income and indirect taxation to describe taxation imposed on consumption. In Canada, the words have the meaning the Judicial Committee assumed was in the minds of the United Kingdom legislators in 1869. In Canada, direct taxation is a tax which a person cannot pass on to another, indirect taxation that which he can. It is therefore possible for a tax on petrol, on tobacco, even on amusements, to be a direct tax, provided it is expressed to be imposed on the person using the commodity or service at the moment when he buys it and therefore at a time when he cannot pass it on further. The retailer is treated as a tax collector, not as a person taxed. It has, of course, taken the lawyers some time to build up this delicate fabric of artifice.

Another feature of the Canadian taxation system is the taxation rental agreements made between the Federal Government and individual provinces. Under them the province agrees not to impose income and corporation taxes on its own account and receives by way of compensation, or "rental", a share in the proceeds of the corresponding federal taxes, with a guaranteed minimum payment. Where a province will not make a tax rental agreement, and Quebec will not, the Federal Government allows a credit to the individual taxpayer in respect of the amount which he pays, on the same tax, to the provincial government. This may still mean that a particular kind of tax may bear more heavily on a man, or a corporation, in one province than in another but, again broadly speaking, the result is that, in United Kingdom terms, the Federal Government imposes and collects the direct taxes on income and earnings, the Customs and Excise duties, and an indirect tax on sales, while the provinces rely for their revenues mainly on indirect taxation, such as taxes on consumption. Even in Quebec, for example, which, in 1950-1, collected $55 million in corporation taxes, taxes on the use or consumption of motor vehicles, petrol, tobacco and liquor, and the general sales tax, produced over twice as much.

PROSPECTS FOR THE FUTURE

Given Canada's present prosperity, what are the prospects for the future of the country?

No trading nation can be invulnerable; that might be put more specifically, today, by saying that no trading nation can expect to remain unaffected by what happens in the United States. Canadians may hope to see their trade with Europe return to its pre-war volume (in their minds the hope diminishes year by year), but they know that they are linked to the United States as closely as one nation can be to another, short of political dependency. For good and ill, in 1952 54 per cent of Canada's exports went across that frontier, 73 per cent of her imports travelled the reverse way. Canada may know very well that the moment difficulties face the people of the United States, or any appreciable section of them, their instinct is to fly to the shelter of protection and the barriers or tariffs and restrictions will go up at once. Canada may know, likewise, that when the United States Government feels a certain policy is advisable in its own best interests that policy will be followed without overmuch concern for any Canadian interests that may be adversely affected. In May 1953, Aluminium Limited contracted to sell half a million tons of aluminium from Canada to the Aluminum Company of America over the period 1953 to 1958. In July 1953, the United States Department of Justice brought a suit under the United States Anti-trust laws on the grounds that the contract would impair the "competitive conditions now prevailing in the domestic (United States) industry". The suit was abandoned this year, but its possible repercussions on the development of Kitimat were never the concern of the United States Department of Justice.

Nor is the contact between the two countries only one of economics, policies and impersonal theory. The industrialists of Canada manage American capital as well as their own, often enough with a controlling voice speaking to them from New York. The businessman thinks in terms of the tone on the New York Stock Exchange. Canada's news comes through American agencies, and her people read twice as many American magazines as any other. Two of the three associations of Canadian trade unions are duplicates of the groups south of the frontier. If business sentiment in the United States is pessimistic, business sentiment in Canada tends to feel that it ought to be pessimistic as well. In short, it is surprising that Canada is not a shadow of the United States. She is not, by any means, but she is within the penumbra.

As a trading nation Canada is dependent on her exports. That is rather an ambiguous phrase. Canada is by no means as dependent on her exports, in the sense that they alone can pay for imports that are essential, as is the United Kingdom. Canada can feed herself, clothe herself (in synthetic fibre), house herself and keep herself warm from what exists in her own country. But she is dependent on exports in the sense that her economy is such that a serious fall in their value would dislocate trade patterns and employment conditions and at once reduce the standard of living. Dr. O. J. Firestone, Economic Adviser to the Department of Trade and Commerce, in a lecture on Foreign Trade at McGill University in October 1952, gave this example:

> Perhaps the year 1929 is an interesting illustration of this experience (of falling exports). In this year, mainly as a result of substantially reduced sales of agricultural products to European countries, overall commodities exports declined by 14 per cent but domestic industrial and commercial expansion continued, with business investment increasing by about 20 per cent. Consumer expenditures rose also though more moderately, up to 5 per cent. As a result, gross national product in 1929 was just a little higher than in 1928—one per cent—in spite of the decline in exports.
>
> Of course what happened after 1929 is only too well known. Most of our major economic indicators declined significantly, exports in 1930 were down 25 per cent over 1929, business investment 22 per cent, consumer expenditures 4 per cent and gross national product 10 per cent. And we were into a depression that, with its slow recovery, would make us remember the 'thirties as a period of business losses, mass unemployment, hunger and misery.

The value of exports from Canada more than halved between 1928 and 1933 (the fall was from $1773 million to $826 million) while personal expenditure on goods and services fell by no more than a third (from $4196 million to $2848 million), yet that transition, in terms of human misery, was almost an absolute one. Half a loaf may be better than no bread, but there is only bitterness in the contrast between half a loaf today and a whole one last week.

Nor is the present pattern of world trade settled for ever. For instance, it costs less to ship cellulose from Vancouver by sea to Tokio than it does to send it by rail to Toronto. In British Columbia they do not volunteer comments on the future of trade across the Pacific while the political implications of trade with China are inconvenient, but they know how important, potentially, to Western Canada the trade routes of the Pacific are. It is in Western Canada that the new industrial output will rise so fast; the polythenes, for instance, from the oil and gas of Alberta. These modern chemical laboratories enlarged into production plants are costly and have an enormous output, far larger than Canada herself can use. A steadily increasing proportion of that output will have to be exported. It will meet a difficult, and a protected, market in the United States. Where shall it go? The answer in the end must be, across the Pacific.

Canadians do not expect progress to be a straight upward-rising line on a graph. Prosperity is not built into the chassis, they say, and while they hope that things will remain the way they have been they do not shut their eyes to the chance that they may not. For the farmer there have been changes already. By June 1953, the prices of farm products were a fifth down on what they had been in July 1951, and this fall had narrowed the gap between the prices the farmer received and those he paid for the commodities and services he bought to the lowest point at which it had stood since the end of the war. In the first half of 1953 the country, on balance, produced or imported more than it could sell. What, then, do Canadians see as the factors which should militate against, minimise, in fact, the effects of any trade recession, readjustment, or shake-out within the next few years or so?

The first factor is the expansion of the home market within Canada. That has grown absolutely, with the rise in Canada's population, and relatively. Over the last twenty-five years, while exports have risen in volume at the rate of 2½ per cent a year, the volume consumed in the home market has risen at the rate of almost 4½ per cent a year. Production for the home market employs, relatively, that many more people each year and is therefore that much better able to take up some of any slack in the export trades should exports fall (that, of course, is only true of the broad national picture; those areas that are mainly concerned with a particular export market, as, for example, on a large scale, lumber in British Columbia, on a smaller scale, apple-growing in Annapolis, Nova Scotia, could be severely hit.)

Secondly, Canadians like to take into account the world shift in the relative values of primary products, particularly food, and of manufactured goods. They point to the ability of the wheat grower to maintain in existence an International Wheat Agreement, and a minimum price for his wheat under it, despite the size of the carry-overs at the end of the 1953 season. They point to the gradual fall in world trade in rice, evidence that the rice-producing countries can afford to eat more and more of their own crop. It may be twenty-five years before the conditions outlined in the Paley Report seriously affect the pattern of American production but even now the United States must buy Canadian wood-pulp and newsprint to supply its presses and some States could now buy oil from Canada more cheaply than from American oil-fields if Canada had any to spare. This development is not wholly to Canada's advantage, for the percentage of exports from Canada which are to some extent processed before they leave continues to rise. But in many things Canada is still a low-cost producer as compared with the United States. She can compete in world markets in price.

A third point is that it would be comparatively easy for the Federal Government to find at home some alternative sources of employment in new projects. Canada's material standard of living is below that of the United States yet not so far behind as to discourage all attempts to catch up. If an American recession held up the Quebec-Labrador iron ore development (and it would have to be a severe recession for that to affect the work actually in hand now) there is still the South Saskatchewan River dam to be built, to say nothing of the St. Lawrence Seaway project itself. Every federal M.P. from Manitoba, Saskatchewan and Alberta could give the Government a list of important roads and railways northwards that are essential to the opening up of those territories. Provided Canada does not lose her nerve and jib at deficit spending in times of difficulty, even a serious recession would give time and opportunity to lay a fresh set of essential stepping-stones onwards. It is inconceivable, within at least a generation or so, that Canada would ever be reduced to setting unemployed to the digging of holes and their subsequent filling in.

Nor should the influence of eighteen years of Liberal Government be overlooked; neither the influence of events on that Government, nor the influence of that Government's policies on political and economic thinking in Canada generally. The philosophy of the Liberal Party has moved a long way from the time, in 1930, when a Liberal Prime Minister, Mr. Mackenzie King, could say in the Commons:

> So far as giving money from this federal treasury to the provincial governments is concerned, in relation to unemployment as it exists today, I might be prepared to go to a certain length, possibly, in meeting one or two of the western provinces that have Progressive premiers at the heads of their governments ... but I would not give a single cent to any Tory government.

(a speech which may, incidentally, have cost the Liberal Party the general election of that year). In his Budget speech on the 1950 Budget, Mr. Douglas Abbott, the Federal Finance Minister, defined the role of the Federal Government in these terms:

> In my mind the proper role of the central government in our federal state is fourfold. First, through its fiscal and general policies it should endeavour to create a favourable climate for healthy economic expansion and development. Second, it should have careful regard in planning its own operations for the best timing and the best placing of its capital and developmental expenditures. Third, it should recognise a special responsibility for the promotion and development of our basic primary industries and other industries of national significance. Fourth, it should be ready to co-operate actively with provincial governments, and through the provincial governments with municipalities, in meeting regional problems that threaten nation-wide economic repercussions.

That speech was made three months before the fighting in Korea broke out, and with the setback of 1949 in the United States in mind. When he made it Mr. Abbott was forecasting no more than a one to two per cent increase in the gross national product for the year 1950. He was defining the terms within which his government would act if such a forecast proved to be too optimistic. There is no reason to believe that the convictions of the Liberal Government have changed in this respect over the intervening years.

For the immediate prospect, perhaps a touchstone is provided by Pine Point, on the southern shore of the Great Slave Lake in the North West Territories. Kitimat and the Quebec-Labrador developments between them will absorb the best part of $900 million. By the end of the 1954 season their initial stages will be so close to completion that it is difficult to see any circumstances in which all work on them would be stopped. Pine Point is still a project.

It has been established that in the vicinity of Pine Point there exists a body of lead-zinc ores some forty miles long, five miles across and up to 100 ft. thick. It is a major discovery in the world of base metals.

The importance of Pine Point is that it provides a species of test case on the confidence with which the mining industry views the future. Pine Point is some 400 miles north of the nearest railway. When the decision to exploit Pine Point is made it will be necessary, as at the other two developments, to provide road and rail connections and to build a hydro-electric plant to supply power for the mine and the concentrator. It will mean a vast capital outlay and that in its turn will require a considerable output of concentrates to make the operation economic. The end of next year's working season should see the finish of the exploratory period. The companies mainly interested in Pine Point are Ventures Limited and Consolidated Mining and Smelting. In deciding when to proceed they must forecast the state of the market, and of supply, at the end of the four years or so which it will take the projected installations to come into production. When they do decide, that will be something of an indicator to the views of at least two extremely experienced companies on how the Canadian mining economy is shaping.

A still less calculable factor in Canada's future is uranium. The latest uranium developments are at Beaver Lodge Lake, in the north of Saskatchewan. The first uranium recovered in Canada came from mines at Port Radium, on Great Bear Lake, in the North West Territories, which were owned by the Eldorado Corporation and taken over, with the company, by the Canadian Government during the war. The Beaver Lodge Lake area is more accessible and a new town, Uranium City, containing, literally, many of the buildings from the now abandoned town of Goldfields transported there intact, is growing on the shores of Lake Athabaska. The Government has installed their plant capable of treating 500 tons of ore a day. The immediate importance of uranium is, of course, for defence. In addition, Canada is producing the "cobalt bomb", or radioactive cobalt, for the treatment of cancer, developed at the University of Saskatchewan at Saskatoon and now being sold to Canadian and American hospitals. Beyond that? No one knows, and there lies the fascination in this section of Canada's future. Will Canada assist in blowing the world to pieces, or will it change the face of its own country by, for example, carrying through my own favourite project, the enclosing and heating of the whole of the waters of Hudson Bay?

8

Present-day Problems

1. Wheat

THE war, of course, produced considerable changes in the pattern of world wheat production. Before the war, taking the average for the years 1935 to 1939, Europe produced 1,592 million bushels a year and North America 1,086 million. In 1947, North America produced 1,718 million bushels and Europe no more than 1,028 million; in production the positions had been almost reversed. Canada herself had increased her production of foodstuffs by some 40 per cent in the period. What the Canadian farmer saw in particular was that the United States farmer had increased his political strength at home and that his country was exporting almost nine times as much wheat as it had done before the war. The United States was both selling more wheat to Europe and giving more wheat to Europe, in the form of aid. The Canadian farmer had no legitimate grounds for criticising either action, but these developments south of the frontier were clear inducement to him to welcome a continuation of the wartime Government-managed wheat pool. He could see that he might very well need the strength that combination on the selling side should give.

In September 1945, the Canadian Government announced that it would set up a five-year wheat pool, and the buying price fixed by the time the pool was in operation was $1.35 a bushel. At the same time the government began negotiations with the United Kingdom Government for a four-year agreement for the export of Canadian wheat to Britain. The impulses that led in the direction of such an agreement were, of course, mixed. There was a real desire to help Britain during the immediate post-war period of

13.   Yukon: The Rockies

14.   Alberta: Drilling an Oil Well

reconstruction by enabling her to count on at least a basic supply of wheat and at a price fair to both parties; for that was how Mr. Wesson, president of the Saskatchewan Wheat Pool described the price ultimately agreed in the house organ of the Pool in June 1946. There was also the desire by the Canadian Government to secure for the Canadian wheat grower a firm market and a settled price for his wheat for that length of time ahead. Both Government and wheat grower had in mind the experiences of the pre-war years and of the years immediately following the First World War. In the 'thirties the wheat grower would have been more than glad of a four-year contract for the disposal at a fair price of half the wheat he exported. Further back, he could remember that wheat had reached its peak price in 1919, with a farm price of $2.21. Four years after the end of that war, in 1922, the farm price had come down to 77 cents. The thought in Canadian minds may well have been that, whilst history does not always repeat itself, there is a chance that it may. However, there were new factors in the situation. One was the chance of this agreement with the United Kingdom Government. The other was the price support programme of the Democratic Administration in the United States for farm produce (which contained an undertaking by the United States Government to purchase that produce, including wheat, at 90 per cent of a "parity" price in return for the right to limit by order the acreage devoted to each particular crop) and that Administration's apparent determination to continue that policy for as long as possible.

The agreement between the two Governments was completed in July 1946. Under it the Canadian Government undertook to sell to the United Kingdom Government 600 million bushels of wheat, 160 million bushels in each of the crop years of 1946–7 and 1947–8 and 140 million in each of the two succeeding crop years. The price for the first two crop years was fixed at $1.55 a bushel: for the two succeeding years it was to be negotiated. The agreement also contained what came to be known as the "have regard to" clause. In that clause the United Kingdom Government agreed that in settling prices for the 1948–9 and 1949–50 years it would "have regard to any differences between the price paid under this Agreement in the 1946–7 and 1947–8 crop years and the world prices for wheat" in those years. At the time the contract was negotiated, the world price of wheat was $1.80 to $1.90.

N

On the day it came into operation 1 August 1946, the price was $2.05.

For the first two years of the agreement with the United Kingdom, the Canadian farmer sold 160 million bushels of wheat a year at $1.55 a bushel. During that time the price of wheat on the Chicago Exchange was well over $2 a bushel, and at its end the Canadian farmer was beginning to say that he had already lost $320 million, certainly that he had sold 320 million bushels at something like $1 a bushel, on the average, below the Chicago price. There remained, he was reminded, the "have regard to" clause for the last two years of the agreement, but "have regard to" clauses in agreement only too frequently represent a sop offered by one side to meet a frustrated hope on the other. Certainly, all the Canadian Government could achieve on the strength of the clause was to persuade the United Kingdom Government to increase the price for the last two years to $2 a bushel, a price that was still a good bargain for the United Kingdom Government. At the start of the 1948–9 crop year the Chicago price was $2.40. Only for two months during the following two years, in June and July 1950, did it fall as far as $2 a bushel. Not only that; Canada had lent the United Kingdom Government a great many of the dollars needed to buy the wheat. Out of the $12,090 million involved in the purchases over the four years, the United Kingdom, from her own resources, had found no more than $118 million. In the meantime, negotiations were on foot for an international wheat agreement.

THE INTERNATIONAL WHEAT AGREEMENT

There had been an international wheat agreement in 1933, designed to allocate quotas for export among the major producing countries. It had been wrecked by Argentina, who had refused to be bound by the export quotas allocated to her. In 1942 an agreement between Canada, the United States, Australia, Argentina and the United Kingdom had produced a wartime working arrangement, and an International Wheat Council, and, when the war was over, negotiations began for a new and more permanent agreement, this time firmly supported by the United States. The 1947 negotiations failed, in part because Argentina, as an exporter, was still reluctant to accept a system of rigid quotas and in part because the United Kingdom, as the principal importer, disliked the maximum and minimum prices suggested. These negotiations were resumed in 1948, again with pressure from the United States. With the farm price support policy hanging over the budget, with the prospect of having to find $56 million for the support of the price of wheat alone, the Administration wanted a solid agreement for the sale of the bulk of American wheat available for export.

An agreement was reached in March 1948, by delegates from thirty-six countries, but without Argentina. The quantity covered by the agreement was 500 million bushels a year, of which Canada's quota was 230 million bushels. The maximum price fixed was $2 a bushel, the minimum $1.50, falling by ten cents each year. The agreement was to come into force on 1 August 1948, provided it was ratified by 1 July. This time it was the United States that failed to ratify it; the grain merchants were reluctant to see such an extension of what they felt was state trading. Congress adjourned in June until January without having ratified and on 6 July, at the first meeting of the new Wheat Council, the United Kingdom representative announced that his government would withdraw, on that account.

The United States Administration was dismayed, but not daunted, by this third post-war failure to obtain an effective agreement over wheat. Conversations, involving even the Secretary of State himself, proceeded during the winter. The main discussions were over price, and calculations on the size of the 1948-9 crop were an important ingredient in the final attitudes of the two sides. The question of "Offshore" purchases also appeared in the discussions for the first time; would wheat become a surplus crop in the United States, and so reduce the right of the United Kingdom Government to use any of the American dollars it received by way of aid to buy Canadian wheat? The Administration took its political courage into both hands and made what can only be described as a most courageous gesture by saying that these dollars could be so spent. The end was an agreement, signed in the middle of March. Argentina (and Soviet Russia, who had joined in the negotiations as a potential exporter) were out. Forty-six countries were in.

The International Wheat Agreement came into operation on 1 August 1949, at the beginning of the 1949-50 crop year. It brought together four of the major wheat exporting countries,

Canada, the United States, Australia and France, and forty-two of the wheat importing countries. The importing countries agreed to purchase 580 million bushels of wheat, each taking a set amount, or quota (the United Kingdom quota was 177 million bushels). The exporting countries divided the total to be sold amongst themselves as follows:

United States	253,128,000	bushels
Canada	235,000,000	"
Australia	88,700,000	"
France	4,089,000	"

The maximum and a minimum price for this wheat were fixed over the four years of the agreement's currency. The maximum throughout was $1.80. The minimum was $1.50 for the first year and fell by ten cents in each of the succeeding years. The price of wheat on the Chicago Wheat Exchange was just over $2 a bushel when the agreement began, rose seasonally in the first half of 1950, but, after the start of the war in Korea, reached the $2.50 level and, over the next two years, fluctuated between $2.25 and $2.60.

The International Wheat Agreement had a currency of four years. It provided that negotiations for its renewal, and for the next set of prices, should begin with the final year, which they did, in 1952. What happened then is common knowledge. All the exporting countries asked for higher prices, and the importing countries, with the United Kingdom and India in the lead, resisted those demands; Britain, as buyer of one-third of the wheat controlled by the agreement, was bound to be the strongest influence on the importing side. After a protracted and Oriental bargaining session, the United States had come down to a maximum price of $2.05 a bushel and the United Kingdom had come up to $2 a bushel. At that point the negotiations stuck, and finally ended. The United Kingdom did not sign the new agreement in the summer of 1953. The remaining importing countries did. The agreement was ratified and came into force. The United Kingdom became a buyer on the free market only.

I have never been able to understand the United Kingdom Government's final decision. On all sides it was agreed that the agreement had worked well; certainly importers had paid less for their guaranteed or "quota" wheat than for their supplementary purchases. The *Economist*, never prone to flatter international commodity agreements, said of the agreement in January 1953: "The virtue of the agreement is that it meets the primary needs of both exporters and importers. . . . Unlike some commodity schemes of the past, the wheat agreement is not run exclusively for producers, nor is it designed as a restrictive scheme." In the first year, importing countries bought 89 per cent of the amount they had guaranteed to buy under the agreement, in the second year 94 per cent and in the third and fourth years virtually 100 per cent. The *Economist*, after recounting these results, added: "Clearly the verdict is that the agreement has been a great technical success."

Only three things could be said to have gone wrong, from the importers' point of view. The acreage of wheat sown in Australia had fallen from 13,800,000 acres in 1947 to 10,200,000 in 1952, and Australia's exporting capacity had diminished in consequence. That was serious, to Britain, because it increased her dependence on dollar wheat. But that was hardly the fault of the agreement. It was primarily due to the fact that Australia had fixed her internal prices for wheat below those ruling under the agreement, and had done so at a time when Australia's wool clip was in great demand. Her farmers had, therefore, tended to switch from wheat to sheep, where they could. The second set-back had been the action of the exporting countries in adding, in 1951, a handling charge of six cents a bushel to the maximum price. In the British view, that was not justified by the agreement and amounted to an arbitrary price increase, made only because the exporters felt powerful enough to enforce it unilaterally. Even so, the action of the exporters can hardly be said to have struck at the root of the agreement, or to have destroyed its virtue as an international bargain.

Finally, there were the actions of the United States Government. The United States Government was inconsistent. It opposed the very suggestion of a price support programme for the commodities it needed to import, such as rubber or tin. It maintained a price support programme for those commodities other countries needed to import, and on a scale which, as 1952 passed into 1953, seemed increasingly unrealistic; it was paying its own farmers an average subsidy of 64 cents a bushel on wheat. Its insistence on a maximum price as high as $2.05 was, the British felt, a demand that the wheat importing countries should use their scarce dollars to contribute to an internal subsidy paid to the American farmers by the government in office for purely party political reasons. All that may be very true. Did it justify the United Kingdom in turning its back on the one international commodity agreement left? "In the Wheat Agreement", an article in the *Financial Times* said, in 1952, "the whole conception of a concerted attempt to achieve an expansionist policy in world food production is at stake."

The United Kingdom Government could not, with any degree of consistency, object to international commodity agreements in principle. It had pressed for something very much of the same kind for quite a number of the commodities exported from within the Commonwealth. It could not, with any degree of consistency, object to internal price support programmes for farmers in principle, either. By the middle of 1953 it was itself becoming increasingly confused by exactly the same kind of trouble with its own farmers as the United States Government was with theirs. It was limiting its purchases of cheaper bacon from Denmark, for instance, because of the higher prices it was due to pay the home producer. About all it could say was that $2.05 was too high a maximum price to fix, but even in doing that it seemed to impale itself on the horns of a dilemma. Either the existing stocks and the 1952–3 crops of wheat were big enough to force the price below $2 a bushel, in which case what would begin to matter under the agreement would be the minimum price, not the maximum, or they were not, in which case $2.05 a bushel was still a price appreciably below that which had ruled on the free markets for the previous three years. Obviously the United Kingdom Government believed that the price of wheat was too high and would fall, for that alone would justify, in terms of internal politics, a reliance for the future on the free markets alone. If so, why did it worry about a $2.05 maximum? Did the United Kingdom Government believe that its refusal to sign the agreement was an essential step in forcing the price of wheat below the $2 mark? If so, it can only have been a supposition, and to jeopardise a commodity agreement that the world had struggled since 1933 to create on the basis of that one supposition alone seems to have been an imperfectly calculated risk.

2. Monopolies

Canada is a good place in which to study monopolies; also legislation against monopolies. A feeling against monopolies is a part of the Canadian tradition. In Britain the public has not felt strongly about them since the days of the Stuarts and today there are as many who defend those that do exist as there are of those who would perpetuate them in the guise of publicly owned corporations. In Canada, generations grew up under the shadow of two great monopolies, those possessed by the Hudson's Bay Company and the C.P.R., and, although those two corporations no longer have the exclusive powers they once enjoyed, there are other giants; monopolies that cover the whole country, monopolies that are local but complete in their locality, and great concentrations of power which do not completely exclude competition but which, as the large tree in the forest limits the size of the undergrowth beneath it, are able to prevent their competitors from becoming serious rivals in any real sense of the word. Electricity is the classic example. The production of electricity can hardly escape being a monopoly. If the generating station is hydro-electric, no one else can use that head of water. Even if it is thermal, who else will build a station alongside one that exists, solely to compete with it?

The bulk of electricity in Canada comes from water power. The plants which make it a business to produce or distribute power for use by others are known as central stations. In 1951, these stations generated 57 billion kWh. as against 6½ billion generated by the remainder. Less than a quarter of the water power available in Canada—of that already known—is at present used for the generation of current (British Columbia has the greatest capacity as yet undeveloped).

The ownership of the central stations is various: in all, 44 per cent of the electricity produced in Canada comes from stations in public ownership. In Quebec, which produces and uses one half of all the electricity in Canada, the largest concern is the privately owned Shawinigan Water and Power Company, Limited, which supplies power in the area west of Montreal to Quebec City and through subsidiaries (one of which is jointly owned with Monsanto Chemicals) manufactures resins and other chemicals.

Other areas in Quebec (including Montreal itself) are supplied
by the Quebec Hydro-Electric Commission, which is publicly
owned. In Ontario, the main supplier is a public commission,
Ontario Hydro-Electric Commission; its plants (which include
those at Niagara) supply nine-tenths of the total power used in
the province. Ontario is still short of power and, if the St.
Lawrence Seaway project goes through, the power dam and
generating station which are a part of it will be operated by the
Ontario Commission. In the west, British Columbia, Manitoba
and Saskatchewan have provincial power commissions, but, in
British Columbia, 85 per cent of the power comes from privately
owned stations.

The principle of public versus private ownership of power
generation in Canada is not a major federal political issue, possibly because the Federal Government may, and does, only generate power in the Territories, for which it is still directly responsible. Alberta, with a Social Credit government, favours private
ownership all through, while Saskatchewan, with a C.C.F. government, is extending public ownership into distribution and retail
sales (and of domestic equipment). Perhaps what takes most sting
out of any campaign is the fact that the cost of electricity in
Canada is low, lower than in the United States. In Canada, in
1951, the average domestic rate was 1·65 cents per kW, in the
United States 2·81 cents, and for the commercial user the rates
were 0·6 cents in Canada and 1·4 cents in the States. At various
times, in various provinces, there have been specific issues over
specific plants (and occasionally provincial politicians found themselves in hot water as a result), but public ownership is a plank in
the federal programme of the C.C.F. only.

But what of the commercial concern that takes the risk of building a power station solely because it is taking the larger risk of
creating a future demand for power that its own station is intended to satisfy? Does it then rate as a monopoly? That is the
situation of Aluminium, Ltd., at Kitimat. Aluminium, Ltd., a Canadian company, is a monopoly in some fields, competitive in others,
and is a mighty creator of demand for electric power. It produces
all the aluminium of Canada and is a major influence in the
world's supply. Its operating company in Canada is Aluminum
Company of Canada, Limited, which owns the Arvida, the Kitimat
and three other smelters. In 1952, Canada produced 25 per cent

of all the aluminium produced in the world (excluding the U.S.S.R.) and the United States 48 per cent. Aluminium, Ltd., has interests in most of the world. It is under obligation to supply the United Kingdom Government with 275,000 tons of the metal a year. It is a partner in the project for the construction of a smelter producing 210,000 tons a year in the Gold Coast, using power from the Volta River. In short, where there is aluminium—indeed, where there is bauxite—there will also be Aluminium, Ltd.

The Aluminum Company of Canada, Ltd. ("Alcan") was once a subsidiary of the Aluminum Company of America ("Alcoa"). The ties between the two companies were formally severed in 1928, when Aluminium, Ltd., was formed to take over Alcoa's holdings in various subsidiaries and the share capital of Aluminium, Ltd., was distributed among the individual shareholders in Alcoa. The resulting identity of shareholdings in the two companies, Aluminium, Ltd., said in its public statement in July 1953, has now been almost eliminated. But the U.S. Department of Justice was not entirely satisfied with the results of the 1928 transaction and the subsequent divergence of the two streams of shareholders. There was an anti-trust action in the United States and a Court order in 1951 which appointed three people (two of them now being directors of Aluminium, Ltd.) to act as voting trustees in the Aluminum Company of America in respect of the shares of individuals who were shareholders in both companies. In 1953 the U.S. Department of Justice returned to the charge, with its claim that a bulk sale of aluminium by Alcan to Alcoa was in itself a breach of the United States anti-trust laws.

The aluminium trust is a classic example of the international combine. It can claim more merit, financially, than the international oil organisation, which forces the rest of the world to pay prices for oil which are based upon the costs of the oil producers in the southern United States, for it can point to an advance in the average price of the metal, from £95 a ton in 1939 to £150 a ton in 1952, this is relatively the smallest advance in price among all the metals in common industrial use. It manufactures a product which requires immense capital outlay and resources before cheap production is possible. Its direction is bold and imaginative. It is acutely aware of public reaction against any mistakes in policy or approach. (Is fear such a bad influence on such concerns? One sometimes wishes that publicly owned monopolies were a little more afraid of the public they are reputed to serve.) It has believed throughout in a constantly expanding market. It presents the classic questions: should such an organisation be judged by what it is, by what it has been, or by what it might become? And how does one impose any sort of effective control which does not at the same time destroy the very qualities that should be preserved?

Aluminium, Ltd., is not the only international combine which is based on and domiciled in Canada; the International Nickel Company of Canada, Ltd. is another. This company produces more than three-quarters of the world's supply of nickel. It is a main supplier to the United States and is under contract to supply to that country 120 million lbs. of nickel and 100 million lbs. of refined copper, deliveries commencing December 1953. It owns some 100,000 acres at Sudbury, Ontario, and operates four large mines there. The Mond Nickel Company Limited in the United Kingdom is now a subsidiary, the Mond interests being a party to the original formation of the international company. In effect, International Nickel is a working partnership between Canada, the United Kingdom and the United States.

The next group of trading monopolies are those whose operations are confined to Canada. A prominent example is Canadian Industries Limited, C.I.L., established in 1910 as a union of the interests of Imperial Chemical Industries Limited and E. I. du Pont de Nemours and Company Inc. The company makes explosives, paints, agricultural fertilisers, chemicals and plastics including nylon and polythene. But the du Pont de Nemours company is domiciled in the United States, which has given the U.S. Department of Justice a grip on its activities. The United States have ordered a severance of the Canadian interests of the two companies and C.I.L. is now formally split. Will competition return?

There are the natural monopolies. Consolidated Mining and Smelting produces about four-fifths of all Canada's lead and zinc, but that is primarily based on the Sullivan Mine, and either you own a Sullivan Mine or you do not. It would hardly be feasible to require that ownership of the mine should be split into two and worked by two competing companies side by side. There are the monopolies by association of trades. The Bell Telephone Company, Ltd. dominates the public telephone service; through a subsidiary, the Northern Electric Co. Ltd., it makes most of the telephone equipment used in Canada, and, through a subsidiary, most of the sound equipment as well. In the meat packing and the vegetable canning industries there are concentrations in one or two hands and such names as the Imperial Tobacco Company and Standard Oil of New Jersey (which controls Imperial Oil in Canada) are names which crop up all over the world. Canadian industry cannot be said to be fully competitive

There have also been price rings and resale price agreements. The Restrictive Trade Practices Commission in Canada investigated the Canadian flat (or plate) glass combine in 1949 and its subsequent report showed that the glass manufacturers of Britain, Central Europe and the United States had, ever since 1928, eliminated competition by sharing out the Canadian market between them in quotas, and had fixed the price at which each square inch was to be sold (even the war did not seriously disrupt the price-fixing mechanism). This was accompanied by a central association, with a registry for contracts, to ensure that all tendered prices were identical and non-competitive, and the withholding of supplies from all glass jobbers (with the exception of a few customers of long standing) who were not members of the association. It is an old and familiar story, certainly not confined to Canada. It cost three of the glass companies fines, the maximum, of $10,000 each. This happens to be one of the few international cartels investigated by the Canadian authorities in any detail during the last ten years. Is it significant that no flat glass was being manufactured in Canada over this period, and so no Canadian manufacturing interests to be upset by a detailed examination of their methods of trade?

THE RESTRICTIVE TRADE PRACTICES COMMISSION

Powers over monopolies and combines in Canada first took the form of a comparatively simple instrument of investigation under a single Commissioner, set up in 1923. But as a result of a new Act of Parliament, a new Restrictive Trade Practices Commission came into existence, on 1 November 1952, to supplement, as the body to hear complaints, the investigatory work of the Commissioner (now the Director of Investigation and Research).

The main features of the 1952 Canadian Act is that it is now a criminal offence, punishable by fine or imprisonment, to be a party to a combine; and combine is defined as an actual or tacit contract agreement or arrangement which limits or reduces opportunities for production or marketing or which fixes a common price, or a resale price for articles or processes, or which otherwise restrains trade or commerce. In addition, resale agreements, and refusals to supply goods if fixed prices on resale are not observed, are specifically forbidden.

The federal agency charged with the duty of investigating combines is the Restrictive Trade Practices Commission, working under a Director. The Commission may take action on the initiative of a Director, if required by the Minister, or if a complaint is filed by any six or more Canadian citizens and residents.

The major investigation so far concluded under the new Act was that into the rubber industry in Canada, and that covered six major subjects, the manufacture, distribution and sale of tyres, tubes, mechanical rubber goods such as conveyor belts, fire, industrial and garden hose, rubber footwear and rubber clothing. The conclusions were that there had been agreements limiting competition and prosecutions followed in which there were pleas of "Guilty" by five of the companies before the Court. The resulting fines, imposed last November, totalled $170,000.

The Canadian system of monopoly investigation arms its instrument of investigation, the Commission, very fully, but it falls short of that of the United States in the powers of enforcement it gives either to the Commission or the Courts. The American system includes power for the Supreme Court to order the legal break-up of the combine, to compel companies to divest themselves of shares in subsidiaries, and to "cease and desist" from monopolistic practices. The Canadian Courts may only punish each offence as and when it is proved before them, and that, in practice, only by a fine, the amount of which may be small as compared with the profits made. The Canadian methods are defended with the argument that publicity is the best weapon against a monopoly and history certainly shows that monopolies in Canada have fought hard to avoid that. But it does look as though the Commission is still ill-equipped to handle what might be called the continuing monopoly, based upon common legal ownership or control.

The proper regulation, the proper degree of regulation, for combines and cartels are matters that go right down to the roots of business activity in the Western World. It is easy to take up attitudes of general condemnation, which may be based on nothing more substantial than an emotion that what is not publicly regulated cannot work to the public good. It is equally easy to swallow uncritically the international cartel's commonest defence, that only by a pooling of knowledge and experience can the results of research be quickly spread, again for the public good. The monopolies may be efficient. They may of their own volition limit their profits to a fair percentage, bearing in mind the risks they take. It is true that, today, the divorce between management and ownership is so complete that, if management is well paid, it feels no strong urge to wring out of the public the last cent of profit solely for the benefit of the shareholder. The fact remains that the structure of economic society is based on the belief that competition will, of itself, check tendencies to exploitation. As the Canadian Commission said in its report on the rubber investigation, once a combine asks a public authority to allow it to continue because its prices are fair and its profits are reasonable it asks that authority to regulate all its activities. "The policy of the Act is . . . to assert that prices shall be determined by competition and not by arrangement."

The international cartel is a horse of another colour as well as one of another size. What the international cartels, such as those that control the marketing of oil, nickel and aluminium, have done is to build up a system of private international law for these commodities to which each unit, or citizen, of that world is subject. Politicians, of course, do not care for these private worlds, for of all things politicians do not relish being placed in positions in which they must of necessity feel non-sovereign, and so inferior, but it is by no means certain that the general public suffers more from the activities of the cartels than it does from the activities of politicians. The true complaint of the public should be directed towards the secrecy with which these private worlds surround their activities; and yet even that is understandable. Does democracy always ask sensible questions? Does not the demagogue always prejudge the case—that is, if he ever bothers to attempt to understand it? Can he resist the temptation to beat up a passion as a substitute for the greater labour involved in thinking out consequences? The witch hunt is a blunderbuss, and it is not surprising that the white witches as well as the black go to ground when they hear the brazen cries of the chase.

But there this argument must stop.

3. The St. Lawrence Seaway

The St. Lawrence Seaway has been a dream in Canadian minds for almost the whole lifetime of the country, certainly since people began to move westwards, for the roads westwards ran over water, and the highway led up the St. Lawrence and on into Lake Superior. To travel by land south of the Lakes meant leaving Canadian soil. To travel north of the Lakes was to face hundreds of miles of broken, tree-clad country and, although the railways now cross those northern parts of Quebec and Ontario, the Trans-Canada highway has yet to do so in the form of a modern motor road. Then came the return journey. The wheat of Canada moving east is first put on board ship at Port Arthur and Fort William at the head of Lake Superior. Why should not the freighters of the world come direct to these inland ports to carry it away? That was the dream.

From Belle Isle, at the mouth of the Gulf of St. Lawrence, to the head of the Great Lakes, is 2,660 miles, rather further than from Liverpool to Halifax, Nova Scotia, and Port Arthur itself is almost halfway between Cape Race and Vancouver. The first 1,000 miles of the Seaway up the St. Lawrence are freely navigable during the open water season. The tides reach as far as Trois Rivières, above Quebec, and there is no difficulty in maintaining a channel thirty feet in depth on to Montreal at all states of the flow of water.

Between Montreal and Lake Superior there are three changes in water level, from the level at Montreal (about twenty feet above sea level) to Lake Ontario, from Lake Ontario to Lake Huron and from Lake Huron to Lake Superior. The channel of the St. Lawrence between Montreal and Lake Ontario is some 185 miles long. The gap between Lake Ontario and Lake Erie is twenty-seven miles and the difference in water levels is 327 feet. These lakes are now linked by the Welland Canal, already deepened to take ships with twenty-seven feet of draught. The passage between Lake Erie and Lake Huron presents no difficulty nor change in level, and Lake Huron is joined to Lake Superior by the St. Mary River, at Sault Ste. Marie. Here there are canals some one-and-a-half miles long, again deepened, mainly by the United States Government. The main problem lies in the waterway of the St. Lawrence between Montreal and Chimney Point and of this stretch 37 miles need no more than the dredging and straightening of the existing channels in the river or the small lakes through which it runs.

From a political point of view, the problem can be still further localised. For some 115 miles the St. Lawrence is the international boundary between Canada and the United States. West of Chimney Point, in the Thousand Islands section of the river, either country could make a navigable channel within its own territorial waters. East of Chimney Point lies the International Rapids section, some 47 miles long, with a fall in water level of 92 feet over its total length. A series of canals now carry vessels through this stretch but they can take vessels of no more than fourteen foot draught and their locks are small and narrow. Canada could, of course, convert these canals, or build another within her own territory, to take larger vessels from Lake Ontario to the sea, but the cost would be prohibitive. The most practical way of providing a twenty-seven foot channel over the whole length is to dam the river at one or two points and so deepen it, but that would both interfere with the flow and flood land on either bank. Can Canada and the United States reach an agreement to build the canal works jointly and flood these lands along either bank, and, if so, how? That is the essence of the St. Lawrence Seaway problem as it stands today.

Relations between Canada and the United States over the St. Lawrence are regulated by a series of international treaties and agreements, any of which could in theory (but hardly in practice) be abrogated. Under the 1871 Treaty, the United States has the right to use the St. Lawrence for ever. The Treaty of 1909 set up an International Joint Commission, three from each country, to deal with all matters relating to the international section of the river. In 1920, the two Governments referred the whole question of the St. Lawrence as a channel of navigation and a source of power to the Commission for investigation and report. By 1927, after two surveys by engineers and a long series of public hearings in both countries, there was unanimity within the Commission that the St. Lawrence could be turned into a seaway taking ships of twenty-seven foot draught, and not very much difference between the two countries' technical experts over how it should be done. By 1932, the two Governments had themselves reached agreement on undertaking the work and embodied their agreements in a treaty, but the treaty, when submitted to the United States Senate for approval, failed to secure the necessary two-thirds majority. A second project was worked out between 1939 and 1941, resulted in an agreement, and again the agreement failed to pass the Senate. The obstruction was too strong.

Until about the end of the war, the inability of the neighbouring governments to co-operate meant, in Canadian minds, a veto on the plan, for Canada could not—or believed that she could not—face the full cost of the works alone. But with the growth in Canada's prosperity the cost of the undertaking shrank, relatively, and at the same time the importance of the power of the water in the St. Lawrence itself increased. The project had begun by being a matter of transportation; even before the end of the war Ontario's shortage of power was so acute that its engineers had been compelled to look beyond Niagara for the next source of supply. This was a double reason why Canada should wish to proceed. Once again the United States Administration was favourable—no President has ever done anything but favour the project—but once again there was never an unqualified "yes" from that side. Bills introduced into Congress seemed to sink without trace, certainly without vote. At last, in December 1951, the Canadian Government announced that it would proceed with the project alone. In a broadcast in Canada on this decision the following month the Federal Minister of Transport, Mr. Lionel Chevrier, said:

> We are not closing the door on United States participation in the Seaway. That participation is still the logical, the desirable choice. But it is results that count. Canada can no longer afford to rely on full United States participation as the only choice. Canada will pursue both alternatives, that is, action under the 1941 agreement and action for the all-Canadian Seaway, until it becomes clear which will be the first to produce results.

The fresh approach to the problem was this: The obstacle to the project had proved to be the United States Senate, because the constitution, customs and methods of working that body gave the maximum opportunity for obstruction to any lobby of interests determined to prevent positive action. The project only needed approval by the Senate if it was cast in the form of an international treaty dealing with the use of the waterway. If it could be cast in a form that did not need an international treaty to give it full sanction, the Senate would no longer have jurisdiction. Could not the project be brought within the existing rights of State and provincial governments? Put more concretely, suppose the Ontario Hydro-Electric Power Commission and the New York State agreed to dam the river to give themselves a fresh source of power? They would need the consent of their respective Federal Governments, of the International Joint Commission and of the Federal Power Commission in the United States: but not that of the Senate. If those hurdles were cleared, if once the power authorities had permission to alter the flow and level of the river, the Canadian Government could add its own works for the seaway channel itself at its own expense and as it willed.

An agreement along these lines was made in 1952. The Canadian Parliament passed two Acts, one setting up the St. Lawrence Seaway Authority, the other the International Rapids Power Development Act, handing over the responsibility for power to the Ontario Hydro-Electric Commission, and in the June of that year the two Federal Governments submitted their plans to the International Joint Commission. The Commission approved them in the October, whereupon the Canadian Government informed the United States Government that it now regarded the 1941 Agreement for a joint development of the Seaway as superseded. The remaining obstacle that held back the final order to start was the consent of the Federal Power Commission (which is, of course, nominally independent of the Administration). By the end of 1953 the position was that the Federal Power Commission had given its consent to the New York State application but that the objectors had not exhausted all their opportunities for delaying activity, both before the Commission and in the United States Supreme Court.

Only this year did Congress at least vote affirmatively in favour of Federal participation in the Seaway as such.

The objections to the Seaway are vehement, even if, to Canadian minds, misguided. What has increased their strength is the fact that competing methods of transportation not only face the loss of existing traffic. They foresee the loss of a great deal more potential traffic, for it is this that has transformed the economics of the Seaway; so much so that, incidentally, Mr. Hughes, the present United States Secretary for Defence once went on the record to

o

say that he would be glad of a chance to build the Seaway as a
private venture, he was so convinced of its future prosperity. The
steel industry of the United States has been virtually built up on
the iron ores of Minnesota, of which the best known are in the
Mesabi Range. They have been eaten away at the rate of some
90 million tons a year and they are not inexhaustible. The steel
companies of the United States have been thinking in terms of
other sources of supply for some time, and the iron ore deposits
in the Labrador trough, on the Quebec-Labrador border, are one
obvious answer. Over 400 million tons have been proved already
in the Knob Lake area and that is but the beginning. When the
Canadian mining operator, Mr. Jules Timmins, of the Hollinger
company, began to interest the Mark Hanna company of Detroit
in this area, he finished with four other American steel companies,
and a dozen and a half insurance companies, four Canadian, joining together to set up the Iron Ore Company of Canada and its
three subsidiaries, the railway company from Sept Isles north,
the air line and the power company, and to provide the necessary
capital for the projects, likely to total $300 million in the end.

The first plans for the Quebec-Labrador mines call for a production of 10 million tons a year, beginning with the first ship-
ments this year. That output should rise to 20 million tons a year
and can move upwards as required. The United States Bureau
of Commerce, basing its estimates on a continuing rise in the output of steel from the foundries of the United States, has estimated
that the potential volume of traffic using the Seaway will be between 57 and 84 million tons a year, of which half will be iron
ore moving west. In 1935, traffic on the St. Lawrence was under
20 million tons a year, of which the bulk moved east. It is this
vast increase in bulk that explains why Canada can face the cost
of the Seaway alone more calmly (the total cost might well be
$1,000 million in the end) for its experts calculate that the esti-
mated income from tolls will pay interest on capital cost and amor-
tise the debt over fifty years. In addition the harnessed power of
the water will supply 12·6 billion kWh. (2,200,000 h.p.).

Some of the objections are based on illusion. It is unlikely that
many existing ocean-going vessels would in fact travel deep into
the Lakes and so cut to nothing the trans-shipment work at Montreal. They are designed for deep water, and salt water, conditions
—in fact, one estimate is that only about one in every ten of the

existing United States merchant fleet could safely use the Seaway. Equally, the existing vessels plying on the Great Lakes are not ocean-going in design and would be dangerous in a winter gale in the North Atlantic. Other objections are more real. If the foundries in the Middle Western States need iron ore from Labrador, they will transport it by some route and if there is no deepened channel along the St. Lawrence the railways of both countries may very well hope for more traffic than they are likely to get if there is. Yet, in the end, none of the objections can survive what, in America, must be the final test; if the St. Lawrence Seaway provides a more competitive method or route for transportation then it must be encouraged, for, if the United States ceases to base her own economy on competition, how can she hope to sustain her present economic strength? She has no belief in any alternative economic system.

If the Seaway had not involved an international boundary, Canada would have taken it in her stride after the war and the work might now be well on the way to completion. Instead, it became a source of political friction between Canada and the United States and left Canadians impatient at the gulf between expressions of accord from the United States Administration and the absence of corresponding action on a practical level. Speaking in New York in April 1953, on Canada's economic future, Mr. C. D. Howe, the Minister of Trade and Commerce, finished by a direct reference to the part the Seaway should play in that future. After reminding his audience that the cost of the existing seaway in the St. Lawrence valley, and of its operation and maintenance, had always been borne by Canada; "Why", he went on, "should your country withhold its co-operation and thus delay this vital Canadian transportation outlet? I must confess I do not know the answer."

Co-operation will probably come; it is a pity it got off to such a poor start.

9

Canadian Politics

BESIDE the politics of Canada, those of the United Kingdom have an engaging simplicity. True, they have also a distressing unreality. "Do you see *that*?" Mr. Aneurin Bevan says, pointing to the Iron and Steel Act of 1953, and it is no use Alice trying to explain that it is no more than an old and broken rattle. "It's spoilt," he cries, and, like Tweedledum, begins to stamp about wildly and tear his hair.

And then Tweedledee appears.

"I hope you're a good hand at pinning and tying strings," the party leaders say in unison. "Every one of these things has got to go on, somehow or other." A general election has begun, and how like bundles of old clothes the party programmes seem.

"A political party in Canada can seldom follow a clear line if it is to get elected, for it must represent all the rival racial and economic interests of the whole nation. It must somehow embrace under one policy the isolated Maritimes, the French Catholics of Quebec, the protected manufacturing interests of Ontario, the free-trade aspirations of the prairie farmer, the almost separate economy of British Columbia. . . . It must be the best kind of compromise possible, while appearing to have a clear-cut plan of its own." So wrote Mr. Bruce Hutchinson, in *The Unknown Country*, putting his finger on one similarity between the political scene in Canada and that in the United States. It is a sobering thought that Canada has the kind of government the United States might have had if Lord Durham and Lord John Russell had been born a century earlier. In which case, what of the French-speaking Canadians? But, then, the political history of Canada has been so much a history of the relations between these two peoples.

The modern history of Canada can be said to begin with the hanging of Louis Riel in 1885. Louis Riel was tried at Regina in July 1885, for high treason. He was found guilty on 18 September, and sentenced to be hanged, but with a recommendation for mercy. As there was some doubt as to his sanity, the execution was deferred whilst a medical commission examined his mental capacity. They could find nothing more wrong with him than a certain number of eccentric and foolish views on religious subjects, and, as good doctors, held that no obstacle in the way of a proper hanging. After two postponements, he was executed on 1 November. Time and the events of the last seventy years have not washed away all the bitterness that execution caused in the minds of the French-speaking Canadians.

Louis Riel was a symbol, of course. He was a "Métis" or half-breed of Indian and French blood, and a Roman Catholic. He had been one of the leaders in the Red River Revolt of 1869 and on that occasion he had become a symbol to the Métis, and the Indians, of their intense resentment of the men from the East who were proposing to turn their hunting grounds west of the Red River, at Winnipeg, into settled farms. In that year Riel also became a symbol to the English-speaking of Ontario, one of a totally different kind, because during the course of that same revolt he tried and executed an Ulster Orangeman named Thomas Scott, and for a Catholic to kill an Orangeman was to bring again before Ontario the whole panorama of the Battle of the Boyne, and one seen through a Red Indian mist. It was said at the time that Donald Smith, of Hudson's Bay Company, had bribed Riel to fly to the United States to avoid capture and trial, believing that by so doing he would spare the Federal Government embarrassment. It would have been better, judged from that standpoint, if he had tied a stone around Riel's neck and dropped him one night in the Red River itself, for fifteen years later Louis Riel came back, to lead another revolt, in almost exactly the same circumstances, but further west, in what is now Saskatchewan. Other Indians were fearing other settlers from the East and were equally resentful of dispossession. This time the C.P.R. brought out the militia far more speedily to put an end to it all. This time, too, Louis Riel did not escape.

When the rebellion began, Ontario and Quebec were equally resolved that it must be put down with firmness, but the militia were a little slow in disposing of the primitive forces against them. By the time Riel was caught, he was no longer a symbol of a rebel in arms against Canada. He had split into two. In Ontario, he was the murderer of an Orangeman. In Quebec he was a Catholic victim of the English ascendancy. If he is reprieved, the *Toronto Mail* thundered, the Conquest will have to be fought again. At the moment the corpse of Riel falls through the trap, the French press threatened, an abyss will be dug between the province of Quebec and the province of Ontario. Riel's body did fall through the trap, and French-speaking Canada noted that the Government in office was Conservative. In the Quebec provincial elections in January 1887, the official Conservative party there was defeated by a new national bloc led by Honoré Mercier. In the Federal Elections the following month, the Conservatives lost the majority of the seats they had held in Quebec. For fifty years afterwards the provinces of Quebec and Ontario chose their political parties as the Yorkists and the Lancastrians chose their roses.

The ghost of Louis Riel walked again in the First World War. The emotions engendered in 1886 did not die. They smouldered and there were always occasions which contrived to feed them with small injections of fuel. There was the Manitoba Schools question, in the 1890's, based on a French-speaking and Roman Catholic resentment that Manitoba was becoming an English-speaking province and not a French-speaking one, as they had hoped. There was the South African War, and Canada's response to the Imperial request for troops, and Mr. Joseph Chamberlain and his wide plans for a British Empire over the world, in the fullest sense of that word. As late as 1912 there was a Conservative proposal that Canada should contribute $35 million to the cost of building British dreadnoughts. All these, to Quebec, were manifestations of Imperialism and the British lust for ascendancy. They were the more determined to resist it.

When the First World War began, Sir Wilfred Laurier, the Liberal French-speaking Canadian whom everyone respected, declared that the war was a war for freedom and justice, and at first the French press supported him. For him, although he later opposed conscription for military service, both that conviction and that emotion remained. The ordinary man in Quebec had little of the conviction and still less of the emotion, and, as voluntary enlistments among the French-speaking fell away, the

English-speaking began to complain. The French-speaking replied and the embers of the past flickered into flame. Feeling
within the Conservative Government, under the pressure of the
patriotic and religious fires in Ontario, began to harden into a
determination to make the French-speaking people of Quebec
see where their duty lay, and that was accompanied by a degree
of ineptitude in the methods used by the Federal (and English-
speaking) Minister of Militia in the recruitment of volunteers from
Quebec that bears a remarkable resemblance to the clumsiness of
the British War Office in its handling of the volunteers from
Southern Ireland in 1915. This deeper issue was exacerbated by
current local issues between the two provinces, over schools and
over land in the Ottawa Valley. There were many breeding
grounds for suspicion.

The Canadian casualty lists grew. In 1916, the Government
introduced a Bill to provide for the registration of man-power.
Early in 1917 the electoral laws were revised in preparation for
the impending general election, and the emphasis was again on
"patriotism". Finally, on 11 June 1917, a Conscription Bill was
introduced. It had passed through all its stages in the Federal
Parliament by the end of the following August, and two months
later the Conservative Prime Minister, Sir Robert Borden, announced the formation of a Union, or Coalition, Government, for
the better prosecution of the war. The Conscription Act and the
election split the Liberals. At the General Election in December,
the Union won 153 seats, its adherents being 85 Conservatives
and 68 Liberals supporting conscription. The Opposition Liberals
won 82 seats, three-quarters in Quebec.

The same issue arose in the Second World War, and once again
it provided the grounds for a battle, the last major battle, between
the Liberals and the Conservatives. But this time it was a different battle and it had a different result. The Government in office
in 1939 was Liberal and the Prime Minister was Mackenzie King.
Mackenzie King was determined that, if he possibly could, he
would divide neither Canada nor his party on the old issue of
conscription. He believed that what the French-speaking feared
was the involvement in Europe rather than the idea of conscription itself. He believed, too, that almost anything was better
than a direct clash between the two peoples with so much emotion
so very close to the surface, and for four years he can be said to

have played for time. He began by bringing forward a National
Resources Mobilisation Act, which required national service from
all men but limited the military commitment to service in the
Western Hemisphere. When the pressure from the Conservative
Opposition began to mount, and when he found its reflection in
the minds of his English-speaking colleagues in his own party, he
met that pressure with another political device, the Conscription
Plebiscite of April 1942. The Liberal Government, Mackenzie
King said, had given its pledge not to enforce conscription for
service in Europe. It could only move away from that stand if the
people voted to release his Government from its earlier pledge,
and the plebiscite he proposed was framed around the question:
"Are you in favour of releasing the Government from any obligation arising out of any past commitment restricting the methods of
raising men for military service?" The question was astutely
oblique and gained a great deal of time. The voting in the plebiscite was 2,945,514 in favour of, to 1,643,000 against, the question
asked; in Quebec the negative won 993,663 votes, the affirmative
376,188. And, when it was all over, Mackenzie King was able to
assure the House that the vote was not a vote in favour of conscription—that issue had not been put to the people—and so to
keep the support of his Ministers from Quebec.

The climax to the conscription issue began in the fall of 1944.
The Minister of War was Colonel Ralston. Normandy had been
invaded, with a Canadian Army at the spearhead, and Canada,
he felt, had entered into military commitments with the Allies
involving the maintenance of the Canadian Armies at a certain
level. By the September he was uneasy that the supply of re-
inforcements available from the voluntary enlistments was insuffi-
cient, and he flew to Europe to find out for himself. He returned
in the middle of October, convinced that conscription for Europe
was necessary to keep the forces for whom he was responsible at
the promised strength. His views divided the Cabinet. Mackenzie
King was still determined to avoid conscription—it is hard to
say if his belief that sufficient numbers could be found from the
existing volunteers was independently formed or a product of his
intense desire to avoid a seeming repetition of the events of some
twenty-seven years back which might now produce a new break
between the French- and English-speaking, one that might never
heal. The debate within the Cabinet continued until 31 October

and Mackenzie King's solution to that was to drop Colonel Ralston as War Minister and appoint General MacNaughton in his place. That was done on 1 November. It did not settle the issue, for General MacNaughton had his own, and an equally strong, sense of responsibility.

The climax reached its peak three weeks later and the circumstances of that climax are still debated in Canada. According to some accounts, General MacNaughton reported to Mackenzie King that the Canadian military commanders themselves would no longer accept responsibility for directing the Army unless conscription for European service were applied immediately, and that, faced with this revolt of the generals, Mackenzie King gave way. According to others, Mackenzie King used some of the arguments from his military commanders to justify, and fortify, his own political decision that he could no longer avoid some measure of conscription in the reinforcement of the Canadian Army in Europe. Whatever the causes, his decision was to apply conscription for Europe to some 16,000 men, chosen from among those already in the forces. On 7 December an anti-conscription motion moved in the House by members from Quebec found 43 votes in support, against the 168 who voted against it, but within three months the war in Europe was virtually over, and with its end came an end to any intention by Mackenzie King to apply conscription to any further overseas service at all.

There is a footnote in Professor A. R. M. Lower's *Colony to Nation* which records Sir John Macdonald, leader of the Conservative Party at the time, as having said this to Brown Chamberlain, editor of the *Montreal Gazette*:

> The trouble is that you British Canadians can never forget that you were once supreme, that Jean Baptiste was once your hewer of wood and drawer of water ... You struggle for Ascendancy. If a Lower Canadian Britisher desires to conquer, he must "stoop to conquer". He must make friends with the French. Without sacrificing the principle of his race or lineage, he must respect their nationality. Treat them as a nation, and they will act as a free people generally do—generously. Treat them as a faction and they will become factious!

Professor Lower himself adds: "Wise words, the beginning and end of our Canadian puzzle, but few indeed taken to heart."

Yet the vital fact remains that, acute as the conscription issue was, sharp as the feelings were on either side, Canada itself never divided. The French-speaking, even in the First World War, lacked the irredentism of the Irish of the same period. There was no Sinn Fein, no shooting at the constabulary, no abstention from the Federal Parliament. They escaped the fate of Eire, and they were saved from it as much by an increase in their own innate sense of balance as by the moderation of their opponents.

The Federal Government of Canada is elected by adult suffrage among British subjects who have lived in Canada for twelve months prior to polling day. Its constitution may be said to be based on the British North America Act of 1867, with subsequent amendments made by the United Kingdom Government, and on the customs and conventions of the United Kingdom constitution of that time, as modified by some eighty-five years of parliamentary practice in Ottawa since. The British North America Act, although passed by the United Kingdom Parliament, was a measure virtually agreed beforehand in Canada, and so have been most of its subsequent amending Acts. The 1867 Act made a valiant attempt to separate, beyond all possibility of future doubt, the powers to be possessed by the Federal Government and the provincial governments respectively, but, of course it failed, in any absolute sense. In principle it was a true federation, defining the provincial powers and leaving the residual powers with the central government, but it left the Judicial Committee of the Privy Council as the supreme judicial body for the interpretation of the Act and the definition of powers, and the Judicial Committee over the years managed to whittle federal powers down and build up those of the provinces (to trace a pedigree of the Judicial Committee's constitutional line of thought back to the lawyers of the Confederate States of America is an interesting study in itself, as is the Committee's own failure to comprehend the forces which were determining both the growth of the Commonwealth and its chances of survival). The Judicial Committee, in consequence, became a thorn in the side of those who wished Canada to have a strong centralised government, and it may certainly have held back the growth of unity within the country. What is a greater misfortune is the fact that the Judicial Committee threw away the opportunity it had of being a positive and helpful force in the shaping of the Commonwealth. However, one political principle remained unshaken throughout; the Federal Government had full control over and responsibility for external relations, defence, taxation and inter-provincial trade.

The Governor-General occupies in Canada now a position corresponding to that of the Crown in the United Kingdom; he represents the Queen in her right as Queen of Canada, not as Queen of the United Kingdom. Until the present Governor-General, Mr. Vincent Massey, was appointed, the Governors-General had been a long succession of figures from the public life of Britain. These reflected their day and age; they ranged from Lord Willingdon—whose wife, so George Ferguson recounts in his memoir of John W. Dafoe, once said of her husband's energetic appearances, "It keeps the people loyal", to the considerable irritation of Dafoe—to an intensely popular character like Field Marshal Lord Alexander, whom every Canadian I ever heard speak went out of his way to praise.

The conception of a Governor-General is in itself in course of transition. He is a symbol, but of what? If he is a representative of a Queen who cannot spend her whole life within the country, then should not a Governor-General be appointed in the United Kingdom when the Queen is in one of the other countries where she reigns? For the United Kingdom Government to preserve the device of a Regency Council is for that Government to claim a different status within the group. That is an aspect of the office that time may modify. But the Governor-General is also a part of the constitutional machine within the Dominion in which he serves, with a duty in some circumstances to act and therefore presumably accountable for his actions. But to whom? That is one of the questions to which it is difficult to give an exact answer. In Canada there is another complication. Mr. Vincent Massey is an English-speaking Canadian. Will there be a demand, or even an undercurrent of feeling, that his successor, if a Canadian, must be French-speaking in his mother tongue? It is already a convention of the constitution that there shall be such an alternation in the individual chosen as Speaker of the Commons.

The Federal Parliament is bi-cameral, the provinces, with the exception of Quebec, uni-cameral. The Federal Parliament consists of a House of Commons and a Senate, which has a maximum of 102 members, all appointed for life by the Government (but with no obligation on that government to fill vacancies as they occur). Reform of the Canadian Senate is as much (or as little) an aspiration in Canada as reform of the House of Lords is in the United Kingdom. In the meantime, it is used, so the Opposition parties say, as a depository for retired Liberal politicians. The function of government itself, in Canada as in the United Kingdom, rests on the Cabinet, which is supreme within the framework of the British North America Acts. Again as in the United Kingdom, that Cabinet consists of men chosen as individuals by the Prime Minister who have in office a collective responsibility to Parliament for what is done, but in Canada there are certain conventions that require the individuals appointed as Ministers to be broadly representative, in the seats for which they sit, of all the ten provinces.

The political situation today following the federal General Election in August 1953, may be summarised as shown in the table on the opposite page.

Government in Canada is a two-stage expansion system. As a friend said, by way of explanation: "We are bound to vote soberly at federal elections; we can enjoy ourselves in provincial ones", and it would seem that they do. Many issues arise locally and some of them generate enough head of pressure to force their way into federal politics. Many more are nothing but local issues and only misfortune can fall on any politician who attempts to force an issue into national politics which the voters sense is no more than a local one. What is true of the issues is true also of the parties and their leaders. The arguments that keep a party alive provincially, the qualities that enable a man to rise to influence within his province, may be too light to carry either to Ottawa. It is significant that neither the C.C.F. nor the Social Credit Party has yet made a real mark on national politics, although, in 1943, it looked as though the C.C.F. were succeeding.

Nonetheless, provincial issues and provincial politics are real because the powers of the provinces are real. It may have been the original intention to give them less power than, say, that possessed by the states in the American federation, but the Judicial Committee of the Privy Council held differently and twenty years ago the Federal Government transferred to the provinces the ownership of the undeveloped resources in each province. The bulk of the Crown lands in Canada, for instance, are vested in the

Province	Number of seats in Federal House	Results of 1953 General Election					Party in office in provincial Legislative assembly
		Lib.	Cons.	C.C.F.	Socred.	Others	
Newfoundland	7	7	—	—	—	—	Liberal
Prince Edward Island	3	3	—	—	—	—	Liberal
Nova Scotia	11	9	1	1	—	—	Liberal
New Brunswick	10	6	4	—	—	—	Conservative
Quebec	75	66	5	—	—	4	National Union
Ontario	85	50	33	1	—	1	Conservative
Manitoba	14	8	3	3	—	—	Coalition
Saskatchewan	18	5	1	12	—	—	C.C.F.
Alberta	17	4	2	—	11	—	Socred.
British Columbia	22	8	4	7	3	—	Socred.
The Territories	2	2	—	—	—	—	
Totals	264	168	53	24	14	5	

The total votes cast for the parties were:

Liberals	2,819,038	Conservatives	1,751,673
Commonwealth Co-operation Federation (C.C.F.)	636,191	Social Credit ("Socred")	305,909
Independents and others[1]	68,333	Labour-Progressives	59,693

(Provisional figures, October 1953)

[1] 54,775 of these were cast in Quebec.

Queen in her right of each province. Each province controls its own development and the prairie provinces, in particular, may in the not too distant future be able to balance a normal budget from the revenues from mineral royalties. The result is that provincial politics in Canada escape the anaemic uniformity of local affairs in the United Kingdom. A county council like that of Lancashire is responsible for twice as many people as the provincial government of British Columbia. It has less freedom to tax far less freedom of action and, not surprisingly, commands far less interest among the majority of the citizens in the county. Politics in Canada cannot be wholly centralised and are all the healthier in consequence.

The Liberal Party has been in office in Ottawa since 1935 and it was led by Mackenzie King from 1919 until his resignation in 1948. It was not a party of his creation but it was a very different party when he resigned from that which he first led. He came into authority within it when the breach between Liberals in Canada made by the conscription issue in the First World War was still wide. The split was healed under his leadership, and he led the party to victory in the General Election of 1921. Save for a Conservative interlude during the depression years, Mackenzie King saw the whole sweeping change in Canadian life from the end of one major war to the end of the next. He held supreme office for longer than any other statesman in the history of the whole Commonwealth.

Mackenzie King is one of the most fascinating characters in Canadian history, and Canadian politics have not been deficient in personalities. He was clear in thought and obscure in speech. In many ways he was timid, but not in his contacts with men. He was not a great statesman but he was a most astute politician. He was a fortunate egoist, because, in Canada, a Prime Minister must impose his personality on his colleagues, and on the public, or fail. He absorbed public opinion as a sponge water and he was rarely wrong in his timing. At home he surrounded himself with a framework, almost a stockade, of material possessions and protective customs. He was a convinced spiritualist, yet managed to keep both his beliefs and his practices virtually a secret. He lacked all consideration for his staff, he had no close friends even among his colleagues, his combat with the Conservative leader, Arthur Meighen, had all the incidental cruelty of a *corrida*, yet he sentimentalised his mother. Politics were his life and he understood them better than any other man in Canada. That, really, could be his epitaph. He made the Liberal Party a magnificent machine for the Government of his country, and his importance to Canada will, perhaps, in the end be judged by the value that machine has for Canada.

The man who succeeded Mackenzie King was Louis St. Laurent

(whose character and achievements will be discussed in the final chapter) a man from Quebec who had followed Mackenzie King's decision to impose conscription for European service in 1944 and who had convinced Quebec in the parliamentary debate that followed that he was a true leader. St. Laurent met French nationalism with French logic and turned narrow provincialism aside with the wider sweep of his mind. Perhaps it is an exaggeration to say that then and there in that debate Mackenzie King saw the man who should be his successor as leader of the Liberals; it is doubtful if Mackenzie King was then thinking of any successor at all in any realistic way. But thereafter Louis St. Laurent stood out as a man who could speak for Quebec in a way that Ontario respected, and that is still the combination of vital importance in Canadian politics. The two victories won by the Liberals under Louis St. Laurent are in themselves assessments of the value of Mackenzie King to his party. He left it a record, and a machine, that were of enormous value in an election; he did not leave it such a towering personal memory that no successor could sustain the mantle he let fall.

Mackenzie King was one of the last of the nineteenth-century Liberals, the last to hold office as Prime Minister in Canada and perhaps elsewhere. His working life began in the assumption that men are reasonable beings, that governments are concerned with politics not economics, and that all international relationships can be governed by conciliation, provided the right machinery is found. His views on the duties of governments changed during the depression years and his views on international relations were sharply altered in 1939, and again in 1945. Yet, doctrinaire Liberal as he was in the beginning, he built up for his country a machine that ran most effectively during one war and which, so he feared in the end, might well be needed for another. He served his time, and that double-edged saying is peculiarly appropriate to such a man as Mackenzie King.

Every political party must have its philosophy as well as its method. To the European, the central core from which he expects the philosophy of a political party to extend is the relationship between capital and labour. The touchstone is the question: do you believe that the two can by synthesis produce a new order of society, or do you believe in their inevitable conflict, followed

by victory for one or the other, or an attrition-produced decay?
Yet the European looking at Canadian affairs cannot feel confident
that the question to be asked there will prove to be anything of
the kind. He himself stands in the aftermath of a century of expansion in which capital and labour did fight it out, and he may
well be convinced that the confusion he sees in his own continent
is an attrition-produced decay. In Canada he is aware at once of a
phase of expansion well into its first flights, but no further. Habit
of mind warns him that the same conflict must underlie all that
he sees, that the end will be an end he is already experiencing.
Hope tells him that one century cannot repeat the pattern of its
predecessor and that he would be a fool to prejudge Canada's
future by what he believes to be his own past. Assuming politics
to be an outward expression of all the hopes and fears, the an-
tagonism and co-operation in a nation's life, what does at least one
European think he sees in Canada?

The Liberal Party claims to march in the middle of the road.
It believes in free enterprise, but it holds that a government
should be prepared to be more than a passive umpire administer-
ing a given set of rules. That must imply an absence of dogma
over the role government should play, which in its turn must
mean that this Liberal Party is a long way from its *laisser-faire*
origins. But the beliefs of this Liberal Party do not lift questions of
public ownership and operation in industry from their proper position as questions of method to the status of political philosophies.
What its attitude seems to amount to is that it believes that the life
of a nation must have balance and rhythm, and that the government
is some kind of governor to the movements of the whole of this
society, intended to correct deviations from some desirable norm.
Judging from its actions, the party considers that a government
should possess both the information needed to detect movements
away from the two essential harmonies and instruments powerful
enough to restore the proper balance. And what is a proper
balance? The practical test seems to be progression towards an
improved material well-being for the whole nation.

Put like that, the Liberal Party might sound to be no more than
a government of intelligent civil servants with reasonably flexible
minds, and that does describe one aspect of the Liberal Government's regime. It has been accused of being dull and it certainly
prides itself on being respectable. It is significant, too, that it has

15. Ontario: Ottawa

16. Newfoundland: St. John's Harbour

felt the need to recruit men like Lester Pearson and John Pickers-
gill direct from the civil service into the Cabinet. But no government can have lasted for so long without some elements of emotion in its composition. What are those, in Canada?

It is here that one senses a contrast between Canadians and the
people of both the United Kingdom and the United States. In
both the United States and the United Kingdom, although for
entirely different reasons, a government is looked upon with resentment. In the United States the resentment is that the government should interfere at all. One of the American myths is that
all governments are by nature evil and oppressive; Americans
have contined the revolt against governments that their Founding
Fathers staged against a particular government, long since dead.
In the United Kingdom the resentments are two. On the one hand
there is a resentment that the Government does not do more, on
the other resentment that what it does do is clumsy and crippling.
Both these are symptoms of frustration rather than objective
judgments on government as such. There seems an absence of this
resentment in Canada. The Canadians are in an extrovert phase.
The energy of most of them is directed towards some positive task,
and one which gives them the emotional satisfaction that comes
from a feeling of conquest. They do not need to look for a scapegoat. They have a feeling of tolerance towards government, which
enables them to judge more objectively, and so appreciate the
more fairly, the Liberal Government's efficiency. A minority, to
the left, of course, believes that the government should do more,
but theirs is more a moral judgment than a cry of desperation.
Perhaps that is why the atmosphere of the Canadian Left seems
to resemble more that of the Fabians of 1910 than the Bevanites
of 1953.

Here, too, one seems to approach the sources of the emotion
on which the Liberal Party, certainly under the leadership of
Mackenzie King, has drawn. Mackenzie King believed that a
party must have a moral ideal, that the ideal must sound attain-
able and that it must appeal to a widening range of people—in
short, he thought, as a nineteenth-century Liberal, in terms of a
spreading democracy and that the party which threw its net wide
enough would get the most votes. But these principles and policies
did not derive their strength in his mind solely from their vote-
catching possibilities. He remained convinced that they are an

P

essential ingredient in the mixtures that gives a party vitality and so leads to success at the polls. He was not cynical over this, nor were his beliefs synthetic. Politics are far too revealing for him to have retained power for so long had he had his tongue in his cheek. Bruce Hutchinson, in his study of Mackenzie King, *The Incredible Canadian*, quotes him as repeating with approval, in the short days of his retirement, John Bright's remark to Gladstone: "The Liberal Party must always be friendly to its rebels."

The moral principle that Mackenzie King applied was that the wealth of Canada must be shared. Is that the same as the concept of a government existing as no more than a mechanical governor, regulating economic conditions so that they lead of themselves to the increased well-being of all the people? It seems to me not, for this reason. The second is a proposition in economics. It pays regard only to the machinery of consumption. It argues that undesirable dislocations will follow (as indeed they do) if the consuming power of the majority falls below a certain level. To state positively that the wealth of a country must be shared is to base a political act on a moral decision. It includes a moral judgment that the people have a right to an opportunity of a fuller and less insecure life. To me that moral judgment must impose on those who make it a moral duty to see that it happens. This duty is one most of the Western countries, including the United Kingdom, accepted when they pledged themselves to the doctrine of full employment. Not all their practices, or methods, have been in accord with their stated principles, but at least let us be clear what I think the Liberal Party in Canada has committed itself to.

The second strand in a party's composition must be the methods it uses to achieve its political ends. Now it seems to me that it is the duty, as well as the fate, of groups on the left to allow their political clothing to be stolen by the government in office. It may be galling, but to complain is to show a sectarian habit of mind, a conviction that an action is only good when it is done by the right people. Equally, governments in office are to be congratulated when they do steal their opponents' clothes, for that shows they understand one of the bases of political method; let the minorities propose, and, when the debate has winnowed what is proposed, do not delay in gathering the grain. And what seems to stand out in the record of the Liberal Party in Canada is its admirable timing in gathering the grain.

Mackenzie King seized his opportunity during the war. The Bank of Canada was nationalised in 1944, and by 1945, when the veterans came back (which is usually the moment when disillusion begins) Canada had a network of social services which includes family allowances, old age pensions and income tax relief in respect of medical and hospital expenses. The Liberals have left the Left wing a great many matters of detail to argue about but they have deprived them of the most effective argument of all, the policy of social welfare itself.

Contrast that with the policy pursued in the United Kingdom. After the publication of the Beveridge Report in 1942 it became clear that the United Kingdom would sooner or later take the next step onwards in the provision of these welfare services. The Coalition Government of the war accepted the principles of this and worked out plans for carrying them into effect. But it had not done so when the war ended. One reason was Sir Winston Churchill's sense of propriety. He regarded party politics as in abeyance for the war period. It may have been that he regarded any wartime action which would redound to the credit of the Conservatives as an unfair abuse of power. Far more likely, the inertia of the Conservatives behind him, allied with his own concentration on the grand strategy of the war itself, effectively killed any action. But the result was to give the Labour Party the verdict in the General Election of 1945.

The majority of the electorate of Britain voted for social welfare on the Beveridge Plan, and it got social welfare plus socialism from the blue-prints of the 'thirties. If the Conservatives in Britain, who are now in aims not so very dissimilar from the Liberals in Canada, had by 1945 brought the level of social welfare and state ownership in Britain up to that prevailing in Canada at that time (for, by then, not only was the Bank of Canada in public ownership; the C.N.R. and the T.C.A. had been for some time) they might well have won power in that year. And, of course, had they been people of that vision, they might well have made a good job of the immediate post-war period as well. However, that did not happen, but the fact that it did happen in Canada is at least an indication of a difference in political awareness.

There is another point of importance. The Liberal Party's decision to share the wealth of Canada was made before that wealth began to expand very rapidly, and that, politically, is the right moment at which to make the decision and to start to carry it into effect. It likewise made it possible for the party to imply (and no party is wholly scrupulous in its propaganda) that the wealth was growing rapidly because it was being shared. It was also a protection to what can only be described as public morality, for, as with a tiger tasting blood, once a majority gets a taste for the evil joys of depriving the minority of the wealth it already has, the habit so formed is hard to kill. Canada has largely escaped the conviction that stalks through Britain today, the conviction that the ownership of wealth, even of prosperity, is a mark of evil in itself.

That, I would say, is the main difference between political feeling in Canadian federal politics and that in the United Kingdom. I would like to believe that the sole motive power behind the left-wing party in Britain is a longing to construct, to do good; events of the last eight years have persuaded me that there is a strong—too strong—admixture of a desire to destroy, that the desire for a change is based more on a hatred of what is than a longing for what should be. I do not think that emotion exists to anything like the same extent in Canada. In Canada, Mr. Butler and Mr. Gaitskell would be walking hand in hand and Mr. Bevan and Sir Waldron Smithers would be yapping at their heels on either side. It is, of course, a matter of preference which scene you find the more attractive; there is no doubt, I hope, about mine.

All this suggests that the Liberal Party in Canada occupies rather more than the middle of the road. It appears to extend leftwards as far as the fringes of the C.C.F. How far does that take it?

The C.C.F., it seems to me, is a party of mixtures as yet far from assimilated. Its more substantial part is an agrarian movement from Saskatchewan, a product of the depression of the 'thirties and one of a long line of farmer-progressive movements. That part is basically co-operative in its ideas. Its provincial programme is one of developing those services, the wheat pool, co-operative or publicly-owned insurance, electricity supply and other such organisations, which will enable the farmer to carry on the more successfully his individual and private enterprise as a producer of food. That section of the party would shy violently at collective farming, even at nationalisation of the land. The Saskatchewan

Government is headed by Mr. T. C. Douglas, born in Falkirk, Scotland, shrewd, fluent, a reasonable and capable administrator and man of business, a man whose social plans would march very well with those advocated by the Lloyd Georgian Liberals in the United Kingdom twenty-five years ago. It seemed to me that he had nothing in common with a British Socialist-cum-economist such as, say, Harold Wilson.

A second element in the C.C.F. is the industrial trade unionist, in the Ontario iron foundries or the Nova Scotia coal mines, for instance, who feels, like some of the C.I.O. leaders in the United States, that the trade unions must have a political wing if they are to exert the full strength of their power. The views in this group seem to range from the total rejection of private ownership and operation (in which case the individual joins, in Canada, the Labour-Progressives, who are Canada's Communists) to rather unformulated ideas of planning control and the defeat of the power of money and capital. Finally, there is a small admixture of the theoretical socialist who gave me the impression of having brought his convictions ready-made from Europe, of talking as Sir Stafford Cripps talked in the 'thirties and of thinking as Philip Snowden did ten years before that. It is this section of the party that contributes the bitterness, the kind of destructive venom, that can condemn in the one breath an industrialist for daring to own the capital in his own business and the bank director for daring to direct a bank without owning its capital. I would say that there is more solid thinking done today on the future of a working-class movement for Canada in the province of Quebec than anywhere else in Canada, and Quebec has almost totally rejected the C.C.F.

The confusion of thought within the party is shown by its election campaign—still more by the points it emphasised in that campaign—for last year's general election. The points made by Mr. Coldwell, the leader of the party, in his eve-of-the-poll speech included a demand for a closer association between Canada and the sterling area, acceptance by Canada of sterling for its sales to the United Kingdom and the remission of interest on the 1946 Canadian loan to Britain. It is not hard to see the groups to whom these proposals were directed; the farmers in Saskatchewan, the lumbermen and salmon fishermen in British Columbia, and the advocates of close ties with Britain and fewer ties with the United

States everywhere in the country. It is not hard to see that a party that could not match the Conservatives' promise to cut taxation by $500 million in the year would feel compelled to think of something else equally startling. But proposals of this kind have a hollow ring in a country which now sells two-thirds of its exports to the United States and buys there three-quarters of its imports. The Canadian farmer may dislike having to pay the tariff on his American washing machine or automobile. Is he prepared to see an import quota restricting his buying of both? It is, perhaps, unkind for an intended beneficiary to make such a comment, but it is the voters of Canada to whom Mr. Coldwell would be answerable. Geography may be inconvenient but cannot be ignored.

On the right of the Liberals are the Conservative Party and the Social Credit Party. The Conservative Party is still a national party. It has not held office since Mr. R. B. Bennett's Government which began in 1930 and perished in 1935. It is now led by Colonel George Drew, of Toronto, who has been Premier of Ontario but has had no experience of federal office.

The Conservative Party of Canada bears many resemblances to the Republican Party of the United States. In the days of Sir John Macdonald the party had mental affiliations with the robber-baron period of development in the United States. It was optimistic and ruthless and it had no inhibitions over how it spent the money (mostly British) that came into Canada to develop the country. With the growth of manufactures it became the party of Ontario, of high tariffs and protection for the manufacturer, and that, largely, it remains. The Conservatives are far less bitter over the social programme of the Liberals than the Republicans in the United States have been over the New Deal, but they used the same arguments at the time of the last election, that a party in power for so long must inevitably have become slack, inefficient, wasteful of public money and, they would imply, to a certain extent corrupt. Their programme in the 1953 election was very much based on two slogans, "Time for a change", and "Anything you can do I can do more cheaply", an atmosphere of "me-tooism" but without the arrogance of the extreme Republican magnate further south. And, as a party, they have suffered the disintegration which a party lacking a moral cause to keep it together experiences when out of office for so long.

The Conservatives are also thought of as the more "loyal"

party, the party that values the British connection. This, I found, was an exceedingly intricate subject to attempt to unravel. I will try, later on, to define what "loyalty" means to a Canadian now, but in the political context in Canada it has certain inconsistencies. It must be remembered, first, that the "British" element in Ontario is more coloured with Ulster-Scots thought than with that of the purely English. Then no one in Canada wishes to see British control, in any shape or form, reintroduced. The British connection now is rather more a consciousness of having come from the British Isles than any deep feeling of ties with the United Kingdom as a present-day political institution. Certainly, in matters of trade and industry the man of Ontario is not prepared to put the interests of the United Kingdom above his own. One can find in this, perhaps, rather composite character traces of the old feeling of ascendancy over the French-speaking Canadians, that being British meant not being French—being a jolly sight better, in fact. There is more than a touch of nostalgia for some of the trappings of life in Britain. There is a feeling that it is a "good thing" to have in Canada more people from Britain—more especially from Scotland and Northern Ireland—to balance the other Europeans who come as emigrants, and there are traces of resentment against what is felt, rightly or wrongly, as a desire in Ottawa to cut down the ties with the old country. All that may seem to add up to no more than a collection of sentimentalities, but sentimentalities is far too unjust a word to use of the generation that fought in the First World War. They then offered their lives for a reality they called "Britain". Their sentiment was real then and I would not believe that, although it may have lost strength, it has lost all its true meaning in their minds.

But, in the meantime, America has grown and America is just across Lake Ontario. In business, the Ontario Conservative thinks as an American. Americans were never less than cousins and it seemed to me that the Conservatives of Ontario might be said to think of Americans as belonging to their own generation, as well as to their own continent, while the United Kingdom is more a part of their past. They are by no means all partners with the industries of the United States—some are, of course—but they all do business in the same street and meet at the same Rotarian lunch. The people of Ontario—and that is the province one has in mind when one thinks of the Canadian Conservative—are a complicated people, generous, friendly and strange, no easier to understand, I found, than the French-speaking of Quebec.

Then, out in the West, is the Social Credit Party, the Socreds. Like the C.C.F. in Saskatchewan, the Socreds of Alberta are a product of the depression of the 'thirties. The C.C.F. gained power in their province on the cry of co-operation; in Alberta the winning cause was that of the social dividend, the "funny money" of Major Douglas's theories. Both were a protest against the money power of the East, against the hard economic fact that, in times of deflation, the burden of a fixed interest rate grows more and more heavy. But, if Mr. William Aberhart, the first Socred Premier of Alberta, ever understood the Douglas Social Credit theory, he soon abandoned any attempt to carry it into practice. Instead, being an astute politician, he tackled the interest rates themselves, which, whether he was successful or not, was a better political battleground for any conflict with the Federal Government in Ottawa.

So, again like the C.C.F., Socreds settled down to give Alberta an efficient, competent and honest government, and the subsequent increase in the prosperity of the province has provided more powerful arguments at each election. "We are in office and look what has happened to your province whilst we have been in office." Mr. Aberhart has now died and his place has been taken by Mr. E. C. Manning, who is tall and slim and still under fifty, and very conscious that if you are to become a personality in the West you must seem to be one already. The disconcerting thing about the Socreds is their ties with some of the curious extremes to which the protestant religions can reach, with such churches as that of the Four-Square Gospel and the Prophetic Bible. The power of the Lord to smite the Amalekites is the real thing in Alberta.

Today, the Socreds are an "Alberta first" party. They are also a party of what might be called the impatient business man, who is not very interested in free speech, for others, who is touched with anti-semitism and who half thinks that communism is a real bogy and half thinks that it is a useful one. The party gained ground in the provincial elections in British Columbia in June 1953, partly because of disgruntlement there over the deficiencies of the former Liberal and Conservative Coalition, partly because the doctrinairic approach of the C.C.F. leaders in British Columbia produced exactly the reaction on the right with which Europe is so familiar. The Socreds did not gain ground federally outside Alberta in the General Election in August.

Government in Canada is based on the two party system and therefore it needs two parties. It is arguable that it needs two parties on the American model, where parties are not exponents of different political theories but are themselves organisations for the settlement, by diplomatic methods, of regional differences and interests. It is, of course, possible, in theory, that the Liberal Party may split, but there are no signs of that, nor does past history make such a happening seem at all likely. Assuming that it does not, will the party in effective opposition to the Liberals come finally from their right or their left?

The answer must to some extent depend on how the Liberal Party develops. The whole history of Canada shows that the vitality of a party comes from the left, or, more exactly, from the rebels and the radicals. It is they who both forecast change and, by their actions thereafter, produce change, and the party that has the wisdom to choose aright from the alternatives in change presented by its rebels gains the advantage. The danger to the Liberals is precisely that of which they have been accused by the Conservatives, that they will cease to think in terms of refurbishing their own content, and appearance, and so lose the support of the electors. No party is so perfect that it can dare allow the voters to believe that it thinks it is. If the Liberals lose the next election, it will be on a vote against them rather than on a vote for anyone else.

Another important element in Canadian politics is personality— one must never forget the vital words of John Dafoe, that all political decisions in Canada are deeply influenced by personal motives and interests. A party must have a leader who is an agreeable personality in the minds of the electorate. He must be someone with whom the voters feel they are at least acquainted. Mackenzie King grew into that position. Louis St. Laurent has gained it rather more quickly and in a more human way. But Louis St. Laurent is now seventy-two and when the party in power comes to choose a leader it faces the difficult task of finding a successor— almost of creating a successor—whilst the Prime Minister himself is still in the centre of the stage. On the other hand, the Opposition party has the equally difficult task of building up a leader against all the natural advantages that office itself gives his rival on the opposite benches.

If the Liberals are voted against, which party will succeed them? Again that must depend on events. The Liberals can continue to steal in perfect safety all the C.C.F.'s clothes, right down to its rather tattered socialist vest. It is difficult to know what socialism can mean in Canada for quite a long time (it is difficult enough to know now what socialism means anywhere). It cannot mean the nationalisation of the means of production, distribution and exchange—at least, not unless the party in Canada is content to remain no larger and no more effective than the socialist party in the United States—for that rigidity in method is totally alien to the North American mind and the pattern of North American development. The C.C.F. will have to go back to the principles of social justice and try and devise a realistic approach to the problems of enterprise and incentive, of the divorce between ownership and control, of the forms of public control, of all the means of producing a harmony between producer and consumer, management and worker. And all the time it will face the thieving propensities of any Liberal Party.

I would have thought that a more advantageous line for a left-wing party in Canada to pursue would have been one based on a closer analysis of the difference between interest and profit. (That is not an exploration any European left-wing party will ever make; the emotional barriers against it are too strong.) Interest is a payment for money lent. Profit is a reward for a risk taken. Of course, all capitalists try to claim that all their capital incurs some risk and is therefore entitled to profit, but it is a very disputable claim. A party which based its political programme on some such proposition, and found methods of confining the earnings of profits to capital carrying a risk, might rapidly improve its position. It would, of course, have to drop its theoretical aversion from the whole ideal of profit-making, but if it did so it would escape the appalling inconsistency of the socialists in Britain, who attack every kind of profit and yet base their whole welfare state structure on the assumption that enough profits will be made to pay for it. Surely, in Canada of all places, there is a hope of moving on from the socialist who broods over the problems of the past, like a Chelsea Pensioner recounting over and over again all the disasters of the Modder River battle.

The parties to the right of the Liberals are, in appearances, more divided. True, these divisions are no wider than those that exist within the Republican Party of the United States, but the Republican Party of the United States has never had to win the province of Quebec.

The conservative-in-mind in Quebec are well placed. They have considerable influence, to use no harsher a word, with the provincial government of Quebec, and the provincial government of Quebec has control of all the natural resources of the province. Because of the importance of Quebec to the Liberal Party, they have considerable indirect influence on any Liberal Government in office. Mr. Duplessis is well aware of this, and he is probably equally well aware of the limits beyond which he should not push his anti-Liberal campaign. He certainly avoided any direct commitment of his party, the Union Nationale, to the Conservative cause in last year's federal elections. If there is a chink in their armour, it is to be found in the fact that the iron-ore deposits in the Labrador Trough lie athwart a singularly inconvenient boundary line between Quebec and Labrador, which brings the Newfoundland Government into the picture, but the present Newfoundland Government thinks of capital development in very much the same terms as does the Government of Quebec. So, before any party to the right of the Liberals can hope to win Quebec it will need to possess great powers of statesmanship, and something of a new approach. It would certainly have to shed all religious sectarianism and intolerance, for instance, since the Four-Square Bible is hardly likely to have a strong appeal in a Catholic province.

A traditionally-minded Conservative Party would face other, equally strong, difficulties in the West. Ontario's devotion to a high tariff cannot hope suddenly to be popular among the wheat growers and it will be a long time before production there is so diversified that high tariff influences are as strong as the others. In the end the Conservatives will have to find a principle that the Liberals cannot, or will not, steal. They may be presented with a victory at the federal polls (although they should not count on any change of luck) and were that to happen it would be a pity if they had not found an effective principle first.

It is important that they should. No country can consider itself free from the risks and the dangers of one-party rule, yet the defences against that growth lie as much in the hands of the Opposition as in those of the party in power. Indeed it can be argued that in a country with a tradition of democratic rule it is only when the morale of the Opposition collapses that the party in power begins to act in terms of perpetual one-party, or totalitarian, rule. A considerable burden lies on the Conservatives, as the bearers of the historic tradition of the second party in the state. It is difficult to attract to a party which seems to have no prospect of office a right mixture of talent and support. The Opposition can always find support—which, of course, may be only the counterpart of the support given with the other hand to the party in office—from those who hope to get something out of their investment, in terms of cash, or power, if ever the tide changes. But a party needs more than a cash box to give it life. It needs fire and enthusiasm.

The Conservatives have also to think of their relations with the Socreds. The Socreds did not strike me as a party deeply interested in the two-party system of government, certainly not on a provincial level. They gave an impression of thinking that they knew best and that opposition to them, of all people, was bound to be factious, almost insultingly unnecessary. Yet there are a number of reasons why the Conservatives ought to be in alliance with them; indeed, one might say that any alliance would be better than none, for it would both compel the two parties to compromise and prevent either from winning an out-and-out victory over the other. One misfortune is that the present Conservative Party of Canada has tended to shrink into becoming a Conservative Party of Ontario, with branch offices in other parts of the Dominion. It would help them if they were able to capture some of the vigour and confidence that comes from Alberta. To achieve any effective union between the parties to the right of the Liberals would require statesmanship of a high order, but that quality of statesmanship has been found in Canada before, in both parties.

Where will the right in Canada find any such new principle, or impetus, one both capable of winning voters from their long Liberal allegiance and of sustaining an alliance with a rather intolerant Social Credit Party? It needs something fundamental, at least something more potent than a mere change in political method or tactics. What the Conservatives search for will not be found in Europe, nor in any of the old ties with Europe, for these have little or no appeal either in Alberta or Quebec. It is not likely to be found in the United States; certainly not from the Republicans of the United States, who seem to be struggling to learn how to catch up rather than how to lead. Still less will it be found in any of the published works of Major Douglas himself (not that anyone in Alberta is likely to look for it, or anything else, there). Nor will it be found in any development of the Conservatives' present election tactics, of criticising anything and everything that the Liberal Party has done or has not done. A party which, as the Conservatives did in 1949, tries to make political capital out of the fact that the engines in the government-owned "North Star" aircraft of T.C.A. are noisy is losing its political acumen. It is trying to score a bull with a charge of buckshot. Even if some pellets do hit the centre of the target, everyone puts that down to chance.

Perhaps their first lessons can only be learnt in the comparatively humble tasks of opposition. They will have to accept the essential elements of a social security state, for a great many people have a vested interest in that now. Above all, they will have to be daring in their ideas for the development of capitalism. After all, capitalism is not an institution designed solely for the protection of wealth that already exists. It is a mechanism for the better deployment of all resources, for the creation and distribution of the wealth that lies as yet unused. Capitalism is not based only on theories of ownership; it is based on theories of application as well. The day may yet come when the Liberals are too flabby to take a risk. If the Conservatives are given the chance to show that they could build again the contemporary equivalent of the C.P.R., and take it, then they will be back again in office, and will have something positive to do when they get there.

10

What kind of People are the Canadians?

THE Canadian, the English-speaking Canadian, is good with machines. Two out of every three live in a town of some size, and they like fishing. As descendants of the Ulsterman and the Lowland Scot, they prefer hard liquor and think of drinking as an end in itself rather than as incidental to some other activity. They do not like either to hear music or to see women in their licensed premises, and they tolerate a degree of what can only be described as hygienic squalor in those institutions that in itself is a tribute to the strength of what they must consume whilst they are there.

This Ulster-Scot in Canada has expanded more than his proto-type in the British Isles, for many of the economic and social pressures that existed in Britain are absent from the Canadian scene. He is hardworking, honest, extrovert, not given to melan-choly, or poetry, thinking of art in terms of decoration and sport in terms of physical fitness. Utilitarians. Practical, reasonable men, except when under the influence of a strong passion, like that brewed in an Orange lodge. Not strongly humorous in the mass, not particularly adventurous on the average. They are bankers, engineers and technicians. They have little interest in women, save for sex, and little interest in leisure, save as a rest from work, and, since it never pays to neglect women in any way, women have come to control a great deal of their lives, in offices as secre-taries, in homes as wives. And that opens a door on a very large subject, one that discretion advises had better be avoided. And yet—? Admittedly, whilst this book is no place in which to

222

attempt a study of the activities and interests of the North American female—it has already been undertaken by far more industrious and inquisitive pens—it would leave a false impression if no comment was made on the total dissimilarity between the relationships between the sexes that exist on that continent and those still prevailing in Europe.

European society still rests on a modified—one might also say a decayed—form of an aristocratic tradition that itself descended from a tribal organisation in which the males contrived to do less and less of the menial work of life. Power came from the ownership of land and land was inherited by the eldest male, and women, as they so easily do, adapted themselves to that system. They worked and they were submissive, and while no doubt on theoretical grounds their status could be challenged, that order of society produced desirable results. Women were compelled to charm their way into positions of influence. They had little opportunity to develop their tendencies towards arrogance and, most fortunately, the shift in the source of power from land to money did not free women entirely from the salutary confines of such social regulations.

In North America this chain of social order was broken sharply, and at an unfortunate time, and the forces that might have prevented, or at least softened, the effects of the break were on the losing side. In Quebec, the French were a defeated people and their conquerors did not show the flexibility of mind of the Normans in England. In the southern States, the aristocratic society had built itself on a basis of slavery and was fatally weakened with the end of that economic order. The triumphant were the Puritans, the people who made a principle of equality and who in their turn produced the settler and the homesteader and finally the horse trader, and that at a time when the basis of power was already becoming money. So in most of North America the female was admitted as a partner, and, of course, now she owns most of the business. It is not so much that she is a better manager; she lives longer. What she cannot collect in her husband's lifetime, she acquires on his death. Today, women own two-thirds of the stocks and bonds in North America and spend three-quarters of the income. And Canada is no exception. Indeed, part of the general superficial friendliness of the urban Canadian in business may well come from this woman-dominated background.

There is about it something of the camaraderie of the prison camp, or of the recreation break in jail. In all the male sessions with drinks, in clubs, at the ball game, or on the curling rink, there is that underlying anxiety: What, they seem to say, can the enemy be thinking up for us now? At least let us enjoy our freedom while we can.

It is all a great pity. It is not for nothing that traffic with woman was one described as playing with fire, for how true it is that they make both good servants and poor masters. Women need some stimulus before they will exert themselves to please; in North America the stimulus has gone, for, on level terms, man is a poor match for woman. He dreams, and imagines that success in business somehow secures his independence. Women dominate the home. They allow sexual relations to become either a manifestation of the reproductive urge or a form of gymnastics. Romance is an excitement to be enjoyed vicariously, at second-hand, not to be sought, still less built up, in the home. The male is not to be wooed; he is to be received. The furnishings of the North American home do not suggest long nights of bliss. The emphasis is on the sanitary fittings; a bed is sold as guaranteeing a good night's sleep. Instead of planning how to entertain her husband, the wife seeks to master the conventions of contract bridge, and is there any more pathetic sight in the world than four women clad as for golf striding down the fairway? Oh, what a serpent St. Andrew bred in Scotland.

What, then, distinguishes the Canadian from the American? There is one immediate answer to that. If the French-speaking Canadians had not existed, it is likely that Canada today would have been much closer to the Americans than she already is, that there might well have been so complete a political tie between the two countries that Canada would have ceased to be a separate nation for all external purposes. She would have become, politically, another Mexico. That is not a statement with which all Canadians would agree, but it is a reason why I would not like to consider Canada's future place in the world without first considering the French-speaking Canadians.

The French-speaking Canadians are North Americans. In the American idiom, they are North Americans, period. Like the Eskimos. The French-speaking have a greater knowledge of

Europe than the Eskimos, a greater understanding, but no deeper feelings for it, for its people, and, perhaps, for its fate. They are right to call themselves *les Canadiens*, and they had justice on their side when they called the English-speaking *les Anglais*. They have no living parents in Europe and they view the activities of their second cousins with a faint distaste. The people of Quebec are the product of a single environment, a firm and closely-knit religion and the traditions that grow within a society that feels itself compressed by an alien majority. In Newfoundland and, to a lesser extent, in Nova Scotia, environment, heredity and circumstance have combined to give a unity of a different kind. Elsewhere, the people of Canada are a product of many environments, different religions and no feeling of constraint at all.

The First World War was a British war in which Canada found herself involved because of a decision made in London. A great many English-speaking Canadians fought in that war precisely for those reasons, and an even greater proportion of the French-speaking Canadians refused to do so, on the same grounds. The Second World War was a war in which the Canadian Parliament decided Canada should join. A great many French-speaking Canadians were reluctant to fight in it because they did not believe that the war threatened Canada. There is one measure of the change in Canada over the twenty-five years, but it also underlines the fact that many of the French-speaking Canadians had changed very little during the same time.

The French-speaking Canadians are the oldest group from Europe in North America. An individual French-speaking Canadian may grow from an inhabitant of the province of Quebec into an inhabitant of the Confederation of Canada. He will not walk backwards in time and become an inhabitant of either France or, still less, the United Kingdom, nor can he begin to feel as one. M. Louis Durant, in an article *Les Canadiens Français et l'Esprit National* in an enquiry into French-speaking Canada made by Action Française before the war, wrote:

One day he (the French Canadian) found himself abandoned in the presence of a stranger who did not speak his tongue who did not worship in his way, and who, moreover, was at no pains to conceal the fact that henceforth it was he who was to be the master. That day Jean Baptiste, letting his gaze wander

Q

over the horizon spread out before him, felt clearly and strongly that this was his home, and that no power, no arrogance, no astuteness could alter the fact that these houses, these fields, these churches, these roads belonged to him, and to him only.

M. André Siegfried, looking at the people of Quebec with the eyes of a Frenchman, was equally, but more sadly, convinced of the same thing. "We lost contact with them after 1763," he wrote in his book *Canada*, "and the French of the St. Lawrence had every right to feel that the Mother Country, henceforward unworthy of the name, had abandoned them." Again, describing the lack of response to the recruiting campaign in Quebec in the First World War: "It is difficult for the French to understand how such matters as the schools in Ontario or the English recruiting sergeants could have been put in the balance alongside the very existence of France, which then certainly was at stake. It was the instinct for local survival, blind but powerful, which determined the stay-at-home attitude." Others besides M. Siegfried have been provoked into damning the French-speaking Canadians as a people in the grip of a powerful but blind instinct. Indeed, it is essential to think of them as French-speaking Canadians, confusing to think of them as French Canadians, for, as M. Siegfried observed, while they may have a respect for the culture of France, and of their share in that heritage, they have no loyalty to France, the political entity.

The French-speaking fall into two groups, those who live in the province of Quebec and those who live elsewhere. Of those who live outside Quebec, the closest to Quebec in feeling are the inhabitants of those areas in Ontario along the provincial boundary into which the expanding population of Quebec has spilled. More distant are the French-speaking peoples in the Maritimes, descendants of original settlers there, who have never been Quebecois. In Quebec the French-speaking have been kept together by their land, their customs, their church and their provincial government. Elsewhere they have their native tongue and their religion, and without the other two defences against the outer world they have the more easily become Canadians. The essence of Quebec is that it is defensive, the attitude of an orphan in an alien and possibly hostile world.

The French-speaking Canadian is usually a Roman Catholic, the English-speaking a Protestant, more often than not a Dissenter. It is not easy for someone outside the Roman Catholic Church to feel that he judges it aright. But at least he can see that for three centuries the Roman Catholic Church in Canada has been as much a part of the lives of the people of Quebec as the air they breathe. It has had behind it a double force; the emotion of the religion itself and the fact that it has been a symbol of the separateness of the French-speaking peoples.

Religion has shaped a great deal in Quebec. Families are large because it is a sin to limit them artificially. Education is essentially a matter for the church, for how else can the young be taught their duties to God and man? Equally, education should be confined to instruction in the classics and the humanities, for they were all that were needed for the established order of society in Quebec and, in any event, nineteenth-century science was hostile to the church. Trade unions are permissible, under the guidance of a priest, for it is the duty of a priest to care for his flock and common industrial action may be the only means in which the flock can win common justice, but communism is a sin and socialism its threshold. The affairs of Caesar are property transactions and best left to political parties that do not mix their proper business with alien social theory. So, if—and when—the young man revolted against such a picture of society, his first battle could only be with himself, and that battle is very painful and may last a lifetime.

Yet, as a result the Catholic has a sense of duty and a sense of responsibility. He has values and certainties. He may even be more light-hearted in life, for there are few sins his church finds unforgivable. All these traits are to be found in the French-speaking Canadian.

The Roman Catholic Church itself, as a world organisation, has always been flexible in the manner of its approach to temporal authority, both from country to country and in its own hierarchies. The central authority in Rome is rigid in doctrine but pliable in its methods of adjusting its worldly relations. The Roman Catholic Church in Quebec is Canadian, recruited from the French-speaking people. Its clergy in the past divided themselves into "Bleus" and "Rouges". The parish priests have led the Catholic syndicates, or unions, even to the point of violence, as in the strikes in the asbestos mines, in 1949, and in that they met with at least a degree of tolerance from the former Archbishop of Montreal. The present Archbishop, Cardinal Paul-Emile Leger, has said: "Only anarchy lies ahead as big business battles to build the empires of monopoly and big unions battle to break down the bulwarks of capitalism." But, underneath, the emphasis is always on religion and the church. For over three years Cardinal Leger has held a daily radio service, the Crusade of the Rosary, on the privately owned Montreal station C.K.A.C. and it is estimated that six out of every ten Catholic families within reach of the station listen to it. There can be no compromise in the minds of the hierarchy over the duties the individual owes to this other world.

The Roman Catholic Church in Quebec has been consistent in its relations with the Government of Canada. It has never been hostile to the British connection as such. It did not, as the Irish Church did thirty-five years ago, allow its priests to countenance, still less to take any active part in, armed rebellion against temporal authority, however alien. On the contrary: "the Holy Scriptures of the Old and the New Testaments expressly enjoin us to respect the person of the Sovereign, and to obey his just laws," wrote the Cardinal Archbishop of Quebec on the occasion of King George V's Jubilee in 1935. ". . . Concerning our religious liberties, for example, it also happens that, by the help of Providence, the Catholic Church is better situated here than in almost any other country in the world . . . ," sentiments which are a graceful tribute to the fact that the British introduced a very practical degree of Catholic emancipation in Canada fifty years before they did at home.

The enemies of the Roman Catholic Church have been and are still the crusading zeal of the Ulster Dissenter and the materialism of the North American continent generally, which corrodes the teaching of the Church itself. The Roman Catholic Church can never be described as wholly defensive anywhere, but, in Canada, it has been intent primarily to protect its existing flock and that consideration has at least modified the shape its propaganda has taken.

The characteristics of the French-speaking Canadians of Quebec show most clearly in the social, economic and political life of their province. The traditional activities have been based on the land, agriculture, lumbering and fur-trapping. The small village was the norm, the town the deviation. Social life was basically feudal, originally founded on a landed gentry rather than a nobility which, soon losing its titular Crown and so lacking either a court or a military tradition, became a middle-class oligarchy. It was a society shot through with defensive reactions to the alien and ascendant people all round. The English-speaking at first dominated trades and manufactures, so some French-speaking developed the arts of collaboration; others kept aloof and attached importance only to literature, philosophy and the cultured professions. Because the government of the province was the place in which a maximum of political independence could be won, provincial rights became a symbol of provincial differences, and, since difference in race was one thing that could not be denied, nor evaluated by any absolute standard, the concept of "Frenchness" was glorified; and of course, with some, that became a conviction of racial superiority.

Quebec and Ontario are still the heart of Canada; in time, perhaps, Alberta will take its place as a centre, but that time is some way off. The relations between Quebec and Ontario may be compared with those between the spouses in a marriage, a marriage of convenience but one which the parties have come to accept, at first somewhat reluctantly but now with fortitude, as an indissoluble union. Both provinces can, on occasion, display the qualities of either sex; Ontario has been the nagging, Quebec the sulking, wife, Ontario the bullying, Quebec the insensitive, husband. Both are capable of hard work, determination, resolution and courage, which are qualities either sex may possess. But such analogies can be pushed too far. Quebec is French and Catholic, Ontario is Ulster-Scottish-American, predominantly Protestant, but with an Irish Catholic admixture only slightly less suspicious of the French Catholics than are the Protestant. Quebec is proud, defensive and conscious that its culture is deeply ingrained. Ontario is proud, aggressive, material, not deeply interested in culture and already half won over to an American pattern of life.

So, in many ways, it became easier for the English-speaking to become Canadians. True, they had this living link with a mother country, but the mother herself was human; she could and did change and in the end she became so different that the English-

speaking in Canada could no longer deceive themselves into
thinking that they were still subjects of Britain who happened to
live in another continent. For the French-speaking, the mother
was a phantasy of their own creation. As they changed, she
changed. She was their reflection, and therefore always perfect;
like Narcissus, how could they help but fall in love with her? The
English-speaking who became Canadians were adjusting themselves to reality; the French-speaking who did so were disloyal
to a dream.

Yet only a minority of the French-speaking can be said to have
based their whole lives on this dream. For every one who has
cherished the dream of a French-speaking Canada withdrawn
from the rest of North America there have been others who have
seen beyond into the reality of the country and the age in which
they lived; for every Bourassa and Duplessis there has been a
Laurier and a St. Laurent. The majority of the people of Quebec
have come to terms with life as it is. They will defend their provincial rights up to a point, but they will not sacrifice Canada for
them, for they are Canada. That is the essential fact. There may
be aliens living in their house, but it is inconceivable that they
should abandon the house itself.

The French-speaking Canadians have helped to keep Canada
North American, as distinct from American, as, to use the hack-
neyed simile, the sand helps to make the pearl, but as with the
oyster there is more to it than that. I would suggest there are five
other major reasons, all of which apply to all Canadians. Canadians did not experience the American Revolution. They retained
the attachments implicit in the Crown. They grew up with a
British legal and judicial system. They acquired, a century after
the American Revolution, a British system of government, considerably modified from that which the Americans had rejected.
They have always been compelled to rely on external trade.

The distinguished historian, Mr. A. J. P. Taylor, has written:
"It is a waste of time for anyone who thinks all revolutions are
wrong to write about Communist revolutions—or indeed about
anything else." I find myself in total disagreement with such a
conviction. It is a disaster when an armed and violent revolution
happens; it is an even greater disaster when such a revolution
succeeds. It is a disaster that any ruling class, or order, should be

so blind as to allow cruelty or injustice to be sufficiently oppressive, and to last for sufficiently long, to drive those they rule into violence, but at least people should think twice before blaming rulers for a lack of foresight they themselves do not always possess. The disasters inherent in a successful revolution are of a different kind. Revolutions are not won by those who wish to build, although those who wish to build almost always take part in them. They are won by men who wish to destroy, and they do destroy, and mankind has so many deep and confused emotions over destruction that, having destroyed, he must at once build up myths strong enough to justify his crime. The Indian Mutiny was an unsuccessful revolution; as a result the people of India were spared the even greater horrors that would have followed its success than did follow its failure and experienced an infinitely more peaceful end to alien rule within a century of the Mutiny itself.

A revolution is a prematurely born child. The delivery is by forceps and the scars remain—for ever afterwards? So it seems, to succeeding generations. A fundamental difference between the United States and Canada lies in the fact that the Thirteen Colonies to the south cut all their connection with Britain by force, while the two to the north were able to cut some of their connections by agreement, and very much in their own time. Looking at India, and Canada, can anyone really claim that it would not have been better for the world if the American Revolution had failed?

The myths built up by the American people to account for their revolution are by now extremely deep-seated. They were needed in great strength to sustain the colonists in arms against the British. They were subsequently built into American history books and there their strength has remained, for few people ever challenge in their minds in later life the emotions they learnt from their history books at school. It was necessary to show that the colonists in the Thirteen Colonies were men who loved the conception of liberty, and who had therefore revolted against tyranny when they found it. They were not lovers of liberty in practice and they rose against stupidity rather than tyranny. It was necessary to say that the colonists revolted against aristocracy and that therefore they must be democrats. They were not democrats (in either sense in which the world now uses that battered word) and they were not super-human enough to abolish privilege. It was necessary to show that the colonists had been oppressed; therefore all colonial powers oppress their peoples and all inhabitants of colonies must be in a state of oppression, unless the contrary is strictly proved. This is a misconception which has caused the American people a great deal of avoidable confusion in their time, and one from which a great many other people in the world have suffered avoidable misfortunes in consequence.

Two of the myths with even further reaching consequences were these: It was inevitable that the colonists should incorporate in their beliefs the conviction that this New World, under their management, was in some fundamental way different from the world they had cast off, and that easily transformed itself into a belief that the New World was good and the Old World bad, that the disobedient children were innocent and that the angry parents were wicked. A great many unfortunate consequences have followed from this division of the world, in American minds, into sheep and goats on a geographical basis. All European political influence that extended into America must be bad, because it came from Europe (if it was not obviously harmful, like the British command of the North Atlantic in times of peace, then it was pushed out of mind altogether). Likewise all European wars must at first be treated as wicked because they were fought between wicked people. All European activities in the rest of the world must be suspect because those of a particular power at a particular time had been condemned in America. And Britain herself could never really change for the better—it was doubtful if she could change at all—because ex hypothesi angels are angels and devils devils.

The second myth is enshrined in the constitution of the United States which, being now a sacred object, must never seem to be changed. It is that political power is always used for oppression; therefore a minimum must be given to those who are governors and the channels through which it is exercised must be split up into many small and seemingly independent tributaries so that the volume of the flood may seem the less. It is a tribute to the political genius of the Anglo-Saxon peoples that they have, in the United States, kept the constitution of that country in continuous and reasonably effective working order for the best part of two centuries.

Canada did not escape the direct impact of these myths. At first, in 1775, in 1812, even as late as 1837, sections of the American people believed that Canada must be in a state of oppression and therefore, if aided to throw off the yoke, would be glad to do so. Again, with that inconsistency of which all peoples are capable, on other occasions, when the concept of "manifest destiny" was uppermost in American minds, Canada could be treated as an extension of Britain and be bullied accordingly. But another consequence of the American myths was that Canada became a closed book to the United States. Her actions had not squared with the myths. She was an inconvenient fact, of that kind that Darwin presented to the fundamentalists, and therefore she did not really exist. The strength of the myth is evidenced by the extraordinary persistency of the belief in the United States that Canada pays taxes to the United Kingdom. Britain drew revenue from all North America in 1775. Canada did not revolt then and so bring that state of oppression to an end. Therefore, Canada must still be paying taxes to Britain now. After 1775, in American textbooks, the history of North America is the history of the United States.

In many ways this collection of folk-lore has been of great value to the American people. It has not only given them a national consciousness capable of absorbing and unifying an astonishingly diverse set of peoples. It has sustained their belief in moral values and helped to preserve in them their sense of obligation to follow the right course and not the one that seems momentarily expedient. It has not weakened their fundamental common sense. It accounts for a great deal of their isolationism, and it has only become a serious handicap to the people of the United States lately, mainly in their understanding of the rest of the world. But, as for the effect of these myths on the rest of the world—! However, so far as Canada is concerned, the point of the matter is that Canada does not, and never has, shared the myths themselves.

To the French-speaking, the American Revolution had few attractions. They had already known years of hostility from the New Englanders, *les Bastonnois*. It had been men from New England who had attacked Louisburg, and who had helped in the final defeat at Quebec. In the Quebec Act of 1774, the United Kingdom Parliament had given them rather more liberty than they could hope to see offered by the Thirteen Colonies. They might dislike the English-speaking but they were the devils they knew better, and at least the seigneurs of Quebec could match the comparative tolerance towards their religion of the colonial officials in their province with the more violent intolerance of the gentlemen of Salem.

With the English-speaking the position was different, because, once the immediate bitterness of the revolution was over, they could divide themselves between the two countries the more easily. Now North America contained the two régimes, the colony and the republic. Those that placed the British connection above everything could find a home in Canada. Those that were attracted to the American way of life could move freely to the United States. There was no natural obstacle between the two, such as language, and no artificial obstacle, such as an immigration statute. Both countries were big enough to expand and so to receive without serious dislocation those who felt strongly enough to make a choice. This freedom of movement and these similarities between life in Canada and life in the United States have helped to prevent friction between the two from raising the temperature of their mutual relations to any dangerous level.

As a result, Canadians have always been able to see the American people as they are, and likewise to see how different, politically, the two countries are. On the whole, Canada has lost by this freedom of movement; every year too high a proportion of her most able young men are attracted south to work in the United States. There are, and have been, Canadians who would like Canada to be a part of the United States because they are attracted by its wealth and strength. Very few have felt any urge towards union because they believed that the peoples were already one.

On matters of trade there has been more, on balance, to keep the two countries apart than to unite them. Manufacture and agriculture expanded in the United States to keep pace with a growing population and American exports have been always been marginal. During Canada's main periods of rapid expansion, in the first and fourth decades of this century, the production of commodities for export played the largest part in the expansion itself. Canada could never isolate herself economically from the rest of the world and could, therefore, never become wholly isolationist in sentiment. Europe was not a tourist region or a political headache; it was the traditional market for Canadian wheat, and Dr. Johnson's observation on how the proximity of an execution sharpens a man's wits is equally true of a farmer with some millions of bushels to sell abroad. Now, the United States is becoming uneasily conscious of the rest of the world because she feels that this outside world will do her some damage if it is not watched. Canada has always had a stronger incentive to pay attention to it; if it does not trade with her she will come uncomfortably close to starvation.

Both Canada and the United States inherited the British Common Law and, in part, the British belief that the judiciary should be politically independent, but the gap of almost a century between the creation of the United States constitution and that of the Canadian constitution made an important difference. It is possible to see, now, that the judiciary in Great Britain in 1775 was politically independent, but it must have been far less apparent at the time. To the American colonists, what stood out was the fact that judges were appointed by the King and held office during his pleasure. They did not see that already the Crown had lost its fight to control the judiciary and had very nearly lost its fight to control Parliament. They were obsessed with the need to establish the supremacy of "the people" and in consequence they gave the people the right to elect their own judges by direct vote and limited the period of office of each judge to a fixed term of years. Another fact of importance is that Canada was given an external judicial body, the Judicial Committee, as the interpreter of its constitution and federal-provincial rights and powers, with the result that the inevitable political repercussions of judicial decisions in that field fell upon Britain rather than upon the Canadian judiciary, and the Canadian judiciary were to that extent—and it is a considerable extent—kept out of current Canadian political disagreements.

Over the respective merits of the United States and the United Kingdom—and Canadian—forms of constitution it is difficult to be objective, and, here, fortunately, not necessary even to make the attempt. We are considering why Canadians are not Americans. One of the reasons is that they have a different legal system and a different form of government and that is that. But it would seem that the Canadians do prefer what they have to what they

see across the border. They believe that they have a deeper
national respect for law and order, and that their judicial system
has helped them to acquire it. They believe that their judges are
more independent, so that they have both a greater authority and
are given a more unquestioning obedience. They say that Americans take the letter of the law as an obstacle to be circumvented
if possible (and claim congratulations over success) whilst they
regard the spirit of the law as an integral part of their social and
economic lives and feel all the better for it. Again, it is the belief
in such a difference that matters more than its truth.

On these issues of constitution and law there is no serious difference in thought between the French-speaking Canadian and
the English-speaking. The French-speaking have become anglicised, in the sense that they accept and value the systems they
have. But there is a difference between them when it comes to an
attitude to the monarchy, and on the French-speaking side it
manifests itself in two ways; the French-speaking Canadian has
never been within that emotion of personal loyalty to the Crown
that is a part of the English-speaking tradition, and, partly in
consequence and partly because of his own habit of mind, he is
hostile to any form of imperialism, to the whole conception of a
physically expanding political system or political sphere of influence. The Quebecois have had to struggle hard to maintain
physical mastery of their own soil. That they will hold against all
comers and on their attachment to that place they have built a
complex of ideas that could not help but have an anti-imperialist
content.

Today, the French-speaking Canadian is more conscious of
American imperialism than of British. It is not only a matter of
the change in the balance of forces in the world; to the French-
speaking Canadian British imperialism has manifested itself as
much through his English-speaking countrymen as it did directly.
In this century this imperialism has taken the form of what might
be called "Round Table-ism", a conception that grew in Milner's
Kindergarten in South Africa, flourished in such men as Lionel
Curtis and left a rather belated blossom in the shape of Lord
Halifax's thoughts in the last war that the Commonwealth should
strive to make itself something of a third force in the world
balance of power. The French-speaking have always rejected that
attitude of mind wherever they encountered it. John W. Dafoe

wrote, in a volume of essays *Our Future in the Empire*, published
in 1917:

> Here in Canada there are certain political facts that Mr. Curtis
> and his supporters should have the moral courage to look
> squarely in the face. Their scheme appeals to only a portion—
> certainly not to more than half—of the Canadians of British
> descent; to the remaining British Canadians it is anathema, as
> a denial of cherished political principles. To the non-British
> elements . . . it makes no appeal. If this question is forced into
> Dominion politics it will swallow all other issues. Until it is
> settled everything else will stand aside. The British-Canadian
> community will be rent in twain. A national party, dedicated
> to the task of preserving Canadian nationality, will inevitably
> arise; and the politics of this party will naturally be determined
> in large measure by the non-British elements, who will con-
> stitute a considerable majority of its membership.

Writing so in 1917, John Dafoe was speaking for the generation
that was to follow him, for the English-speaking Canadian has
himself changed. He accepts a greater, more adult, responsibility
towards the susceptibilities of the French-speaking than his
father did forty years ago. The long period in office of a Liberal
Government has both softened the suspicions of the French-
speaking and changed Ottawa itself. It has even influenced
thought in Ontario.

American imperialism—it is a clumsy and not very self-expres-
sive phrase—is another matter. It is no longer a direct threat to
Canada's political independence, although Canadian history
books have examples enough of occasions on which Americans
have talked in terms of annexation (it is impossible to write of
Canadian-American relations without quoting the famous sentence spoken by Sir Etienne Pascal Tache: "The last cannon
fired in defence of British sovereignty in Canada will be fired by
a French Canadian," but the remarkable thing about it is that it
was spoken as long ago as 1846). American imperialism, in the
minds of the French-speaking, presents a two-fold threat to
Canada. It might drag Canada into conflicts which the French-
speaking would feel no impulse to join. It does present all Canada
with a prospect of submergence by the American way of life,
which derives so much force from the happy American confidence

that it is the best possible way of life in the world. The French-speaking Canadian sees at least a negative protection for his own way of life in the continued existence of the British Crown. But, as one French-speaking Canadian said to me, of the Royal visit, "Do not forget that to us it is a show, and we, like you, judge shows by whether they are good ones."

The attitude of the English-speaking Canadian to the Crown, his "loyalty", is a real emotion, but a complex one. It is not uniform over Canada nor from one generation to another. With some immigrants from Britain it is heightened—almost exaggerated—by nostalgia. To other Canadians it is not a Canadian tradition at all; it is a part of history, accepted because it has always existed and there seems to be no urgent reason to change it. There is a broad division between the generation that fought in the First World War and that which fought in the Second. In the First they fought as British, in the Second as Canadians. To Canadians it is now more important to create unity of feeling inside Canada than to preserve unity of feeling with the United Kingdom. It was impossible to feel in Canada during the Coronation period that the majority of people in Canada were sharing in the ceremony. They were spectators. Equally, it was hard to feel that they were meant to share in it. Too much of the ceremony was a medieval display. The dedication by the Queen of herself as a person in the sight of God to the service of her people was real. The vows of the peers were, to Canadians, no more than actions of dimly understood characters in a pageant.

To the Canadians the Crown is a symbol, but of what? The Canadians are realists. They will not let the past overshadow the present, for to them the present is immensely superior to the past. Matthew Halton, one of the younger generation of Canadians, made this assessment of the strength of the Commonwealth link in a B.B.C. broadcast in 1952: "Our nightmare is Anglo-American rupture. Canada loves and cherishes the Commonwealth connection, but she could not survive a break with the United States. If the terrible choice ever had to be made, geography would dictate it." The choice may never have to be made, but nothing is more important in international relations than a realisation that there are such things as breaking-points, and the making of correct estimations of where they are.

.   .   .   .   .   .

The French-speaking are not too difficult to label; isolated rather than isolationist, devoted to their conception of Canada and gradually widening it to include something more than Quebec. The English-speaking more difficult; American in some ways, yet not American because there is always Quebec; very well aware of the fact that they are not American, and understanding pretty clearly why they are not, where they differ. Neither British nor French-speaking are European and so lack something which is a part of the British. Not American, not British, yet with kinship to both. Is this country then, a separate nation?

I wrote that question because I thought I knew the answer and when I had written the answer I tore it up, because it seemed to me that the question really could have no direct answer within the terms of what the European has for so long meant by the word "nation". I wrote the following chapter instead.

11
External Relations

On 10 September 1939, after a parliamentary debate and direct contact between the Prime Minister, Mr. Mackenzie King, and the King, Canada declared war on Germany, a week later than did the United Kingdom. No arbitrarily chosen moment in time can make a satisfactory starting point for such an evolving process as the external relations of a country, yet that date in September 1939, has its advantages. It certainly was a turning point, both for Canada and for Mr. Mackenzie King. Canada launched herself into a European war by her own independent act. For Mr. Mackenzie King it was the moment when he finally turned his back on one policy, "No commitments in advance", and moved outwards into the external world with the positive intention of influencing its history.

Canadian Governments had spent the first ten years after the First World War in establishing Canada's right, in as legal a way as possible, to have a separate foreign policy if she wished. They had spent the next ten years in ensuring, so far as they could, that Canada's actual foreign policy did not venture beyond the lowest common denominator of agreement between the policies of the United Kingdom and the United States. With such a determination in mind, and with Mr. Mackenzie King in charge, Canada had little difficulty in avoiding anything positive.

Mr. Mackenzie King adopted the formula that no commitment over foreign policy—he was referring specifically to sanctions to be applied by members of the League of Nations—"could be made without the prior approval of the Canadian Parliament". He had, earlier, repudiated the speech by the Canadian delegate to the League of Nations, Mr. W. A. Riddell, in which Mr. Riddell had argued in favour of adding oil, coal, iron and steel to the list of sanctions to be imposed on Italy because of her actions in Abyssinia. Mackenzie King's formula was an evasion; Canada was not the United States and no government of Canada needed, as a matter of constitutional practice, the approval of Parliament to make a binding decision on foreign policy. Mackenzie King had deliberately discouraged debates on foreign policy in Parliament while he was protesting that he would make no commitment without Parliament, from which, perhaps, it is not unfair to draw the conclusion that, before 1939, he must have believed that his country did not need a separate foreign policy. His view was probably based on the conviction that it would be politically dangerous for his government to attempt to formulate a positive foreign policy of its own when there was no evidence that a majority of the electorate required any such thing and a good deal of evidence that, whatever the policy adopted was, very many of them would disagree with it. Mackenzie King certainly built up the machine, an External Relations Department, by which he might be informed. Informed, he kept his oars within the boat.

And from there one might almost jump to the present day, for the foreign policy that Canada has now is the foreign policy based on all that she has learnt in these fifteen years. Canada did start with virtually a clean sheet, so far as commitments were concerned. Her present policy, therefore, is likely to be a straightforward assessment of her interests, intentions and aims, for, after all, the foreign policy of a country is based ultimately on an appreciation by its government of what the needs of the country are and of the strength the country has in their fulfilment or defence. Further, the strength of a country as an international force is a product of that country's own unity and strength multiplied by some proportion of the strength of those other countries she knows, or believes, will support her in securing her own ends. The proportion of that on which she may count varies according to circumstances, but it will always in some measure depend upon the strength she herself can add to the common pool.

The words "National Sovereignty" stand in the world like a vast totem pole, like some incantation that has power to defeat warlocks and summon the angels of light. They are the suit of

R

clothes the Emperor wore and that only the small boy in the crowd could not see. "Cry—cry God for Harry, England and St. George!" Cry again for National Sovereignty, and men who the hour before were cold and timid and cursing the day they were ever pressed into service become bold, resolute and cunning, and intent on the destruction of—? Other men who cry "National Sovereignty", of course.

In the last twenty-five years two nations have attempted to carry the concept of national sovereignty to complete fulfilment, Germany and Japan. The concept assumes that nations inhabit a world of total anarchy, recognising no external legal restraint upon their actions and only those moral restraints that their rulers cannot wholly suppress in their own peoples. Any commitment that a nation has at any time made to another is a mere expediency, to be repudiated as and when the supreme political power in that country thinks it advisable in its own interests. Today, it is possible that three nations alone, the United States, Soviet Russia and Communist China, could maintain for any appreciable period an attitude to the rest of the world based upon the logic of national sovereignty. No other nation could, yet a great many of them go through the motions of absolute power and pretend that any decision limiting it is an act of grace on their part.

Every nation that accepts a treaty surrenders some of its sovereignty but that is of small importance because sovereign nations can also tear treaties up. What is important is that virtually every nation has had its sovereignty clipped by changing circumstance, and that is far more difficult for them to accept. Persia under Dr. Moussadeq beat her wings against the bars, for a time. Egypt has pretended that the bars were not there, and a great many Egyptians were convinced that they did not exist, but at least her rulers have kept one eye on the United States, in the hope that she would help to pull the bars apart. Italy sent her Italian men, and her American equipment, to beat the bounds of Trieste, but did the idea of talking it over first with the American Ambassadress in Rome never enter the head of Signor Pella? There are times when the United Kingdom Government clears its throat and gives the impression of a man about to speak his mind to Mr. John Foster Dulles, but there would have to be a very big wheat harvest in Australia (and a non-smoking pledge by most of the inhabitants of the British Isles) before it could actually do so. National sovereignty, in that expressive phrase, is not on, yet it remains the totem pole at the bottom of so many nations' garden.

I doubt if either Mr. St. Laurent or Mr. Lester Pearson sees any such object in his.

They say of Mr. Louis Stephen St. Laurent that until he was ten he thought that all children spoke one language to their fathers and another to their mothers, that bilingual family life was a natural order of society. This story appears in all accounts of St. Laurent's life, partly because it explains so simply his stature as a Canadian and his acceptance by all the people of his country, and partly because there are so few stories to be told of him at all after the age of ten.

Louis St. Laurent was born in 1882 in Compton, in the Eastern Townships of Quebec province, where his father, French-speaking, had moved, as that part of Quebec, first settled by the Loyalists, had become increasingly peopled by the French-speaking. His mother's family, Brodericks, had come from Galway, in Ireland, and both his parents, of course, were Roman Catholics. The St. Laurents kept the general store in the town. From school, Louis St. Laurent took a law degree at Laval University, began to practice as a lawyer in Quebec City, and became known—to those whose interest it was to know—as an extremely capable and successful advocate in the Canadian Courts and before the Judicial Committee of the Privy Council. He might still have been that—save that, by now, he would probably have retired—if he had not been appointed to the Rowell-Sirois Commission on federal-provincial relationships. His work there became an element in the public life of Canada. When Mackenzie King's Minister of Justice, Ernest Lapointe, died in 1941, someone suggested to the Prime Minister that St. Laurent would make a good successor in that office.

In Mackenzie King's mind, St. Laurent had three important attributes as a Cabinet Minister. He was solidly in favour of Canada's war effort (one of his sons was in the Royal Canadian Navy and a daughter was serving in the Air Force). He was known and respected in Quebec by the French-speaking. Even though he was not a member of the House, he was not likely to be accused of seeking personal advancement if he accepted

Cabinet appointment as Minister of Justice, for that Ministry was not among the highest of Cabinet positions and everyone would know that a successful lawyer could only accept it at some personal financial sacrifice. Mackenzie King put his proposal to St. Laurent in the form of an appeal to his sense of duty and after some hesitation St. Laurent accepted. Two months afterwards, at the age of sixty, he was elected to Parliament for the first time, for Sir Wilfred Laurier's former seat, Quebec East.

The next turning point in his career was his determination to support—positively and with all the force of his character—Mackenzie King's decision in the fall of 1944 to extend compulsory military service to cover service in Europe, and the appeal his sincerity made to Parliament, and to both his province and all Canada, when he did so. From that followed the decision to appoint him leader of the Canadian delegation to the San Francisco Conference in 1945 at which the Charter of the United Nations was settled, and to the first General Assembly in London in 1946. And from his work on those occasions it followed that, when Mackenzie King finally decided to separate the office of Secretary of State for External Affairs from that of the Prime Minister, St. Laurent was the man he chose to succeed him in the management of foreign affairs. In 1948 Mackenzie King resigned and St. Laurent was elected to lead the Liberal Party. He has since led that party to two considerable victories at the polls. He is a man of whom, the Canadian journalist, Blair Fraser, has said, all men speak well, and they do so earlier than is commonly the case, in the funeral oration.

What St. Laurent has given Canada, and through his government to the world, is something more than a first-class legal brain. Those are not exactly plentiful, but they are not invariably accompanied by the other qualities that make a man a successful leader of a party or a country. St. Laurent has contributed his character and his sincerity. He is a Canadian, without prefix or suffix. Because he came to politics late in life he has escaped the tricks of mind and speech that politicians sometimes use as substitutes for principle or thought. He is deeply religious. He has seen the forces at work in the world at first hand and he has made his own decisions over which to support and which to counter.

Mr. Lester Pearson is a man of a different background. He is a career diplomat turned politician. It is revealing that he likes to be called "Mike" and that he is called "Mike". He was born in Ontario in 1897, a son of the manse, and he flew in the First World War as a pilot with the Royal Flying Corps. He graduated at the University of Toronto, spent two years in business, with Armour and Co., of Chicago, and then won a scholarship to St. John's College, Oxford. In 1924 he returned to Toronto, to teach history, and in 1928 he was drawn into the government service when Mackenzie King took a hand in the establishment of an effective Department of External Relations, and he served there under Dr. O. D. Skelton. As a First Secretary he saw the Naval Disarmament Conference in London in 1930 and the League of Nations in 1932 and 1933. He was in the High Commissioner's Office in London from 1935 to 1941, in Washington in 1941 and 1942, and the Canadian delegate to U.N.R.R.A. in 1944. In 1946 he became Under-Secretary in his department and Secretary of State with a seat in the Cabinet when St. Laurent surrendered that office to become Prime Minister. In a profile of him in the United Nations Bulletin in 1952 he was described so: "In his habits he is well-known for his punctuality; in his attire, for his bow-tie; in his personality for his friendliness, as outwardly expressed in his grin; in his relaxation, for his fondness for baseball." He is, in short, very much as the Canadian business man likes to think himself, realistic and practical but not unidealistic, having the common touch, not naturally prone to flights of emotion, imagination or oratory. Lester Pearson still leaves observers undecided on whether he is likely to be as successful a politician as he was civil servant.

His policy has been a continuation of that of his two mentors, Mackenzie King and Dr. Skelton, whom he succeeded as permanent head of the department—and one must remember that Mackenzie King was deeply disillusioned over the United Nations as a result of all he saw at San Francisco. The policy of no commitments in advance has gone, but the commitments now accepted as inevitable are at least to be thought of as limited. Of the provisions for collective action in the United Nations Charter, he has written that they "are not a cast-iron commitment to resist aggression anywhere it may occur with unlimited military force." But behind the international agreement a statesman feels he can secure there always lies another, that which he would like to make if he could. In the case of Canadian statesmen, what are these agreements?

It is inconceivable that Canada would of her own volition have aggressive aims—her situation, her people, her whole economy negative that as strongly as those of any country could. It is likely, therefore, that Canada's own influence would be asserted away from aggression, away from any attitudes that might invite aggression. It is equally clear that Canada's geographical position welds her to the United States and her history ties her with the United Kingdom, and through the United Kingdom to the Commonwealth, so that the basic strategy of defence in Canada must rest on two major provisions:

> (a) a complete military union with the United States for the defence of the territorial integrity of the North American continent, *and*

> (b) political associations with other countries, including Commonwealth countries and the United States in particular, in terms of the United Nations Charter, the North Atlantic Treaty Organisation and so on, for international action elsewhere.

In so far as the political consequences implicit in those two rather different conceptions can be kept from conflict, the resulting situation can only be described as one admirably suited to Canada's needs.

But they cannot always be so kept apart and when they do conflict it is instructive to see which Canada puts first. She will not take any action which could jeopardise her ability to defend her own territories. In 1950 she refused to release her most effective single defence unit, that trained for fighting in Arctic conditions, for the war in Korea, despite considerable American pressure to do so and considerable adverse comment in the United States after her refusal. Canada reacted to that pressure to some extent later, in 1951, after China's intervention and when the war had taken a different shape, and raised another brigade unit for service in Korea, but throughout her Government was determined that Canada's own defence should never fall below being a joint affair, never become wholly dependent on the strength of the United States.

The military defence union with the United States dates back to the agreement made at Ogdensburg, in August 1940, between Mackenzie King and President Roosevelt, under which the two countries agreed to set up a Permanent Joint Board of Defence. The Board was given the task of considering the defence of the whole of the northern half of the Western Hemisphere. It was advisory, not executive, but its wartime plans, which included the Alaska Highway and the airfields in the north-west and the east, were generally accepted. Since the war the original agreement has been supplemented by a renewal of the pact, announced in February 1947. The Ogdensburg Agreement was criticised by some at the time it was made as being too close an association with the United States, and that criticism has been repeated since, notably during a debate, in June 1947, on a Canadian Bill to give United States courts jurisdiction over their own men in Canada, but, as with so many other decisions, geography has triumphed.

The result of this partial surrender of sovereignty (which can be matched by parallel action by the United Kingdom Government over U.S. bomber bases in Britain) is a close integration of American and Canadian training methods and equipment and the building of a chain of airfields, bases, posts and warning devices that cover the northern lands towards the Pole. This is not a book on military strategy or tactics, but one cannot spend any time with any of Canada's defence forces without being very conscious of how their minds have turned to all the problems of action in that terrain.

In such a position, it is hard to see at first what flexibility Canada's own foreign policy can have, and yet it does move. Mr. St. Laurent described Canada's dilemma in these terms in 1948:

Canada will be expected by some to follow the United Kingdom, by others to follow the United States. Unfriendly observers will write us off as a satellite of both. . . . It will not be easy to secure credit for independence and honesty of argument and decision. Nonetheless, we will continue to make our decisions objectively, in the light of our obligations to our own people and their interest in the welfare of the international community.

After five years his government may not have convinced everybody that it is behaving in that way, but the evidence would suggest that it is.

If the essence of Canadian policy is defence, what is Canada to defend—besides, of course, her own frontiers? Clearly peoples and ideas, not empires and dominions; the way of life of Europe, not a colony in Africa or a balance of power in the Middle East. There was a generation in Canada that thought of Britain as the centre of an Empire and that what Britain did was necessarily good. That generation has almost died out and it has not been replaced by like-thinking people. If Canada is to have a foreign policy that is supported by all her people, it must be one of defence for things they can all wish to defend, and that confines it, in reality, to a defence of Western Europe, the North Atlantic Treaty area. Of course Canadians can see that the defensive battles may be fought further afield, but that is a matter of tactics, not strategy, and it is strategy, not tactics, that is the name for foreign policy projected into military action. The agreement that came nearest to that which Canadian statesmen most wanted to complete was the North Atlantic Treaty, setting up N.A.T.O.

It would be too much to claim for Canada the basic conception of a defensive alliance reaching across the Atlantic; the idea was mooted during the war, notably by the American commentator, Walter Lippman. Nor could the pact have taken the shape it did before the communist seizure of power in Czechoslovakia in February 1948. That was felt as an electric shock throughout Europe and became a decisive factor in, for instance, the decision of Norway to join N.A.T.O. and commit her future to a specific group of powers. But Canada took the initiative in 1948 and began a series of negotiations in Washington, and among the five powers who had concluded the Brussels Treaty in Western Europe, intended to bring together this group of like-minded nations and to secure for them both a specific American commitment over defence and the weight of American arms behind that. There was a significant change in emphasis in two speeches of Mr. St. Laurent, one to the University of Toronto in January 1947, the other in Parliament in April 1948. In the first, he declined to commit Canada, as a member of the Commonwealth, to a reduction of that association to "the formal terms of specific commitments". Fifteen months later he was advocating just such a specific and written commitment in the North Atlantic area.

The North Atlantic Treaty was signed in Washington in April 1949. It contained fourteen articles, and all of them were drafted to fit into the framework of the United Nations Charter. The principal articles dealing with defence were Articles 5 and 6, which declared that an armed attack on one signatory should be considered as an armed attack on all (the wording followed that of the Rio Pact for all-American defence) and defined the area within which the Treaty operated. The machinery for implementing the treaty was to be a council, but the treaty in its final form was silent on how the council was to vote and otherwise manage its affairs. The original signatories in Washington were Canada, the United States, the United Kingdom, Norway, France, Belgium, the Netherlands and Luxemburg, and Italy, Denmark, Portugal and Iceland joined shortly afterwards (Eire was invited but declined). The *Tribune*, in London, called the treaty "A Pact made in Moscow" and in a sense that was true. It was ratified by the United States Senate by 82 votes to 13 and in the ratification debate there Senator Mundt, of South Dakota, said: "I am going to vote without enthusiasm, and with a great fear that it will be but a futile gesture"; American observers at the time agreed that his attitude of mind was shared by a large mass of his fellow countrymen. They were, perhaps, despairing of Europe's determination to defend itself; Canadians were more inclined to think how important it was that Europe should be defended.

But Canada then, and since, has emphasised Article 2 of the treaty, which is worth setting out in full:

The parties will contribute towards the further development of peaceful and friendly international relations by strengthening their free institutions, by bringing about a better understanding of the principles upon which these institutions are founded and by promoting conditions of stability and well-being. They will seek to eliminate conflict in their international economic policies and will encourage economic collaboration between any or all of them.

These words may sound to be no more than a pious expression of hope, yet it is remarkable how exactly they set out the

main elements that the Canadian feels should be present in
a true and effective international relationship. Those are the
standards by which the Canadian would judge not only the
North Atlantic Treaty Organisation but also the Commonwealth
itself.

The motives in Canadian minds over the treaty were not without self-interest, of course. No national commitment should be
free of self-interest; if it were, it would lack all strength. Canada
has her own vulnerable areas in the North Atlantic, but at least
there she already had a full military alliance with the United
States. Again, Canada had always been under pressure from the
United States to join the Pan-American organisation and had
consistently refused; the existence of a North Atlantic Treaty
Organisation could make an effective reason for further refusals to join. More important, there was, too, in Canadian
minds a desire to bring the United States within a formal coalition that would not only commit her to positive action in case of
trouble but would also act as a brake on incautious action likely
to provoke trouble.

Mr. Lester Pearson has made that very clear. Speaking of a
policy of destroying Communist Governments in Asia because
they are communist, and of preventing them from emerging, if
that is possible, he said to the Harvard Alumni Association at
Cambridge, Massachusetts, in June 1953:

> I believe—and firmly—that there can be no effective or suc-
> cessful collective action or policy on the basis of this policy.
> It would mean that we would have to extend our specific obli-
> gations to the defeat of the Communist Governments in North
> Korea and Peking, and not merely to the defeat of military
> aggression. There are few countries inside our Western alli-
> ance willing to accept this obligation, especially in the terms
> in which it is sometimes presented in this country . . .

(and he was speaking in the United States). Two years before in
Foreign Affairs, he had written:

> Before the last war, the spectre haunting Canadian policy-
> makers was that the United States would remain aloof from
> British and French efforts to protect the peace against Nazi
> and Fascist aggression. Today the spectre is that the United

States may feel it necessary to pursue policies inside our coalition which the other members cannot wholeheartedly follow, or that inadequate co-operation from the other members may discourage American effort and leadership to the point where Washington may decide to "go it alone".

Yet, transcending these calculations of caution and defence was the basic Canadian belief that her destiny was to be a member of exactly this group of nations of Western Europe and North America, of peoples to whom the Atlantic was a common highway of history. Just as Article 2 defines the kind of Commonwealth in which Canada would prefer to live, so the original members of N.A.T.O. are the peoples who she feels share her blood. The Organisation may be as yet little more than a military alliance and events since June 1950, have checked its growth into anything wider, but, if the hopes have been buried, Canada has carefully marked the spot.

In those circumstances, the expression "National Sovereignty" has no true meaning in Canada—it would be the equivalent of asking if music were red. So, too, with the question: "Is Canada a nation?" In the sense that Europeans have used that word "nation"—and too frequently still think of that word "nation"—Canada is not and never will be one.

This conception of group activity is, I believe, the key to Canadian foreign policy. It is hard for Americans to think of themselves as members of a group co-equal in the formation of policy, partly because of their own strength and partly because of their constitution, partly because of the tradition of isolation among them. Canada may have had the good fortune to have been able to watch her power as a nation rise in a smooth curve. She certainly has not, like the United Kingdom, been compelled to make the uncomfortable adjustments that relatively diminishing strength imposes on a people. But her increase in power has come at a time when the world was already palpably inter-dependent. She has had, too, the realism to see that her increase in strength has carried her no further than the ranks of the middle powers, and that it is never likely to carry her beyond them—not, that is, within the time during which such expressions as "middle powers" will have any meaning.

The kind of association Canada envisages is a form of self-governing guild. Such a guild must have a common philosophy, a common acceptance of general ends and a common intention of avoiding certain lines of conduct, but its discipline must come from within and what each nation lacks in independence—by surrender or because it never lost some degree of dependence—is made up by strength through association. That, I am sure, is Canada's conception of N.A.T.O.

There have been occasions in the past, when the strengths of the United Kingdom and of the United States were less disparable, in which Canadians have taken advantage of their chances to play off one country against the other. Was it not John Hay, the American Ambassador in London, who said, in reply to Lord Salisbury's comment that Canada was like a coquettish girl with two suitors, that she might with greater justice be called "a married flirt, ready to betray John Bull on any occasion but holding him responsible for all her follies"? But that was nearly sixty years ago. The difference between the Canada of today and that of no more than twenty years ago is that she knows she is no longer a country that lives in a fireproof house and which, therefore, needs no more in the way of a foreign policy than that provided by extracting the lowest common denominator from the policies of two other powers.

For, when it comes to the policy itself, history does count. The United States severed her original ties with Europe nearly two hundred years ago and spent the best part of the following century and a half shielded by the belief that no further ties of that kind would be needed again. Only within the last few decades has America, reluctantly, begun to explore political Europe again and the ties she is prepared to make with this Europe are fewer in number and of a very different kind. She mistrusts Europe; she has the resentments commonly felt by a person towards someone to whom he once did an injury. She would turn her back on Europe if she could with safety and from Chicago westwards a great many Americans feel that she could, with safety. But Americans have a deep sentiment over China, and this the communists have outraged. So much of the idealism and sense of Christian duty that is inherent in the American character was poured into the China missions and when the communists overran them and expelled them that, in many American eyes, was a crime against the Holy Ghost. One consequence of this is that the United States has come to think of the Pacific almost in terms of Mare Nostrum.

Canadian sentiment is quite otherwise. The French-speaking did not sever their ties with France by their own act; the causes lay in France. Nothing has ever happened to the English-speaking in their three hundred years in Canada to create any serious conflict between their ties of feeling with Europe and their bonds of interest within North America. Each of them seems to think first, naturally, of the Atlantic Ocean before the Pacific; they could each agree with the thought expressed by Hr. Lange, the Norwegian Foreign Minister, in the debates in Norway on the North Atlantic Treaty: "The people of Norway have the best of reasons for knowing that the ocean connects, not separates." The majority of Canadians have not developed any great interest in the Pacific or in the Pacific countries. In British Columbia, yes; that is a Pacific province. In Alberta there is a growing interest because there are possible markets the new Alberta will need. East of, say, Regina, there is very little interest at all. It was surprising, to me, to find no one in the east who volunteered any comment on Australian or New Zealand problems, or on the A.N.Z.U.S. pact. The politically minded are aware of the importance of India and Pakistan; there is a kind of liberal tradition that welcomes them as newly "liberated" countries. But I found no general emotion about the Far East of the kind that is apparent in the United States.

In consequence Canada did not share the United States' emotion that the war in Korea was a Holy War, just as she did not experience the emotions that came from the three-year long list of American casualties. She had opposed from the first, in 1948 (opposing both the United Kingdom and the United States in doing so), the plan to constitute and recognise South Korea as an independent and sovereign state. She regarded the war as a police action against a single act of aggression, not as the opening campaign in a Crusade against Communism. She was very close to a parallel de facto recognition of Communist China (geography there made a difference to her actions, not her views) at the time when the United Kingdom Government made that decision. Ottawa is not an echo of Washington. Canada has to be persuaded to come; she cannot be dragged along by the hand, like a small child.

But, where?

There this book must stop. It is not an attempt to describe what Canada's foreign policy should be; only an attempt to describe the kind of country that Canada is and the kind of influences that compel her people to choose one road rather than another.

The trouble is that the unanswered questions of the world today cannot be solved by the United Nations, not even by N.A.T.O. They go deeper than matters of national sovereignty and written treaties. They are even deeper than questions of Communism and Russian Imperialism. They relate to the end of civilisations and the births of those that will replace them. Is the mainspring of Europe finally broken?—I defy anyone to read, say, Czeslaw Milosz's *The Captive Mind* without realising that it has been in a great part of what was, in 1939, still culturally Europe. Can the white races come to terms of living with the coloured? Is the Commonwealth the world's best chance of creating a synthesis from this conflict of colour—and how good a chance is it?

In an address at Chatham House, in London, in June 1948, Professor Arnold Toynbee, in discussing the prospects of the survival of our civilisation, put the unanswered questions in this way:

Can we find a middle way in international affairs between the old anarchy of independent states jostling against each other—an anarchy which, I believe, cannot go on much longer in its old form—and the extreme opposite régime of a world peace imposed by some single power on the rest of the world? . . . And can we find some middle course, not only in the arena of international politics, but also in the social fields, between the old inequality of classes, leading to subterranean class warfare, and a social revolution leading to the forcible abolition of class, which is the programme for which Communism stands?

I do not know the answer to these questions but I think it fortunate that the guardians of this great storehouse of resources and power in the North American continent should be sober and intelligent people, not given to bursts of impatient emotion, cautious and resilient. What an opportunity they have to think for the world!

12
Envoi

THE bar at Gander Airport is called the Big Dipper. It never closes. My 'plane back to London was due to leave at 4.45 a.m. local time and I saw no point in going to bed the night before. Jim Paton, who is Gander's doctor, and Howard Kilpatrick, the T.C.A. Station Manager, who flew in Mosquitoes during the war and who hopes, so he said, to retire to some lost village in Devon or Cornwall, kept me company, abandoning their rest to me.

There's been only one fatal crash to a civil airliner at Gander in the last seven years, they said, to give me comfort. It came down just about twenty miles from the field, as the crow flies, but it took three days to bring in the last of the survivors. Eighteen died; we could have saved another five, Paton added, if we'd known then all we do now. Their graves are in a clearing by the wreck and that clearing has been named "St. Martin's in the Woods". The widow of one of them was through here a few weeks ago. She wanted to see the grave of her husband. They were from Liége.

Ten hours from Gander to Brussels; another three on to Liége by road. From the empty woods of Newfoundland, where trees live out their seventy or eighty years of life, fall, decay, and are no more than a soft platform from which others will grow, to history-ridden Liége—

My first acquaintance with any European history had been the 14-inch Austrian howitzers battering the heroic forts of Liége into submission, in August 1914. Until then, history had been confined to books and had virtually ended with Waterloo. In that summer holiday week, it began again. I had seen Liége itself, in 1945, battered by another set of weapons, and already

256

each of those battles seemed as outmoded as those Vauban himself had planned to dominate with his line of fortresses across
France and the Low Countries. Outmoded? That is not how
generals would describe changes in tactics, but generals are
serious people.

Thirty-five or forty people came into the airport waiting room.
A K.L.M. airliner had just landed, Kilpatrick said. Immigrants.
Twoscore Netherlanders. One very old lady, the others families,
the parents between twenty-five and forty; two small boys who
still had all the energy in the world, a baby that cried despite all
its mother could do to pacify it. Real people; in contrast to their
surroundings, for all international airports are unreal. The passengers are freight. They must be watered and allowed to stretch
their legs. They are offered standardised food, trash at the
souvenir counters, and are then shipped on. The permanent inhabitants of the airport watch them as we do traffic through a
freight yard.

We had another round of Canadian rye whisky. I should not
be drinking that again for some time, I thought.

I go back to Ulster, Paton said, once in a while; to see my
mother and my brother and sister. An uncle died some time back
and left me a fair sum and since I can't bring it with me I go
back and spend some of it. It's good to see the places you knew
as a child—so lovely, so unchanged. But—live there again? With
so much to do here?

Paton's hospital had been named in memory of Sir Frederick
Banting, who died off the coast of Newfoundland during the war
when the aircraft he was in crashed in the sea. It is the hospital
for an area as large as all Yorkshire, for a population perhaps no
bigger than that in Rutland. The staff must cope with everything,
from those who survive a 'plane crash to tonsils. An outpost—not
of Empire.

Outside it was a fine night, with the stars clear and the air
fresh and cold. The Netherlanders a few yards away were probably unconscious of that. When you fly, it is the sky that is unreal, and Gander, an hour's stop-over in the blackness of the
Atlantic, would be even more unreal. They were still in the long
tunnel of night from Europe to America. But they had all made
their decisions. That was why they were there.

But, to give up Europe, its civilisation, its—? I could see again

s

the Labour M.P. standing with his back to the fire and saying, smugly, that the British were the most adult people in the world. Speaking against him in the debate in my mind had been the voice of the man in Montreal who had returned from London on the eve of the Coronation: "Now I know what Imperial Rome must have been like in the days before its collapse—"

Leave Europe, the home of Western culture? What could bring more contentment than retirement to a village in Devon, Kilpatrick had said. He was a Canadian. Provided, I might have reminded him, you were able to keep clear of all the officials, from the Rural District and the County Council, from the Commissioners of Inland Revenue and those of the Customs and Excise, from the Ministries of Agriculture and Fisheries, Food, of Housing and local Government, of Works—

Why is there no Ministry of Faith? Has no one any left?

If your children grew up here, Paton said, they'd mature against a different background. Their technical education would be better. They'd be expected to know more techniques about their jobs. They would, too.

And the background? I asked; not vaguely, for he knew what I meant.

There are two answers to that, he said. They could go to Europe to find again the background you have—I have. If they wanted to, that is, and if there was any Europe left to give it to them. Or they could become a part of the process of making a new background here, for themselves, amongst the people of Canada. They could do worse.

They could, indeed, do much worse.

All my life a book-title has haunted me: "The People of the Ruins". The book was written by Edward Shanks not long after the first war and the ruins in which his people lived had come as much from decay as from disaster. I remembered seeing Diocletian's palace at Split, in Dalmatia, a honeycomb of life built up and contained within the framework of a Roman palace as the hive, and I remembered reading at the time, because in the 'thirties it became a sudden topic of interest, the condescending descriptions of that warren written by those who re-discovered it. And now, I thought, I live in Belgravia, where the present-day inhabitants of Britain are making a Diocletian palace out of the ruins of Mr. Cubitt's Victorian Empire.

It seemed to me that we had become too fond of our ruins, that while we may hope for progress we do not really want change. There is a tradition in every acre and we would rather worship the tradition than work the acre. No new buildings in London can be permitted to dwarf St. Paul's; not because it would be an insult to God but because it would offend the Royal Fine Arts Commission. We may not dig for the open-cast coal we need if it will spoil the view from an eighteenth-century house. We do not like to co-operate with a boss because Keir Hardie was all against it. We dare not carry an overhead power-line through the Lake District because that was where Wordsworth saw the daffodils. We are becoming custodians of a museum, and even our right to alter or discard the exhibits is atrophying.

By then, the decision, for me, had become simple enough, for this was at the end of my exploration of Canada. If you emigrate, you emigrate. You abandon what you have, you accept what you will find. You abandon, you find. You leave the ruins, you start to build. Diocletian or Frank Lloyd Wright. In a sense this book is an account of all that went into that change of mind.

It was just four o'clock and the rising sun was dazzlingly bright in the window opposite the bar. It would be nearly setting by the time I was back in London.

London: July–December 1953.

Appendices

APPENDIX I

ESTIMATES OF POPULATION, BY PROVINCES AND TERRITORIES, INTERCENSAL YEARS 1931-53

NOTE.—At every census the previous post-censal estimates, made at 1 June each year, are adjusted to the newly recorded population figures.

Year	N'f'ld.	P.E.I.	N.S.	N.B.	Que.	Ont.	Man.	Sask.	Alta.	B.C.	Yukon	N.W.T.	Canada[1]
	'000	'000'	'000	'000	'000	'000	'000	'000	'000	'000	'000	'000	'000
1931..	..	88	513	408	2,874	3,432	700	922	732	694	4	9	10,376
1932..	..	89	519	414	2,925	3,743	705	924	740	707	4	10	10,510
1933..	..	90	525	419	2,972	3,512	708	926	750	717	4	10	10,633
1934..	..	91	531	423	3,016	3,544	709	928	758	727	4	10	10,741
1935..	..	92	536	428	3,057	3,575	710	930	765	736	5	11	10,845
1936..	..	93	543	433	3,099	3,606	711	931	773	745	5	11	10,950
1937..	..	93	549	437	3,141	3,637	715	922	776	759	5	11	11,045
1938..	..	94	555	442	3,183	3,672	720	914	781	775	5	11	11,152
1939..	..	94	561	447	3,230	3,708	726	906	786	792	5	12	11,267
1940..	..	95	569	452	3,278	3,747	728	900	790	805	5	12	11,381
1941..	..	95	578	457	3,332	3,788	730	896	796	818	5	12	11,507
1942..	..	90	591	464	3,390	3,884	724	848	776	870	5	12	11,654
1943..	..	91	606	463	3,457	3,915	723	838	785	900	5	12	11,795
1944..	..	91	611	461	3,500	3,963	727	836	808	932	5	12	11,946
1945..	..	92	619	467	3,560	4,000	727	833	808	949	5	12	12,072
1946..	..	94	608	478	3,629	4,093	727	833	803	1,003	8	16	12,292
1947..	..	94	615	488	3,710	4,176	739	836	825	1,044	8	16	12,551
1948..	..	93	625	498	3,788	4,275	746	838	854	1,082	8	16	12,823
1949..	345	94	629	508	3,882	4,378	757	832	885	1,113	8	16	13,447
1950..	351	96	638	512	3,969	4,471	768	833	913	1,137	8	16	13,712
1951..	361	98	643	516	4,056	4,598	776	832	939	1,165	9	16	14,009
1952..	374	103	653	526	4,174	4,766	798	843	970	1,198	9	16	14,430
1953..	383	106	663	536	4,269	4,897	809	861	1,002	1,230	9	16	14,781

[1] Estimates for Newfoundland prior to union with Canada, which took place on 31 March 1949, are not included in Canada totals.

Taken from *Canada Year Book 1952–3.*

APPENDIX II

NATIONAL PRODUCT, SAVINGS AND NATIONAL DEBT.

Figures in millions of dollars.

Year	Gross National Product	Savings			Capital Expenditure	Balance of National Debt [2]
		Budget Surplus	Corpn. Savings [1]	Individual Savings		
1946	12,026	133	1,329	988	1,703	18,960
1947	13,768	773	1,765	426	2,489	17,698
1948	15,613	746	1,943	1,009	3,175	17,197
1949	16,462	440	1,925	1,005	3,502	16,950
1950	18,203	648	2,556	645	3,815	17,751
1951	21,450	1,044	2,546	1,386	4,577	16,923
1952	23,011	214	2,709	1,419	5,122	17,522
1953	—	—	—	—	—	17,918
Totals	—	3,992	14,474	6,878	24,383	—

(Figures supplied by the Federal Bureau of Statistics.)

[1] Including depreciation.   [2] Fiscal years ended 31 March.

APPENDIX III

NATIONAL PRODUCT AND ITS EXPENDITURE, 1952

(Figures in millions of dollars)

Agriculture	2,181
Forestry	367
Fishing and Trapping	62
Mining, Quarrying and Oilwells	718
Manufacturing	5,365
Construction	1,008
Transportation, Storage and Communication } Public Utility Operation	1,880
Trade:	
Wholesale	917
Retail	1,613
Finance, Insurance and Real Estate	1,286
Service	1,412
Government	1,593
Non-Residents	267
Sub-Total	18,135
Add:	
Indirect Taxes less Subsidies	2,687
Depreciation Allowances and Similar Business Costs	2,070
Residual Error of Estimate	119
Total	23,011

It was spent as follows:

Personal expenditure on consumer goods and services	14,334
Government expenditure on goods and services	4,216
Investment:	
(*a*) Plant, equipment and housing	4,138
(*b*) Increase in stocks	278
Surplus of exports over imports	164
Residual error of estimate	119
	23,011

(Figures supplied by the Federal Bureau of Statistics.)

APPENDIX IV

AVERAGE WHEAT CROP FOR TEN YEARS 1940-9

Figures in millions of bushels.

	Total Crop	Carry-over at 1 July	Domestic Consumption	Exports	Percentage of Exports to Total Crop
Canada	394.4	275.3	154.2	259.3	65%
United States	1701.3	319.3	838.2	217.8	13%
Australia	145.6	54.7	76.6	74.0	51%
Argentina	215.2	88.9	133.4	82.6	38%

Figures from *The Story of Wheat*, by L. D. Nesbitt (Alberta Wheat Pool, 1953).

APPENDIX V

COMPARISON OF RAILWAY OPERATING RESULTS, 1953

	C.P.R.	*C.N.R.*
Average mileage operated	17,018	24,368
Operating Revenues	$470,443,857	$696,622,451
Freight Revenues	$389,443,857	$553,618,614
Percentage of total operating Revenue	83%	79%
Passenger Revenue	$37,210,362	$45,916,272
Percentage of total operating Revenue	7¾%	6½%
Operating Expenses	$441,686,799	$659,049,086
Net operating Revenue	$28,884,572	$37,573,365
Ratio of net to gross earnings	6.1	5.4
Other income	$16,802,501	$10,292,041
Interest of fixed charges	$14,236,161	$28,087,326
Capital Liabilities:		
Ordinary Stock	$345,174,925	Equity Capital:
Preference Stock	$137,256,921	$1,556,564,557
Funded Debt	$418,662,888	$931,951,738
Revenue tonnage carried	$59,256,634	$86,523,327

Figures from the published accounts of the undertakings.

APPENDIX VI

NOTE ON A COMPARISON BETWEEN CANADIAN AND BRITISH COSTS OF LIVING

THE most important thing about Canada that many will want to know is how its cost of living compares with that in the United Kingdom. This is the most difficult of all aspects of the Canadian scene on which to say anything which will not be misleading, yet it would be dishonest to ignore it. I would make this tentative answer, conscious that it may be thought to be very inadequate.

For a manual worker without very much special skill—there are no manual jobs which do not require some skill—the hourly wage in Canada is not likely to be below a dollar. On the official exchange a Canadian dollar is worth 7s. 3d. From what I saw in Canada I would say that it takes about four Canadian dollars to buy in Canada what an English pound will buy in Britain. On that basis the lower semi-skilled rates of pay in Canada are in the neighbourhood of five shillings an hour and that, I think, is a reasonable measure of the advantage in the cost of living that the Canadian worker has.

Beyond that point it is very difficult indeed to make any comparison. For instance, in Canada it is cheaper both to own and to run a car, but outside the towns the distance a worker may have to travel in that car to work may compel him to spend more on transportation than would his opposite number in Britain. But he has the advantage of the car at the week-end and on vacation. Where does the balance of advantage lie? In the towns, a Canadian worker will almost certainly have to pay more, either in rent or in purchase instalments, for the living accommodation his equivalent in Britain would obtain in a Council house, but he will usually accept a lower standard of accommodation (in floor space, not in domestic fittings) until such time as he can improve his job and his earnings. In most of Canada an occupier will have to spend more in heating his house than does an occupier in Britain (but he will have a well-heated house as a result). To set against these higher costs, he will have greater opportunities to change and improve his job as his skill progresses. In Britain the worker seems to expect that his pay will increase while his work remains the same. In Canada the worker is more inclined to see a closer relationship between pay and work and to accept that if he wants to change the one he may have to change the other.

Over clothing, I would say that the Canadian has the advantage. Over food, the Canadian factory worker does not often have the benefit of a works canteen; management does not always provide one and certainly does not subsidise it if it does. But there are many jobs in places in which management must provide both accommodation and food (for the worker; not for his family) and in that case it does so at cost. Again, in many parts of Canada it is not practicable for an individual to have a garden or an allotment in which he can grow some of his own food; the climate rules it out. But, in general, the individual in Canada is more free to set his own style and standard of living. He has a wider choice in his diet. He may buy more meat and butter if he wishes. He may, of course, do nothing of the kind and live entirely on tinned foods and ready sliced and wrapped bread (and Canadian bread is refined to a remarkable point in tastelessness).

The fact is that comparisons confining to nothing but the cost of living must be false because the only true comparison that can be made is one between the whole pattern of life in one country and that in another and, in this case, that is not a comparison of like with like. If an immigrant from Britain wishes to import intact into Canada all his habits and tastes he becomes, in Canada, an eccentric, and the cost of living for an eccentric is usually higher than for the norm. But, if he is that kind of man, he had better stay at home. Canada is no longer a place to which one can import with success a routine of life from outside. To enjoy it, the settler must become Canadian, at least in the mechanics of living. If he does, he is likely to get as much from his life there as most Canadians do.

Index

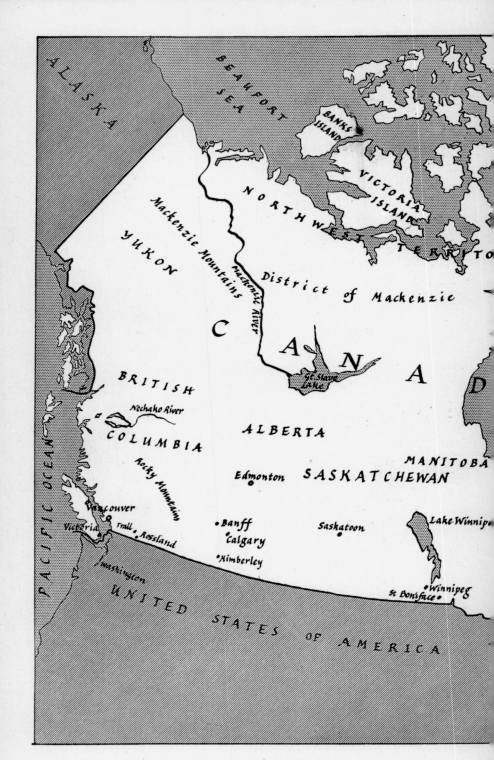